# TRAVELLING LIGHT

# TRAVELLING LIGHT

Edited by Sarah Webb

PAN BOOKS

First published 2004 by Tivoli, an imprint of Gill & Macmillan Ltd,
Hume Avenue, Park West, Dublin 12

This edition published 2005 by Pan Books
an imprint of Pan Macmillan Ltd
Pan Macmillan, 20 New Wharf Road, London N1 9RR
Basingstoke and Oxford
Associated companies throughout the world
www.panmacmillan.com

ISBN 0 330 43203 6



3 5 7 9 8 6 4 2

A CIP catalogue record for this book is available from
the British Library.

Printed and bound in Great Britain by
Mackays of Chatham plc, Chatham, Kent

# CONTENTS

# ACKNOWLEDGMENTS

I would like to take this opportunity to thank all the writers involved in *Travelling Light* for their generosity of time and spirit, and Marie-Louise Fitzpatrick, Lucinda Jacob, Mary Murphy, Nicola Sedgwick, Niamh Sharkey, and Kate Webb for their wonderful illustrations. There would be no book without you; thank you, one and all.

Special thanks must also go to Alison Walsh, Michael Gill, Deirdre Nolan, Imogen Taylor and the dedicated team at Tivoli, Gill & Macmillan, and Pan Macmillan for their support of this book from the very beginning. I would also like to thank my agent, Ali Gunn for all her help with this project.

On a personal note I would like to thank Martina Devlin for her valuable input into the planning of *Travelling Light*, Archdeacon Gordon Linney of St Paul's Church, Glenageary, and Richard Emmens in Kisiizi for their help, and all at Kisiizi Hospital for doing their best to make the world a better place to live in.

*Dedicated with love to my mum and dad,*
*Melissa and Michael Webb*

# SARAH WEBB

## INTRODUCTION

Everyone loves to travel, whether literally or metaphorically, and this collection is for every traveller – from the most dedicated armchair traveller to the most intrepid jungle explorer. And there's certainly something for everyone in this book – from Martina Devlin's hilarious search for the perfect amber necklace in St Petersburg, to Marian Keyes's moving Ethiopian Journey, and Julie Parsons's unforgettable voyage from New Zealand to Ireland. In fact, it's the ideal travel companion.

I get ideas for new books every week and most are forgotten about by the following week. But some ideas take hold and refuse to let go, like this book. What started life as a collection of short stories with a travel theme, after some thought and reconsideration, became the collection of real-life travel adventures you now hold in your hands. But what never changed was the *raison d'être* behind this book – the children's ward of the Kisiizi Hospital in Uganda.

Kisiizi Hospital is situated in the Kigezi Hills in southwest

Uganda. The hospital is still relatively isolated and patients travel from a large area to receive treatment. The hospital deals with the whole spectrum of medical, surgical and obstetric problems, and for many patients Kisiizi is their only hope.

Among its many community outreach programmes is a support scheme for thousands of AIDS orphans, providing material as well as medical aid.

The hospital has strong links with St Paul's Church in Glenageary, where my family and I are active members. Currently, a civil engineer from the parish and friend of the family, David Barrett, is supervising the completion of the new children's ward.

That is why I decided to put together this book – to help children in Uganda to get a better start in life. And by buying this book, you have also helped to change the world in a small way. If you would like to find out more about the hospital and its work, turn to the back of the book or check out www.kisiizi.supanet.com

# MARTINA DEVLIN

## AMBER ALERT

I'll let you in on a secret: the chief reason I wanted to go to St Petersburg was to buy an amber necklace. Obviously, I knew better than to admit this to anyone, aware that it left me looking suspiciously shallow. I shop therefore I am.

So when pressed for a reason why St Petersburg was this year's holiday destination, I crossed my fingers behind my back and claimed I was going to visit the Hermitage's art collection, or I longed to see the city that inspired Dostoevsky, or I'd heard the architecture was breathtaking in its magnificence.

I knew Russia was the place to buy amber because I'd been to Moscow the previous year and spotted it in all its siren splendour. Unfortunately, I'd already frittered all my cash on twenty-three babushka dolls and a fake fur coat, soon to inspire a priest in my home town to remark that the Devlins were getting above themselves. That was a triumphant day – we waited far too long for people to start getting above themselves in Ireland.

But back to Moscow, where I fingered amber rings the size of a Central European statelet, and debated trading my jeans to finance the purchase of one. Regretfully I realised this idea was a non-starter. Every Russian I laid eyes on was wearing a pair of Levis already, so they were unlikely to swap a year's salary for my tatty old pair. All that glasnost and perestroika had much to answer for. I left the baubles behind me, but I didn't forget them.

For a year and a half I fantasised about opulent chokers from the Baltic, which could be bought for a pittance. I holidayed in California and Madrid, both fine destinations but, frankly, challenged on the amber front. Russia remained at the top of my wish list, because I knew beyond a shadow of doubt that an amber necklace would transform my life – I'd be more rounded, sensitive, caring, fulfilled.

The problem was finding a reason to go there which didn't include admitting the real one. I hinted about Russia from time to time to my young man but he was unenthusiastic, claiming that nobody spoke English and the street signs were in the Cyrillic alphabet, so we'd get hopelessly lost. Then, curiously, he'd suggest, as an alternative, a trip to China where nobody spoke English and the street signs were in Mandarin.

One day I heard that St Petersburg was celebrating its tricentenary and the hotels were offering special deals, and I treated it as a sign. Peter the Great was intervening personally to expand my jewellery collection.

Special deals from five-star hotels overrule all uncertainties about whether you actually want to visit the country in question, so tickets were booked and my companion bought a new Swiss army knife for the trip. Any excuse. He also purchased a Russian dictionary because of his conviction that even the St Petersburgers who could speak English would decline to do so as soon as they saw him. 'We have to memorise the Cyrillic lettering for the name of the street our hotel is on – it's our only hope,' he insisted, pointing to a geometric squiggle that included two back-to-front Ns. I left him to it.

In addition, he acquired a guidebook and every so often, in the weeks preceding our trip, he'd bombard me with details about how many staircases there were in the Hermitage art gallery – 117, don't say I never share esoteric data – or the distance between the Winter and Summer Palaces, or how many bridges cross the River Neva. He seemed to have formed the impression that I yearned to admire Catherine the Great's art collection, and allow the Kirov Ballet, performing on home turf, to nourish my soul, and I hesitated to admit how superficial I really was. I could always nip out and buy the perfect necklace while he was still savouring his breakfast coffee on the first morning, I reasoned. Then we had the rest of the week to be culture-vultures and he'd never guess how trite I really am.

We landed in St Petersburg late on a Sunday night, and after pounding into the bathroom to purloin the tiny sewing kit – a particular weakness of mine when staying in hotels – and sucking our teeth over the criminal cost of everything in the minibar, we retired to bed.

Incidentally I regard myself as a seasoned traveller, but was taken aback to discover that in the Nevskij Palace Hotel's minibar, nestling alongside one of those quarter bottles of red wine you wind up drinking despite the fact they cost the equivalent of a three-day-old Lada, there were two packets of condoms. And one of the packets was open. The carton describing itself as 'American Quality' had been rifled, while the Russian quality alternative had been left intact. Probably wisely.

Inevitably their discovery set me wondering about who'd occupied the room before us and why they'd opened a three-pack of condoms but only used one. Economising? Shortage of time? Change of heart? In no time at all I had a bodice-ripping scenario steaming through my imagination, involving a Russian sailor in one of those irresistible striped shirts they wear, throwing caution to the winds and urging, 'No, Svetlana, let us not use contraception – let us use this one night we have together to make a baby.' I could have speculated endlessly if the day's travelling hadn't caught up with me and I hadn't fallen asleep.

Zombie-like the next morning, en route from the hotel bedroom to the breakfast buffet, the edge of my gaze brushed against something glittering inside a glass case. It was a collection of amber necklaces. My body craved caffeine but I was in the grip of a power beyond my control. I paused to admire them.

'We can come back and look at the amber after breakfast,' negotiated my young man, alerted, even at that early stage, to a certain fanaticism in my bearing.

I was about to agree when three Russian ladies bore down on us with the determination of women on commission. Before you could say toast and marmalade, or in this case caviar and sour cream – Russian breakfasts are in another league, and not one you can adjust to in the space of a week – they had kidnapped me. Well, propelled me at high speed, anyway. I found myself inside their shop with amber dripping from my neck, wrists, ears and fingers. You have never seen a creature so comprehensively festooned.

The quest for the perfect amber necklace was under way.

The saleswomen didn't speak much English, but nobody needs words to express rapture when a customer is wearing the most expensive string of jewellery on the premises. There was a torrent of language that sounded like 'take this preposterous woman outside and feed her to the street-cleaning machine' – Russian is an accusatory-sounding tongue – but which appeared to convey unqualified admiration.

'What do you think?' I asked my companion.

He claimed the pieces of jewellery were all equally gorgeous, and asked would I ever hand over my credit card so he could have a peaceful cup of coffee and another read of the guidebook.

Now, here's a lesson that men have wholly failed to grasp

about women, no matter how often it's drummed into them. When we're debating a purchase, no two items are exactly as desirable as each other – one is always marginally superior. The quandary lies in resolving which it is. So if he'd pantomimed indecision before pinpointing one of the necklaces as infinitesimally preferable, I'd probably have gone along with it. But every woman knows she's being humoured when her partner says, 'Yes, that's lovely, and so is that', in-between sneaking furtive peeks at his watch and whimpering about wanting food.

Naturally I left empty-handed, although with promises to return for a further preening session, and we adjourned for breakfast. This was spent in a delicious haze of pondering which necklace to buy. I still hadn't made a final decision after a glass of the Russian champagne served with our eggs. It was sweet and warm, but I polished it off anyway. I don't have many rules in life, but never turn down free champagne has to be one of the fundamentals.

Still irresolute about whether to plump for the traditional amber rope or the milk-and-garnet-coloured amber mélange, I consented to be organised into a plan for the day. On the agenda was an acclimatisation stroll, followed by a visit to the Church of the Spilled Blood. This turned out to be a joyous carnival of multicoloured onion domes, despite the dour name. And predictably, blood has been spilled there – royal blood, in fact – by a group of nineteenth-century anti-monarchists called the People's Will.

We pottered off along Nevsky Prospekt, the main road that runs through the centre of St Petersburg, with me covertly memorising amber-shop locations and my young man searching in vain for a plaque mentioned in his guidebook. 'Citizens! At times of artillery bombardment this side of the street is most dangerous!' Craning for the stencilled warning, camera in hand, he made a discovery that threatened to destabilise the holiday. All the street signs were in incomprehensible Cyrillic lettering, as he'd predicted they would be, but with a perfectly intelligible translation underneath. So all that brainpower expended on memorising back-to-front Ns was redundant. There was weeping and wailing and gnashing of teeth, assuaged only by coffee and cake in the Gostiny Dvor department store, which had a balcony for watching street life.

There is no power on earth that could make me sit and watch St Petersburgers go about their daily business when one floor below me lies a series of in-store jewellery shops. The building was awash with amber. So with the companion settled at a table, a huge chocolate confection in front of him, I bolted downstairs to study the form.

Russian department stores were a revelation. They trundle endlessly along for what feels like miles, housing hundreds of small concessions, each one the same as the previous one. So while there were numerous jewellery stalls, all their wares were identical. Furthermore, inspecting them is time-consuming, because the Russian system requires job creation. It is one assistant's responsibility to remove the necklace from behind a glass case for a customer to view it, another models it and a third rings up the purchase. They take these roles seriously. At the first stall where I lingered, the girl whose job was to model the amber wouldn't allow me to try it on. 'It looks better on me than on you, you bourgeois foreigner,' she pouted – I may not be able to understand Russian but I can read body language. Of course, I sulked and wouldn't buy anything from her, transferring my acquisitive streak to another stall.

It was here that, in a rare burst of insight, I acknowledged my pursuit of a piece of jewellery was going to overshadow the holiday, even though it was my clandestine reason for being there. So I flung vacillation to the winds and chose a necklace. Simple as that. I felt quite proud of myself for being so decisive.

When I tried to pay, however, the shop wouldn't accept euro. Now, every other shop, restaurant and hotel in the city was happy, indeed eager, to relieve visitors of their foreign currency, but Gostiny Dvor was a state-run store and roubles it had to be. No decadent euro, comrade. I left the trinkets behind, secure in the knowledge that there were dozens of identical necklaces in stock and I could pick up one any time, provided I paid a visit to a money exchange. Then I doubled back to collect the man with the guidebook and cake crumbs on his chin, to see something of St Petersburg.

We looked at bridges, we walked across bridges, we had our photographs taken beside bridges. We favoured the wooden bridge suspended by cables emerging from the mouths of gold-winged griffins. Then we went home for dinner.

One of the most gratifying aspects of a holiday is sauntering past restaurants, delaying to inspect menus and toss around possibilities of where to eat that night. But we had our evening meal in the hotel's rooftop restaurant, basically because the *maître d'* sank to her knees and pleaded with us to come in as we passed by en route to the leisure centre. (Not to use it, mind you, just to check that it really existed. We've done this ever since Madrid, when the hotel claimed to have a leisure complex, but we discovered a gaping hole where the facilities would one day be located, perhaps in three years' time.)

One other table in the restaurant was occupied, containing two business people and a supremely bored interpreter. But it was swarming with staff and they were desperate for diversion. We had no choice but to supply it. Naturally we were put right beside the other diners, despite a yawning chasm of tables around the room, so we eavesdropped on their conversation. It was all terribly formal – 'It's a pleasure for me doing business with you'; 'On the contrary, my friend, it's a pleasure for me doing business with you' – and it was a relief when they paid the bill and removed all that mutual pleasure from our vicinity.

Meanwhile, our waitress looked at us with incredulity

when we ordered Russian champagne – 'But we also stock Moët et Chandon,' she protested – and for the remainder of the evening a knot of staff gathered to gaze in wonder at us. The tourists who were voluntarily drinking shampanskoe. It's not bad once you get used to it, we felt like reassuring them. But we didn't; we just bore their scrutiny meekly.

The following day we headed for the Hermitage, five linked palaces containing a collection that amounts to a history of Western art. Rembrandt, Titian, Rubens, Picasso, the Impressionists and the post-Impressionists are all featured in a series of awe-inspiring marble rooms. I promised myself I'd immerse myself in art and avoid amber for one day.

Initially we couldn't find the entrance, because an army of workmen was swarming all over the buildings, preparing for Russian Federation President Vladimir Putin's visit later that week. We stopped a couple walking away from it, who looked like tourists, to enquire how to gain access. They were French and engrossed in a savage and expletive-ridden argument, which, with any other nationality, would signify irrevocable sundering of all future ties and immediate division of the saucepan collection. But they were probably just debating where to go for lunch. They paused in their diatribe to pronounce the museum closed, with an air of absolute certainty. Then they said, 'Have a nice day', and resumed lacerating one another.

We resigned ourselves to missing all those Renaissance masterpieces and ambled over to the side of the building to watch the workmen instead – where we found the entrance. And a babushka collecting admission fees according to the usual system of one scary price for tourists, another less scary charge for Russians. Actually it only sounded frightening in roubles; once you converted it, you didn't mind.

The Hermitage was sumptuous, magnificent and lavishly ornate – within minutes it was clear to us why the peasants had revolted and the tsars had been deposed. These rulers literally had diamonds on the soles of their shoes, to plagiarise Paul Simon. But credit where credit is due, they had impeccable taste in art. After the revolution, the state confiscated aristocrats' collections, boosting the displays still further, so we wandered contentedly for the rest of the day.

Except I found an amber shop. Truly. In the souvenir section, where I thought to buy a couple of postcards, I stumbled across a glass case with a selection of amber necklaces in it. An Italian woman was handling several, while her husband infuriatingly muttered bellissima at each one she pointed to – even Italian men are clueless. I manoeuvred myself into the tiny gap beside her flailing arms and pored over the merchandise, and was relieved to discover that I preferred the necklace in the department store. Imagine if I just kept finding more and more fabulous amber chokers, it would reach sensory overload.

'You were a long time buying postcards,' remarked my young man, when I retrieved him from the café, where he was ploughing through his second Danish pastry.

'Massive queues,' I fibbed. 'Sure you know how bureaucratic the Russians are.'

We trundled home, picking our way with care along the lunar landscape footpaths. Compo culture is obviously unknown in Russia.

Since drinking in culture is thirsty work, we stopped off in the hotel bar for some refreshment.

Later, as we paced beneath lime trees in the Summer Garden, feeling like a couple who'd stepped from the pages of a Tolstoy novel – in fact, I positively mourned the lack of a parasol – my companion shared snippets from his guidebook. He had supplemented it by the purchase of a map, but I wouldn't let him read out street names, even if he spoke in a smoky Russian accent with K sounds at the end of words, like darlink.

Nearby, Russian pairs walked arm in arm, most of the women carrying bouquets of red roses presented to them by their escorts, some even with red heart balloons attached. Russian men are romantic, despite their predilection for long leather coats, shaven skulls and a general demeanour that implies 'one crossways look from you, pal, and you'll find my flick knife buried in your ribs'.

The last day rolled around. I'd put by enough money to purchase the amber necklace from Gostiny Dvor that I'd spied on the first morning, and I determined to buy it. I had been methodical about evaluating every other necklace I'd chanced upon during the week, but none had measured up. So I left my companion eating at a café, and went off to conduct the transaction.

But – talk about a malign twist of fate – I was robbed within feet of the stall. Possibly by a romantic man who yearned to buy his girlfriend roses and a scarlet heart balloon. At least I hope that's what he spent my money on. If I discover he bought a long leather coat and had his head shaved with it I'll be extremely aggrieved.

Robbed. Just as I was about to buy my amber necklace. Destiny was toying with me, I thought, in an explosion of Russian fatalism. I staggered back in a state of hyperventilating sorrow to interrupt my young man's cake-eating, relaying the sorry tale of how I was now rouble-less and amber necklace-less. My holiday was utterly spoiled. He laid aside his half-munched custard slice, went straight to a money exchange, swapped his emergency stash of euro for the price of the necklace and bought it then and there. The business was completed in a matter of minutes.

Then he swept me off to the Mariinsky Theatre, with me sparkling in amber and him wearing his last clean T-shirt. I'm not even sure which ballet it was, because there was nobody to translate it for us, but it was brimming with energy and ego, it even featured a mechanical elephant, and we loved it. We'd have loved it even more if it had lasted two hours instead of three, but Russians prefer to get their money's worth from a night at the ballet.

We strolled home afterwards through the White Night of a long summer's evening, smiling at the prostitutes, smiling at the boarded-up shop fronts, smiling at the bridges and statues and the potholes in the pavement. Smiling at St Petersburg.

# JULIE PARSONS

## CROSSING THE LINE

The flying fish hung suspended above the ship's deck, its iridescent wings catching the light and spinning it into a silken aura of colour. Then, as suddenly as it had appeared, it collapsed and lay panting on the bleached wood. Its small mouth was wide open, its transparent gills stretching out to try and net the air. I squatted down beside it and watched its dying moments. Soon it was joined by others. I touched them tentatively with my bare toe. Why didn't they know? I wondered. Why didn't they realise that when they shot high up above the Pacific Ocean's blue vastness, they might land somewhere they could no longer breathe? That the desire to fly would bring them to their moment of death.

It was April 1963. Just before my twelfth birthday. It was the second week of our six-week journey from New Zealand to England. We'd left behind the choppy waters of the Tasman Sea and were now steaming through the Pacific, heading next for the Indian Ocean. It had been days since we had seen proper land. Occasionally a smudge of green suggested there might be an island somewhere out beyond the horizon. But it was easy to forget that there was another world beyond the confines of the rust bucket of a cruise ship, the MV *Fairsea*, in which we and twelve hundred other passengers were travelling from the southern to the northern hemisphere.

It's difficult to explain to people now at the beginning of the twenty-first century, but back then, forty years ago, travelling by boat was commonplace. It was the way people moved from one side of the world to the other. Air travel was only for the very rich. Our fellow passengers were mostly young New Zealanders and Australians, heading for the 'old country', as they quaintly called it, for adventure, fun and excitement for a year or so, before returning home to settle down.

But it wasn't like that for us. We, that's my mother, my sister Gay, and my two brothers Simon and Rory, were moving lock, stock and barrel from what had been our home in New Zealand to what had been our parents' home in Ireland. At last, after seven years, my father, who had disappeared into the same sea over which we now floated, had been declared legally dead and my mother was free to sell our house and make the decision to leave. Down in the ship's dank hold were the six trunks that contained every bit of our New Zealand life that my mother had deemed fit to bring. Everything else had been left behind, including, as we were to realise, a large chunk of our past.

But that was still to come. For the time being all that mattered was here and now, the MV *Fairsea*, pride of the Sitmar Line and home to us all. The Sitmar Line was an Italian shipping company. Hence, the crew were Italians. They were, to a *signore*, dark-haired, dark-eyed, and mad for it. I was too young to be the object of their attentions, but with a keen interest in sex and the sexual antics of my elders, I was fascinated by all the goings on. Passenger ships are perfect for liaisons – dangerous, secretive and mysterious.

They are filled with narrow corridors, tiny cabins, and all kinds of nooks and crannies. Below deck, below the water line, the air is hot and stuffy, heavy with innuendo and barely suppressed desire. No one was immune to it. Not even the ship's nurse, sent to bring me, pale green with seasickness, to the doctor.

We lurched together down steep staircases and ever-narrower passages. I tried desperately to focus on her spreading hips, conscious that I did not want to disgrace myself by throwing up. But suddenly she disappeared into a large walk-in linen cupboard. I tried not to look but I could not avoid the scene in front of my eyes. Nurse and cabin steward, locked in a passionate embrace. I waited, nausea gone, as large brown hairy hands gripped wads of white-coated flesh. There were fervent sighs and groans, muttered expressions of adoration and desire. I shrank back against the wall, clutching my faded dressing gown around me, and waited. Eventually they parted. Hair was patted back into place, uniforms straightened, buttons slipped back into button holes.

'*Andiamo*', the summons was flung back over the nurse's shoulder, and I meekly bowed my head and followed her once again, this time to the doctor's quarters, where I was prescribed that very continental of treatments: the suppository.

'The best for seasickness,' the doctor said, as he gestured to me to turn over on my side and pull down my pyjamas.

On the return trip I was unaccompanied. Holding on to myself, I scurried back to the safety of my cabin and my bunk and lapsed into a fitful sleep, punctuated with dreams of linen cupboard encounters and heavy breathing. Florence Nightingale *Fairsea*-style – you can keep it.

Life on board had a surreal Alice-in-Wonderland kind of quality. As children, we were expected to live in a world apart from the adults. We ate at different times. Lunch was at eleven thirty in the morning. It was the same food every day.

The printed menus promised much, but delivered little. Each meal began with what was described as 'cold consommé in cup', which was little more than a pale, Bovril-type liquid. This was followed by a pasta dish, or as we called it in those days before TV chefs and *The Sopranos*, spaghetti. It was decorated with a few squiggles of Parmesan cheese. Weird stuff, we muttered to each other, and pushed it around on the plate. Surely spaghetti was always coloured bright orange and came out of a tin? Still to come was a meat dish of indifferent quality and a few limp-looking vegetables.

And as for entertainment. Again much was promised. The small cinema presented a film every evening. The first night it was *The Three Stooges in Orbit*. The next night was the thriller, *The Box*. The third night, well, guess what? Larry, Moe and Curly Joe fetched up again in a space ship that looked like it was made from Meccano, the 1950s version of Lego. And the night after? Right again. *The Box* opened its creaking lid once more. Soon the audience of under-fifteens was reciting in true *Rocky-Horror-Picture-Show* style. We shouted out the words in unison and mimed the actions; caused an uproar and were banned from the movies.

Not that that mattered. There was plenty to occupy us all on that old boat. My mother had discovered a group of people who wanted to play with the Ouija board. Soon she was hooked.

'I'm sure I'm going to find your father,' she announced over mid-morning coffee and delicious Italian fruit cake sprinkled with icing sugar. 'Definitely. There's a lot going on down there,' she said with a meaningful look, as she put on her dark glasses and disappeared for the day.

And there was a lot going on up on deck too. There was a swimming pool to splash and dive and laze in. There were acres of deck on which to lie and dream. There was an ocean to gaze at and dolphins to watch. And then there were the ports we sailed into with increasing regularity the further north our course took us.

Singapore, Colombo, Aden, Port Said and Naples. In my mind's eye a dotted line connects them one to the other. They all have the same kind of smell. Heat radiating from cobbled docks, littered with cranes and ropes and dark men, rendered small by my vantage point high up on the *Fairsea*'s deck. Crowds of people in white clothes and huge straw hats, thronging the gangways that crept down the ship's smooth steel sides. The cries of hawkers and sellers, flogging everything from cheap watches to hand-made dolls. Paper cones filled with nuts and seeds, and long, unripe bunches of bananas. The huge engines down in the bowels of the boat throbbed. Now they were familiar and as constant as my own heartbeat. They idled, a soft rhythmic vibration, until it was time for the giant anchors to be hauled up and the pilot boats to guide us out into the open sea once again.

We passed over the equator and there were the customary celebrations. Old Father Neptune ruled for the day and there were parties and fancy-dress parades. I went as Brigitte Bardot. I have photographs to prove it. I'm wearing the bikini my mother made for me. It has multicoloured stripes with a fringe around the bottom that dances as I move. My long hair is back-combed into a candyfloss bouffant on the top of my head. My lips are scarlet, my eyes are ringed with black liner, and a cigarette holder, complete with a Craven A king-size, droops from between my fingers. And there was scandal. Mario, one of the most gorgeous of the waiters, who bore a strong resemblance to a young James Garner, was escorted from the boat at the next port. The whispers ran around the decks. He had been found in a cabin with a girl, a very young girl. Lucky thing, I thought wistfully. Oh for an afternoon with Mario, or anyone else.

But it was not to be. I spent my days in a lethargy of longing, sprawled on my towel, watching young lovers cosying up to each other. I was waiting. For what, I don't really know. Waiting perhaps for our voyage to end. Knowing that the sense of suspended animation couldn't last forever.

That all of us, rocking and rolling on the ocean's swell, would soon have to face the outside world again. But for now there was my twelfth birthday party to look forward to. The girls in my class at school in New Zealand had arranged a surprise. Again there are photographs. I am sitting in front of a huge, elaborate cake decorated with candles and iced flowers. My hair is brushed to a sheen and held back with a broad pink ribbon. My teeth shine whitely in my sunburnt face. Around me, gathers my family, singing 'Happy Birthday'. I lean forward, close my eyes and blow. The candles flicker then simultaneously go out. I wish. I wish. I wish.

What do I wish for? Suddenly I wish I were back at home in the house on the cliff top above the beach, where I've lived since I was born. I wish we had never left it. I wish we weren't travelling all these thousands of miles across the ocean. I wish for the security and familiarity of childhood. I wish I never had to grow up.

We're like the flying fish, I think now. We're driven to leap beyond what we know. But where will we land? When I look at the pictures of my twelfth birthday party, I can see behind the brightness of my smile. I can see the fear for what lies ahead.

# MORAG PRUNTY

## THE HAMMAM EXPERIENCE

After my three-day bus trip across the Atlas Mountains to the edge of the Moroccan desert, I felt like I was sweating grains of sand. I was weary. I had spent four days away from home already and had another three to go. My Marrakesh landlady, Jalila, and Heja, her maid, were perfect hosts; the Riad Jilbel, with its resolutely feminine atmosphere – candles and petals floating in the courtyard's gently simmering fountain, bowls of local sweet-cakes in the bedroom continually refreshed – felt like a home of sorts. But I was craving my infant son.

I had decided I needed to get away, to 'find myself' after the intense emotional shock of being a mother. I needed to take stock, make a bit of space for myself. What I learned from almost the first day was that I never wanted to be away from my child for so long again. I missed my husband but was angry with him. That's the way it is whenever I feel afraid or alone. I didn't want to get in touch with myself after all. I wanted to be back home with them.

The desert trip had been extraordinary. I had bonded with strangers in French; sung sean nós to a handful of goat-herders in the Moroccan equivalent of the Bates Motel; and led a train of camels into the Sahara, shared a tent with twelve adults and a lot of dung beetles, then led them back out again. I had learned some new things: the true value of the Boots Wet Wipe; that kohl keeps your eyes watering so that sand never gets into them. And relearned some old ones, most significantly that no mountains, even the magnificent Atlas Mountains, will ever match the brooding brown mounds of County Mayo. It had been a feat just sitting in a suspensionless bus on a narrow mountain road for as long as five hours at a stretch. My body, never mind my soul, needed, deserved something special.

Jalila suggested I visit a hammam – the public baths where most Muslim women go on a weekly basis, as much a meeting place as a 'spa' experience. She arranged to put me in the hands of Mamam, one of the old women who worked there. We walked deep into the core of the kasbah, down identical alleys, high-walled and narrow, Jalila marching fast and calling brief greetings to passing tradesmen and neighbours. I dawdled behind, searching for landmarks – a 1960s soap advert melted onto a red sandstone wall; cheap straw 'shoppers' in primary colours dangling from a shop doorway – so I might find my way back.

We stopped at a building with the kind of simple sandstone exterior that almost always hides magnificent mosaics, mirrors and filigree. Not so the hammam. The décor was something you might expect of a prison interior: plain concrete with high ceilings and no windows. Parts of the walls were tiled in an institutional shade of yellow and the only furniture was a couple of wooden benches and a counter, behind which sat two very ancient and very cross-looking women. Jalila gave money to one of them and took off. My multilingual landlady was widely travelled and had correctly guessed that my interpretation of a hammam was likely to be the Turkish hotel version, which involved fluffy white towels and massage tables. In hindsight I am glad she left me before my shocked expression had the chance to offend her.

Mamam urged me to get undressed where I stood, which felt something like getting naked in the waiting room of a train station. As I folded my clothes and fussed over the contents of my small cosmetics bag, this woman, who was a good deal older than my own mother – perhaps in her seventies – stripped also. She carefully took my pile of belongings from me and hid them behind the counter. Then, rather than waiting for me to follow her, she grabbed my hand, tucked it securely beneath her armpit and led me into the furthest chamber of the hammam.

It was dark and wet. The roughly tiled floor was roasting underfoot, the hot pipes servicing the wall taps running beneath it. There were no seats, and the few women already there sat on protective rubber mats. My old woman took one out of the small bucket that Jalila had given me earlier and which I had duly filled with local purchases. A slab of pure soap wrapped in foil from my landlady's kitchen, a coarse, synthetic loofah glove, the rubber mat, as well as my own toilet bag. She put the mat on the ground next to a tap and indicated for me to sit. I was all limbs, trying to find a way to preserve my propriety whilst kneeling naked on the floor. My minder filled a bucket from the hot tap at my back, threw it over me, then sat down open-legged opposite me and began to scrub at my arms and torso with the loofah.

My unwitting primness at my own and this old woman's nudity became amplified with her touch. I felt – not violated – but certainly invaded, as she vigorously rubbed the loofah over my nipples, sloughing off maggots of dead skin, then rinsing them away with a bowl filled from the constantly running tap. She rubbed and rinsed, moving and manipulating my limbs so that she could reach every part of me; holding one arm aloft as she scrubbed at my armpit; wrenching my knees apart as she went to work on my thighs.

Her touch was far from sexual, but there was something both strange and familiar about it that was, in equal parts, alarming and comforting. She was so intent in the business of washing me that there was a peculiar privacy about our proximity. As if I were suddenly nothing but my body. All the other women were washing each other's hair and throwing water over each other's backs. Some of them had firm beautiful bodies, which I was shy to have noticed, and while many of them looked over, none would hold my own faltering eye.

There was water gushing from the taps and flushing across the floor in grimy waves from dozens of buckets and bowls. I found myself overwhelmed with an emotion that felt like loneliness but was probably just straightforward homesickness. So I cried. My old woman continued to wash me but then I noticed that she was looking at my face. Immediately I worried that my tears might have offended her; that they might be construed as an indication that she had done something wrong. Worse – that this podgy pale-skinned Westerner's urbane sensibilities were being offended by the basic nature of what was going on around her, and to her. Then it seemed that the old woman's touch was not invasive but rather a privilege, and that it was *I* who was invading *her* privacy with my lack of understanding and therefore enjoyment. And still I cried, although my neurotic line of thinking made me give her a wide smile through the tears to let her know I was okay.

She smiled back, toothless cute, despite the rheumy eyes, and then she did something extraordinary. She tickled me. Moved one hand up suddenly from the lower leg she was massaging, and gave me a quick chuckle-making pinch on my side. I giggled – and she did it again. She laughed and I laughed – then she seemed satisfied that her work was done and continued her silent massaging as if nothing had happened. I continued to cry a little, but now we both knew it was all right.

In that quirky incidence of physical contact between us I felt very close to her. She had handled me with the confident, pragmatic care of a mother. The same way I bathe my own son; in the way I know my mother bathed me as a child. I wished then for a moment that my mother had been there washing me, instead of this old Arab woman. And I felt a pang of grief for the day when I will no longer be able to enjoy such intimacies with my own son, and briefly wished for a daughter that I could sit and bathe with until I too am seventy.

Over the next twenty minutes or so she tackled my hair and my feet – which made me wince and giggle in turn. She grimaced at the handfuls of dirt (fake tan, if she but knew it) coming off my skin. I tried to indicate the purpose of hair conditioner. When she was finished, she stood up, and patting me on the shoulder, she walked back through the baths to her work counter. Her gait was slightly stooped, as one would expect from a woman of her age. My maternal grandmother lived with us and I had never seen her naked. I wonder what difference it would have made if I had.

As I was getting dressed in the reception area, a young Arab woman arrived and asked if I needed help. Her face was full of concern as she tried to explain that I might need a local to accompany me into the hammam. I told her that I was just leaving, and held out my arm to her so that she could touch my skin and see how soft and clean it was. It felt like butter.

As she did so, some misaligned corner of me clicked back into place, and I was, in that moment, satisfied.

# CAUVERY MADHAVAN

## THE RELUCTANT WIFE

Like a tea-taster swirling a mouthful of the brew before expertly discharging it into a spittoon, I took in several breaths, slowly and deeply, expelling each when the pungent cocktail of smells overpowered my senses. The Central Bus Station at Egmore in Madras wasn't enveloped in the malodorous air that choked the city's nearby Central Railway Station. For, unlike the railway station, the bus station was almost entirely roofless, with no dingy, soot-coated walls to contain the sharp rankness that emanated from the incessant ebb and flow of humanity in transit. No, the bus station smells were not days, months or decades-old accumulations – the nauseating smell of diesel was only as old as the last bus to belch out off its platform. Strong, fishy whiffs, which came from the stacks of Thermacol boxes packed tight with ice, were wafted away briskly by the hot and dusty blasts of breeze that constantly swept through the open-air concourse. The heady fragrance of fresh jasmine buds could be detected too, drifting in from the direction of the flower-seller who sat cross-legged, deftly hand-tying her flowers into long strands, stopping only to flick drops of water on them to keep them from wilting in the heat.

The wind changed direction and in the next breath I was able to discern lentil patties deep-frying in rancid week-old oil, combining with the sour stench from the toilets opposite the platform where I stood and the heavy muskiness of the Ayurvedic balm massaged into the hair of the woman who stood a few feet away from me, waiting, as I was, for the driver and the conductor of our bus to finish their smoke and allow us in. The two men drew intently on their beedis, pursing their lips as they exhaled. The harsh, overpowering smoke was finding its way out of the bus and quickly smothering all the other smells around.

Every once in a while the moustachioed conductor walked up and down the length of the empty bus peering through the barred windows, looking out at us, a growing line of very patient passengers with our numerous bags and bundles. When he went back to his lengthy companionable discourse with the driver, I looked at my watch. Fifteen minutes to departure and it would surely take an hour to load us all up, I thought, checking the queue behind me: about forty people and at least a hundred odd-sized pieces of luggage waited to be packed into the belly and onto the roof of the bus.

'You needn't worry, they are experts at stuffing. Normally there are twice as many passengers but it is the Adi Masam, so people don't like to travel. The inauspicious month – you know of it?'

I turned around to look at the middle-aged man behind me. When he had joined the queue, I had taken an aversion to what I was sure was the cloying perfume of Brylcreem, and so I was taken aback to note that the man was, in fact, nearly bald. Now I disliked him instantly for his delusional and futile application of the hair cream and I smiled at him non-committally, thinking about the eight-hour journey from

Madras to Bangalore and not wanting to end up sitting next to him.

'However, a very auspicious month for us, don't you think? We can travel in comfort. No standing passengers leaning heavily on our shoulders. One time a fellow put his bedding roll on my lap – all the way from Madras to Hyderabad! Your bag is small, best to keep it on the luggage rack above your seat.'

I nodded, smiled weakly and looked away. But I wasn't to lose him that easily. Aboard the bus he took the window seat right behind me and immediately proceeded to fiddle with the shutters.

'The sun will be on our side till midday. It adds to the strain of this journey. The glare is not good for the eyes.'

I pretended not to hear him and busied myself instead with an exaggerated rearranging of the contents of my rucksack. I took out the large bottle of water, the cucumber sandwiches wrapped in a double layer of damp napkins and four loose jacket oranges that my mother had got ready for me at five o'clock that morning, and then I took my time putting them back just as I had found them. My father had dropped me at the bus station in time to catch this six thirty bus to Bangalore and on my insistence had headed off home once he had seen me to the correct platform. In Bangalore I was going to meet up with cousins I hadn't seen for a couple of years, since I had got married and left India for Ireland in 1987.

Outside, on the platform, the last few passengers milled around the door of the bus looking on anxiously as their belongings were hoisted towards the roof by two gaunt, young men who were being supervised by the conductor. He hurled abuse at them, alternating between twirling his moustache into elaborate hooked curlicues and spitting vociferously against a pillar sporting a faded sign that said 'Cleanliness Is Next To Godliness, No Spitting Please. By Order.' Every few minutes the two young men flung up a few of the smaller bags, which arrived on the roof with loud thumps, accompanied first by cries of apprehension and then groans of resignation from the owners.

The whole loading operation had indeed taken barely twenty minutes. The two men clambered down from the roof and then hurriedly ran along the outside of the bus beseeching the passengers for tips. To those who threw them a few coins through the windows, they muttered back in what the donors liked to think was gratitude.

The conductor hacked out a final hefty expectoration, and giving the side of the bus a massive double thump with his fist, followed by a piercing shout of 'Rriiight!' he jumped aboard. The driver, who had been watching everything nonchalantly until then, chose that very moment to let out two excruciating blasts of the horn. Simultaneously a candle-shaped electric bulb burst into light, throwing a reddish glow over the framed print of the god Ganesha, which graced the corner of the dashboard. The bus roared into life, and the double row of plastic jasmines that festooned the windscreen shuddered crazily.

The men now switched to loudly cursing the tight-fisted passengers and as the bus pulled out of the station, they ran alongside giving everyone vicious one-fingered salutes. When they could no longer keep up, they simply turned away, laughing at their own temerity, their arms around each other's shoulders, counting in their open palms their very meagre earnings.

On my father's advice, I had picked a window seat almost dead centre of the bus, where he said the effects of the poor shock absorbers would be felt the least. My mother wished I had gone by the Shatabdi Express train, unable to understand why I would want to travel by the most uncomfortable mode of transport between the two cities. But it had been over ten years since I had journeyed within India and I wanted to refresh my memory and restore to all my senses the experience of travel in the sub-continent. The air-conditioned, sanitised version was not what I was looking for.

Even before we had reached the suburbs, however, I wished that I had listened to my mother. The diesel fumes from the steady stream of heavy goods vehicles heading out of the city onto the national highways, combined with the jerky stop–start way in which our bus lurched forward every few hundred yards, brought on waves of nausea. I dug into the rucksack for a pull of tissue and held it to my nose, a makeshift filter that was also to double up as my first line of defence if I did throw up. My discomfort hadn't gone unnoticed.

'Would you like to have your shutter down?' Brylcreem man asked.

'No, no, I must have some fresh air,' I replied without turning around fully, my answer muffled through the tissue.

'Fresh air will come after Sriperumbudur,' he stated knowingly, leaning forward in his seat before adding, 'Try some chit-chat – it will pass the time.'

I nodded in a vague fashion and considered my fellow passengers. Many of them had fallen off to sleep in awkward positions that would no doubt cause them much agony when they awoke. The two seats in front of me were empty, as well as the seat beside me. Across the aisle, a woman poured hot coffee from a flask and offered the cup to her husband, who accepted it wordlessly, never once taking his eyes off the view from his window. The woman peered into the flask longingly and I wondered if there was any left for her.

A few seats ahead, six women who had talked incessantly since the bus left the station were now in animated conversation with the conductor. They were fruit vendors, whose jute-covered baskets of mangoes and bananas had been loaded onto the roof with more care than had been afforded anyone else's luggage. It was obvious that they were regulars on this early-morning bus and that they knew the conductor fancied himself as a bit of a ladies' man. They nudged each other discreetly as he ran his hands through his hair in film-star fashion and proudly twirled his moustache.

They smirked when he showed them his digital watch, goading him on to play the various alarm tones he could set it to. They pandered to his ego, laughing at his jokes and admiring his take on popular catch phrases from the latest Bollywood blockbuster to hit the movie screens. The conductor lapped it all up unsuspectingly. Mesmerised by their collective deviousness and his singular vanity, I was surprised when the bus pulled into Sriperumbudur in seemingly no time at all. In his window seat behind me, Brylcreem man was snoring gently.

No one got off at Sriperumbudur, and perhaps no one would have been able to, for the stampede towards the bus resulted in a desperate crush of bodies, bags and screaming babies. The conductor left the company of the fruit vendors reluctantly but with a look that promised them he would be back. He treated all those who had approached his bus in riotous fashion with equal contempt. Standing at the top of the narrow steps of the vehicle, he calmly flailed his intending passengers with his fat leather ticket dispenser. The mêlée broke up instantly, with people retreating swiftly, this time using their bags as protective shields, which minutes earlier had been employed as battering rams. While they regrouped, now in a ragtag queue, the conductor twirled his moustache thoughtfully and then examined the ticket dispenser for any damage.

When he permitted them to board, the new passengers darted around the bus like dragonflies, quickly grabbing the first available seat and then looking around to see if any better could be had. But very few changed their minds – it was obviously too risky a move to chance. The driver, who had been summoned to the control room, returned to his steering wheel and had a lively chat with the conductor, who indicated by his vehement emission of a sizeable spit globule that the news was bad. The information filtered down the aisle within minutes. Our bus had been forced to take on passengers from a mofussil service, the rural village-to-village route. Their bus had broken down and, en route to Bangalore, we would have to make one small diversion off the national highway. Many men and all the fruit vendors took their cue from the conductor and spat their disgust out through their respective windows.

The seat next to me was now taken by a rather stout man who, when we pulled out of Sriperumbudur, was still panting lightly from the exertions that had preceded the final orderly boarding. The young couple who occupied the seats in front of us were making themselves comfortable, she cradling the infant and he putting their four small bags in the overhead rack.

As we roared down the highway towards Kanchipuram, I was struck by the change of scenery. Gone was the ugly semi-industrial eyesore of garages, truck stops, welding units, small factories, brick kilns, puncture-repair specialists, tanneries and warehouses that had stretched in a hideous fashion from the outskirts of Madras city to Sriperumbudur. The road ahead was tunnel-like, shady and cool under the canopy of huge trees that lined the highway. Flame-of-the-forest, ablaze with their bright orange flowers, and tamarind trees, heavy with their brown pods, stood side by side with majestic banyans and the dark-leaved medicinal neems. Beyond the trees, on either side of the highway, lay villages – some dissected by the road itself, some visible just in outline a good few miles away. As Brylcreem man had promised, the air was fresh and clean. This was rural south India as I had remembered it: small fields, modest coconut groves, cool mango plantations, reddish earthen dams and drying river beds with scrawny buffaloes lolling in stagnant green pools. And then suddenly the green cultivated belts would end without warning to be replaced with miles and miles of unpopulated, dry scrubland, dotted with thorny acacia bushes and enormous rocky outcrops with 'Jesus Saves' painted in foot-high letters.

The stout man next to me had kept his distance, making

sure there was a respectable few inches between us. For this I was grateful and I asked him in Tamil if he wished to store the bag he had on his lap under my seat.

He replied in English. 'I am thanking you, but in this bag is my daughter's wedding sari. I am taking it to Bangalore to be blessed by Sai Baba. We are devotees, great believers in his divine powers. You see, my daughter did not agree to this match initially. But when Sai Baba himself appeared to her in a dream, urging her to marry the boy her parents had chosen, she changed her mind. The groom is a chartered accountant, non-smoker, in a non-transferable job, and the only son. His two sisters are married and settled abroad, so there will be no interference. My daughter is a lucky girl. It is all Baba's blessings.'

'Excuse me, sir, you are Baba's devotee? So am I. I carry him on my key-ring. He opens all doors for me.' Brylcreem man dangled his key chain over my shoulder and the stout man examined it with devotion.

Before the bus reached Kanchipuram, I was offered the opportunity to examine the sari in its box and, curious, I accepted. It was woven with pure red silk shot through with orange and gold thread, a combination that dazzled and shone every which way the light fell on it. The sari had a woven *zari* border and I was assured that the *zari*, the gold thread, was pure gold.

'You will understand now why I have to keep it with me at all times.'

I nodded, and behind me, Brylcreem man clucked sympathetically.

In Kanchipuram the bus conductor announced a five-minute halt. Many disembarked to stretch their legs and have a quick cup of coffee, steaming hot *idilis* and crispy, fried *vadas*. I stayed in my seat eating an orange and envying their cast-iron stomachs. From my window I could see Brylcreem man chatting with the conductor.

The young man in the seat in front of me had stepped out

and now returned to ask the woman if she wanted a cup of tea or coffee. She declined, saying she would wait till the baby fell asleep. He persisted. What about some water? She held up the full bottle she had beside her. He smiled and headed out to have a cup of coffee.

'She will be married soon, my daughter, as soon as the Adi Masam is past. Then before we know it, there will be grandchildren.' My stout neighbour rapped his fingers on the sari box excitedly. 'I hope my son-in-law will show the kind of concern for my daughter as this fellow in front of us.' Then after some thought, he added, 'Would you like a cup of tea, coffee?'

I showed him the bottle of water in my rucksack and he smiled knowingly. 'NRI, Non-Resident Indian?'

'Yes,' I replied.

'Only NRIs buy bottled water. Excuse me, but with your dollar power, why are you not flying by air? Are you not married?'

Only in India, I thought, and plunged into explanations. But our chat did not last too long, for I realised that the man who had asked me the questions was not nodding but had nodded off to sleep. Hoping that Brylcreem man had not noticed my gaffe, I quickly looked out the window. I didn't feel any different from when I had first left India and yet a bottle of water had given me away! It was a relief to realise that the many enormous changes that had confronted me on my return to India were merely cosmetic. In her heart and soul India had stayed the same. Nosiness remained a friendly virtue, and indulging in a bit of frank conversation with a perfect stranger was still the best way to avoid the tedium of long journeys.

We were by now driving through Wallajahpet, onwards to Ranipet. The baby in front had become restless and had started a pathetic non-stop whimpering. The young woman cradled it and patted it to no avail. After a while, the young man offered to take the child, but the women said she would try standing in the aisle; maybe that would calm the baby down. So they exchanged seats and for a while the rocking did seem to soothe the child. The man suggested she take off one layer of clothing; it was obvious the child was too hot.

From behind me, Brylcreem man added his agreement. 'The child looks too hot.'

The young woman did as she was advised and the child quickly quietened. Soon the mother sat down again, and nearly everyone on the bus slept till we pulled into Palmaner. The conductor announced a twenty-minute lunch stop.

I took my place in the queue of people waiting to get down from the bus. I had my cucumber sandwiches with me and I ate them standing in the shade of the cement canopy, keeping a close eye on a troupe of white-faced langur monkeys that were watching the proceedings with care. As a child, I had had too many school lunches hijacked by monkeys not to know about their cunning, opportunistic behaviour. Despite the many passengers standing around, the langurs made several quick charges down the young banyan tree they were sitting on. However, their every attempt was thwarted by a young boy armed with a heavy stick who had clearly been employed by the owner of the lunch stall for that express purpose.

With ten minutes to spare and flies swarming everywhere there was food, I decided to get back into the bus. The young woman was eating with one hand what smelt like rice and potato curry, and holding the baby with the other. When she finished, the young man offered to hold the baby while she got off the bus to wash her hand at the tap next to the stall. She hurried back and busied herself with rummaging around two bags she had taken down from the overhead rack. It was the baby's food and she quickly and expertly mixed it, and, armed with a small, stainless-steel spoon, she sat down with the child once again on her lap and began to coax it to eat. The conductor had meanwhile positioned himself at the top of the steps, from where he loudly berated the latecomers, and then once again, with two loud thumps from his fists to the side of the bus, we were off, heading for Kolar.

'An extra twenty-six miles we are being forced to divert, the conductor himself told me. This mofussil route we have to take to Kolar will delay us,' the stout man grumbled. 'If I am too late I will miss Baba's public appearance this evening and I will have to wait an extra day.'

Soon we were leaving the highway. A left turn took us onto a much narrower road and the surface deteriorated dramatically, the bus raising a plume of dust that probably could be seen for miles. The driver had decided to make up for the extra distance by driving even faster than he did on the highway, and on this smaller thoroughfare, where might was certainly right, he knew he was the undisputed king of the road. After a hair-raising few miles, my cucumber sandwiches had begun to lurch dangerously in my stomach and I made a concerted effort to distract myself. I looked out towards the deserted crossroads we were approaching. At first the junction appeared to be in the middle of nowhere, until I spotted a little village at least a mile away to the left. The young man in front stood up and signalled to the conductor.

I felt sorry for the young couple who had this distance to walk to their village. I assumed they would take turns with the bags and the baby. I smiled at the young man as the bus stopped and he gave me a small wave.

As he gathered all their things, the young woman stood up, looking very flustered. 'He is taking my bags,' she said to no one in particular.

'Please don't start that again – you promised your father you wouldn't do this to me.' The young man walked back down the aisle to her.

The woman instinctively clutched her baby close to her. 'Give me my bags back. This man is stealing my bags, my baby's food.'

The young man turned to the conductor. 'Please excuse her

– she has had difficulty since the child was born. It will just take a minute; please let me talk to her.'

'I have another twenty miles of this useless mofussil road before I get back on the highway; sort out your problem within the walls of your house.' Having arrived at the crossroads, the driver was not going to tolerate any unnecessary delays.

'I will – I had sorted it – in her father's house. I have just spent a week in Sriperumbudur persuading her to return home with me. Her father and brothers had promised me they had succeeded in making her see reason. She imagines things, suspects even her own family. I have told her I will not hold any grudges at all.' He put his hand out to the woman. 'Come, we have reached home.'

She shrank away from him and fell back into the seat shaking. 'This man is not my husband. I am going to ... to Bangalore. My husband will be waiting there for me.'

'I wish I had allowed your father to accompany us.' The young man looked at the stout man and the Brylcreem man. 'I did not want to trouble him – he is frail. Her erratic behaviour doesn't help either.'

The fruit vendors had walked up the aisle to be close to the action. They grumbled to the conductor. 'We will miss the evening market at this rate.'

'You can see we are delaying the bus; come on now before they throw us out.' The young man pulled her to her feet.

She flinched. 'How dare you touch me?' Then, looking wildly around, she shrieked, 'I had never seen this man till he boarded this bus. Can somebody not do anything? My husband will be waiting for me.' She began to shake violently.

'Let me take the child before you drop him.' The young man reached forward and grabbed the baby.

With a deep guttural scream, the woman made a lunge for her child.

'Here, I will take the baby while you take care of your wife.' The conductor had decided to intervene and take charge. 'Why don't you write to her mother to come and stay with you for a while? A girl needs her mother when she is as troubled as this.'

'Are you stupid? Are you deaf? Are you all deaf? My father will take this complaint to the highest level. My husband will be waiting for me. Give me my baby back.' The woman clawed the air towards her baby as she spoke.

'See the gold bangles she wears? I bought them for her when she went for her confinement to her father's house. That gold necklace I purchased from Madras when our son was born. I have been generous, tolerant, forgiving. What more can a man be?' The young man looked around the bus. He could see many people shaking their heads and tut-tutting sagely.

'Get the fellow and the baby off the bus; she will follow quietly,' the driver yelled to the conductor impatiently.

The young woman began to scream again. 'I don't know this man. Give me back my baby! Tell them! Tell them! Someone tell them to give me back my baby!'

She followed them out of the bus onto the crossroads, where the young man had put down the small bags. She looked at the baby, now crying loudly in the conductor's arms, and suddenly fell at the young man's feet.

'Take my bangles, all my gold, I have money as well. Just give me back my baby. Let me go. I don't know you.'

Some passengers got down from the bus. The driver yelled at them to get back on, but they remained passive, standing in the cool shadow of the bus, looking on, waiting for something conclusive to happen. A couple of the passengers wandered around to the other side of the bus and proceeded to relieve themselves against the culvert.

It was stiflingly hot in the stationary vehicle and there were impatient shouts from the passengers in the bus.

'Let's go, enough is enough.'

'These marital problems can't be sorted at a crossroads.'

'Look how the child suffers because of the parents.'

'Don't blame her alone; he must be beating her regularly.'

'Ask him if he got a decent dowry.'

From where I sat at my window, frozen to the spot, I could see that the baby had nearly cried himself blue, while his mother threw the contents of her purse out onto the road at the young man's feet.

'Look, at least I know my son will recognise me,' said the young man and took the screaming baby from the conductor. The child stopped crying instantly and everyone sighed and smiled in relief. The child knew its father and the matter was resolved. The young man rocked the baby lovingly and made soothing noises. The driver tooted his horn and everyone got back on. The woman ran to the door screaming and banging on the side of the bus. The young man sat on the culvert, still talking to the child in his arms. The woman ran back to the young man, shaking. The fruit vendors were the last to board, having waited until the last minute in order to direct several spurts of their red, tobacco-stained spittle at the whitewashed culvert. As the bus pulled away, I watched with relief the young man give the baby back to its mother and then pick up all the bags.

The rest of the journey to Bangalore was subdued, even though the consensus was that the matter had been concluded satisfactorily. Some people thought it was obvious that the woman was spoilt. By her brothers and her father, for wasn't it very clear she was an only daughter? The fruit vendors suggested that this is what happened when a city girl married a man from such a rural backwater. Why, the nearest cinema was fifty miles away! The bus conductor laughed that explanation off. The trouble, he said, was that the husband had spoilt her and was now ruing the day. Why would a man buy anything for a wife like that?

Once back on the highway, we stopped as scheduled at Kolar and Hoskote. An hour later, people on the bus were still discussing marital problems of every sort, with solutions, both practical and far-fetched, being offered.

'Nothing new – perhaps she is afraid because he beats her, but then maybe she is a difficult wife. One thing I can tell you, this kind of drama happens all the time.' Brylcreem man and my stout neighbour were arguing about the frequency of such strange domestic incidents on public buses.

'My daughter has been brought up in a very responsible manner. Anyway, if she has problems, she only has to ask for help in her prayers. Sai Baba will watch over her always.'

'Baba watches us all.' Brylcreem man had the last word.

We arrived in Bangalore forty minutes behind schedule. I waited beside the bus and soon spotted my cousins weaving their way through the throng of people at the city's enormous Kalaspalayam Bus Station. As I waved to them, I saw a man tap the conductor on his shoulder. Trepidation had me rooted to the spot even before he spoke.

'Have you seen a woman with a child – my wife and child? They were to have travelled on this bus.'

Then, before I knew it, my cousins descended on me and I was enveloped in several bear hugs, warm embraces and gentle reprimands for having put on a bit of weight. When I was finally able to disentangle myself, the man and the conductor were nowhere to be seen.

For the next few days, I remained obsessed, scouring the papers, even getting my cousins to buy the regional Kannada language dailies to see if anything untoward had been reported. Nothing was ever mentioned about a missing woman and child and I was urged by my cousins to stop thinking about the incident.

'Scores of men come to meet their wives and children off the buses. It was just a coincidence – the husband you saw must have been at the wrong platform,' one cousin said.

'Enough now of scanning the news. You are on holiday, remember? And anyway, this is India not Ireland. Single casualties never make the headlines,' said another.

More than a decade on, I often wonder about the fate of the young woman and her child. Was she a victim of the callous indifference of her fellow travellers or were we all innocent – the gullible and trusting prey of an audacious and cruel con man? Or was she, as I will always hope, just a reluctant wife, a victim of my imagination?

# MARIAN KEYES

# TELL THE PEOPLE IN IRELAND: AN ETHIOPIAN JOURNEY

In September 2002, I was asked to visit Ethiopia with Concern. This is the diary of my trip.

*Thursday 5 September*
Myself and himself visit Concern's Dublin office for final briefing. Suddenly I realise how tough this trip is going to be, wish I wasn't going and curse myself for ever saying I would. Despite their assurances that we'll have a great time, and that there's a lovely market just outside Concern's Addis compound, I'm not convinced. Himself also has the fear.

*Monday 9 September*
9 a.m. Leave for airport to fly to London, then to Alexandria, then on to Addis Ababa. Delays in London; more delays in Egypt.

*Tuesday 10 September*
3.30 a.m. (two and a half hours late) We land at Addis Ababa airport, then hang around the carousel for a very long time until it becomes clear that our suitcase hasn't made the journey with us. But it'll be on the next flight, the nice man tells us. Which is on Friday. But today is Monday, I protest. Tuesday actually, he says.

All we have are the clothes we stand up in, a copy of *Vanity Fair* (read) and a selection of snacks purloined from an airport lounge. Nothing for it but to go and meet our poor driver, who has been waiting outside since one thirty.

4.45 a.m. Arrive at the Concern compound.

5 a.m. Head hits pillow.

5.01 a.m. Cock crows.

5.02 a.m. Another cock crows. Then four hundred of his closest friends get in on the act. A sound system kicks into life blasting Ethiopian pop. Ah yes, the market just beyond the wall.

9.30 a.m. Wake up, put on our dirty clothes and go to introduce ourselves to the Concern staff. It's a gorgeous morning, with blue, blue skies. In the distance I see lush green hills – surely some mistake? Where are the sun-bleached deserts?

Concern staff very nice, offer to loan us clothes and suggest the market beyond the wall would be a good place to buy underwear, etc. A mixture of fear and curiosity propels myself and himself though the gates and into downtown Addis and, I swear to God, it was like going back to biblical times. A dusty red-earth road teeming with life – tall, elegant men in robes and wellingtons, women with babies tied to their backs, a man wearing a sheep around his neck like a scarf, donkeys laden with enormous bundles of firewood, mad quavery music coming from somewhere. The only non-biblical note was the minibuses, beeping like mad as they struggled through the packed street, trying to disperse the herds of goats loitering in their path. (And the wellingtons.) Blankets spread on the roadside were offering all kinds of things for sale: onions, tomatoes, batteries, lengths of twine, chickens (live and unplucked), firewood and – oh great! – socks and knickers. The socks were fine, the knickers less so – baggy and funny-looking. But what the hell! When in Rome. The price for two pairs of socks and two pairs of funny pink knickers? Twenty birr – about two euro. Excellent value. We'd been told to haggle but how could you? On to the next stall, where we purchased two pairs of underpants for himself, a T-shirt for fifty birr, and a pair of plastic sandals for me for eighty birr.

12.30 p.m. Decked out in our new and borrowed finery, we set off to see some of the Concern projects. Addis is a city constructed almost entirely of corrugated iron; miles and miles of shanty town, holes in the rotting iron patched pitifully with rush matting and polythene bags. Almost all roads are untarmacked: just bare lumpy earth like boreens, which I've never before seen in a city. And everywhere there are people – it's incredibly densely populated. An estimated five million people live in Addis.

Our first stop was at a community-based urban-development programme, where Concern is working with the poorest of the poor – households headed by women and households with more than ten members – to construct houses, communal kitchens (one between three households), water points, latrines and roadways. Concern provides most of the funding but the community provides the labour and becomes responsible for maintaining the common areas.

One of the many people I met was a beautiful woman called Darma – by and large the Ethiopians are extremely good-looking. Darma has nine children, her husband is 'gone', and she's younger than I am. With great pride, she ushered us into her new house – a ten-by-ten room with a packed-earth floor, no electricity and no running water. With a smile she indicated the roof – 'no holes, so no rain gets in', which would turn the mud floor into a quagmire. I was beginning to understand. The sturdy walls provoked another smile – 'secure against rats'. Gotcha.

Darma's day begins at six, when she prepares breakfast for herself and her children. This is harder than it sounds. The staple diet is injera: a bread that's made from a grass called teff, which has to be pounded into a paste – a process that takes up to two hours – and then cooked. Before Concern funded the communal kitchens, Darma had to light a fire in her chimney-less home, which filled it with choking smoke and upset her children. After breakfast, Darma walks half an hour to the wholesale market, buys potatoes and onions, then returns and sells them in her own neighbourhood. At six in the evening, she comes home and once again pounds teff until her hands blister. She goes to bed around midnight.

But life is so much better, she says. She has the kitchen, the communal water point – which saves an hour a day walking to buy water – and most of all, her house. I was humbled by her positivity and hoped I'd think twice the next time I wanted to say, I've had a hard day.

Before I left, I was invited to admire the latrines, which I did as best I could – I mean, what do you *say*? – and then it was on to a clinic that feeds and treats thirty-six malnourished children. By the time we arrived, they'd left, which I was shamefully glad about. I didn't think I was able for the sight of three dozen malnourished babas.

Back in the Concern house, I suddenly remembered that today was my birthday. Himself's present for me was in the awol suitcase. However, he gave me a celebratory Club Milk he'd nicked from the Aer Lingus lounge in Dublin. I was very happy.

*Wednesday 11 September*
New Year's Day. And 1995, no less. Something to do with a dispute over the date of the birth of Christ. Great hilarity (at least on my part) as himself dons his Ethiopian knickers – very little and snug, Bruce Lee *circa* 1977. Great hilarity (at least on his part) as I don mine – baggy and mad, like a granny's.

11 a.m. Visit a Concern-funded project which aims to educate and train girls. This is a very macho society and I'd been told that Ethiopian women would have a better life if they'd been born donkeys. They have much less chance of receiving an education than a man, yet often end up being the main breadwinner, as well as doing the 'invisible' work like childcare, taking care of sick relatives, cooking, carrying water and tending the animals.

This project nails its colours firmly to the mast: the sign on the office wall reads, 'God created man before woman. The reason why? Every artist does a rough draft before creating a masterpiece.' Right on, sisters!

We visit a girls' school they're building; it will provide education for two hundred pupils when it opens in late September. Dozens of amber-eyed children appear from nowhere to shake hands (even the toddlers do it) and have their photos taken.

2 p.m. Then on to the training project, where thirty young women are taught to sew, and learn silkscreen printing and batik. They're also taught basic business skills and – best of all – computer skills.

3.30 p.m. Next we went to a vocational-skills training project for street children. There are an estimated sixty thousand children and young mothers living permanently on Addis Ababa's streets, where they're at the mercy of anyone and everyone, including the police. This project aims to make them employable by training them in all kinds of disciplines – from driving to metalwork to office skills.

I was introduced to a twenty-year-old girl, a graduate of the programme. She looked like Lauryn Hill – like, *exquisite* – and asked me not to use her name. Both her parents died when she was sixteen, and she had to take care of her three sisters and two brothers by washing clothes and gathering and selling firewood. Her income was so low that prostitution was the next step, either for herself or her younger sisters. But instead, she managed to get a place on a training course. Now she earns 340 birr a month as a cook (good money, honestly), is able to rent a house for herself and her siblings, and is going for lessons in computer skills, and paying for herself.

When I asked her what her parents had died of, she bowed her head, began to cry and didn't answer. Later the director of the programme told me that she has never said, but he suspects they died of Aids. Despite the fact that at least one in ten and maybe as many as one in six adult Ethiopians are HIV positive, few will admit to being affected by it.

Two ex-street children are among the many other success stories of the project. They are working for Ethiopia's previous president as a cook and a housekeeper.

It was an uplifting and energising day. Back at the ranch, we watched *The Young and the Restless*, a spectacularly awful American daytime soap, and spent a happy hour trying to figure out which ones were the young and which ones were the restless. It was strangely compelling.

*Thursday 12 September*

5.30 a.m. Several of us travelled in a packed four-wheel drive to Damot Weyde, a six-hour journey to the south. This area was the scene of a famine in 2000, and this year the rains didn't come, so the maize harvest has failed and once again the people are facing a famine.

On the drive down, we passed field after field of burnt

dead maize. But otherwise, the countryside was spectacularly beautiful: it was surprisingly green, with lots of trees, and high mountain ranges layered against the blue sky. When I asked why the trees were not cut down to free up the land for food, I was told that they prevented soil erosion, already a huge problem which further exacerbates drought. Also contributing to the appearance of lush vegetation is a plant called insett, or 'false banana'. It's a slow-growing but drought-resistant plant, which has the large wax leaves of the banana plant but only the roots are edible (after being pounded for three hours). So although the area is facing a famine, it's called a 'green famine'.

Always the roadsides were swarming with people; even though it's a rural area, it's densely populated – 250 people per square kilometre. Twice we passed people carrying a stretcher, making their way with a sick friend or relative to the nearest clinic.

9.30 a.m. Stopped for breakfast in Shashemene, a town which has a large Rastafarian community. I had to restrain himself; he's always nursed a desire to run away and become a Rasta.

12 noon. Arrive at Concern's compound, twenty kilometres off a tarmacked road and no phone line. But there is electricity and as everyone kept telling me, their faces aglow, there's a shower, a *hot* shower. And a toilet? I asked. Yes. Well, an outside latrine, which is the same thing really. I'm not really an outside-latrine kind of girl. But I was about to become one.

1.30 p.m. After a quick lunch, we head off to visit a well that Concern had built. However, it had been raining and the four-wheel drive got stuck in the mud. We all had to get out, and as I clambered down, I landed on a donkey, which gave me a patient, I-won't-hold-it-against-you look and carried on up the hill.

We turned back and instead went to visit Itanish, a local woman who'd been trained by Concern to teach her community about nutrition and hygiene, but, most importantly, how to take care of malnourished children. Previously if a child was malnourished, the mother would take it to a Concern feeding centre, where mother and child would stay until both were healthy. This could take up to three weeks. Meanwhile, no one was at home to take care of the mother's other children; nor could the mother earn money during that time. This scheme helps to avoid those problems by returning control and responsibility to the community. All of Concern's work is about 'sustainability' – they are enabling the people in the community to do things for themselves, so that when Concern leaves (all NGOs have to move on after three years), the locals will be well able to look after themselves.

But Itanish was nowhere in sight – they'd all gone to 'the weeping' – a lyrical way of describing a funeral. Right so, we said, girding our loins. We'll visit the Kerchech health clinic.

Back into the four-by-four and after another bumpy hour on muddy roads, we arrived at the three-roomed clinic, just as a young woman called Erberke was arriving with her husband, Bassa, and their sick baby girl, Jelsalem. They'd walked for forty minutes in their bare feet to reach us because Jelsalem was passing blood; she was fifteen months old, but she was so stick-like and shrunken that she looked like an infant of three months. Bassa, was wearing what might have once been Farrah slacks but which were now a collection of rags held together with yellow twine. I'd seen so many sad things but, for whatever reason, this was the one that did it for me. I couldn't stop crying.

Doctor Degu Tinna, who runs the clinic and visits patients on the motorbike purchased by Concern, examined Jelsalem and found she was seventy-five per cent of the weight she should have been, but she wasn't showing signs of oedema, which is caused by protein deficiency. He gave her antibiotics.

The local method for dealing with an infant with diarrhoea is to burn the baby's stomach. (Likewise, eye infections are 'treated' by branding the temples.) It was horrific to think that if the clinic hadn't been there, Jelsalem would have died.

8 p.m. Dinner that night was the famous injera bread. It was grey and looked like a rolled-up sponge but it had a pleasant taste. Had to get up twice in the night to use the outside latrine. Didn't get eaten by leopards.

*Friday 13 September*
7 a.m. Set off to visit another well but once again got bogged down in the mire. This time we pressed on and arrived at 9 a.m. Yay!

The well was a godsend – clean water for washing, cooking and, most important of all, for drinking. Before the well was built, the only option was the dirty water from the nearby river – so filthy that a glass of it looked as opaque as drinking chocolate.

It was all go at the well. Ofusi, a thirteen-year-old stunner, was washing her family's clothes, scrubbing like billy-o with a bar of soap. Salem, a ten-year-old girl, was filling a five-litre container of water for her home an hour's walk away. But what I noticed most was that a lot of the children clustering around me looked sick. Their teeth were brown and most of them seemed to have an eye infection. Flies were landing in babies' mouths, and some of the children's skin was patchy and piebald-looking. I thought I remembered reading that this was an indication of oedema. The effects of chronic food deprivation were staring me in the face. They pressed closer and closer to me but remained silent, and for the first time since I'd arrived in Ethiopia, I felt slightly freaked out.

On the way back, we passed several women working in the fields, including one called Tefari who was seven months pregnant. Then we got to meet Itanish at last; the work she was doing with the women in her area would ensure that the malnourished children would recover. This news cheered me up.

11 a.m. Drive back to Addis.

5 p.m. Our suitcase has arrived! Because I'd had a week living with just the basics, I'd suspected that I'd have no interest in it, but I'm sorry to say how wrong I was. I fell on it like it was a long-lost friend and marvelled at my lovely things. My face cream! My sunglasses! My anti-malaria tablets!

6.30 p.m. Attended an open-air concert to raise awareness of HIV/Aids among the young and homeless in the Merkato area, a huge market that has a lot of prostitution. I wasn't expecting much, but I swear to God, I've never seen anything so wonderful. On stage, three slender, elegant boys and three gorgeous girls in traditional dress were dancing like Irish people wouldn't be able to dance if they practised for a million years. Imagine people receiving electric shocks, but *gracefully*, and you get some idea of how extraordinary their performance was. And they were having such fun, it was a delight to behold. The concert (a monthly event) is the brainchild of Anania Admassu, a very energetic and intelligent man who runs a Concern-funded project that helps Aids orphans. There are a huge number in Addis – one thousand in the Merkato area alone.

*Saturday 14 September*
9.30 a.m. Visited Concern's Street Vendors' Programme, which gives basic business skills and low-interest, collateral-free loans to the poorest street traders (nearly always women). Hundreds of women have had their lives changed by this programme, and most of them have even managed to start saving.

Part of the programme has involved the construction of

several latrines and I was invited to visit a couple. Well, one latrine is much the same as another, as far as I'm concerned, and though they tried to persuade me to view the facilities, I stood my ground, despite their obvious disappointment.

2 p.m. The last gig. A visit to Mekdim, an association run and staffed by HIV-positive people, who provide education, medical help, counselling, home nursing, and funeral expenses for those with the virus.

HIV/Aids is an enormous problem in Ethiopia. Because of extreme poverty, many women have no choice but to become prostitutes – it's either that or let themselves and their children starve. Nor is the situation helped by the attitude of the government, which until recently was denying the spread of the disease. Now, rather late in the day, it has admitted that the problem has reached epidemic proportions.

Mekdim is run by Tenagne Alemu, a charismatic man who has lived with the virus for thirteen years – 'drug free', everyone kept telling me. Like an eejit, I thought he was drug free for some valid reason. But not at all. He is drug free because he can't afford the drugs. The miracle antiretroviral drugs, which are saving the lives of the thousands and thousands of HIV-positive people in the developed world, are far beyond the reach of Ethiopians.

I met one of the home-carers. She was a beautiful and articulate twenty-nine-year-old who discovered she was HIV positive when her three-year-old daughter became sick and died. No one could tell her what her daughter had died from, but she'd heard about 'the sickness' and suspected the worst. Her husband had been her first sexual partner, so she'd caught it from him. As you can imagine, her life fell apart. She divorced him and was going to kill herself when she heard that Mekdim were looking for people to train as home-carers.

This woman is constantly coming down with infections. She is ostracised by her peers. (She wouldn't let me take her photo because she was harassed enough, she said.) There are antiretroviral drugs which can help her but they aren't available in Ethiopia because they're so expensive. And the number of those infected with the virus – particularly women – continues to escalate.

'I'm angry,' she said with vehemence. 'I'm always so angry. Will you tell the people in Ireland we need their help?' she asked.

So I'm telling you.

# CATHERINE DUNNE

## RICHARD NIXON AND THE PAST IMPERFECT

I am sitting in the middle seat of three. Even before take-off, I am feeling squashed, wedged uneasily between two large bodies. On my right is an elderly gentleman whose toupee is to be the object of endless fascination during the three-and-a-half-hour flight. Right now, it is sitting comfortably, all bases covered. At a discreet distance from this head, you could almost be fooled. Up close and personal, however, the texture is a dead giveaway. Smooth, shiny, flat – too even, too groomed and too *compact,* somehow, for hair. Then there are the coarse tufts of real stuff which sprout eagerly from everywhere else, perhaps in compensation: ears, cheeks, nose and neck – or at least, the couple of inches of flesh visible above a none-too-clean collar – all are randomly planted with sedge-like growths of grey. I am careful not to make eye contact. This man needs no company; he is already deep in nervous, fractured conversation with himself.

To my left is a thirty-something Spaniard trying desperately to look twenty. The insistence of his cologne vies for attention. Occasionally it vies for attention with the heady hum of black tobacco, a darker note below the sharp fruitiness of scent and perspiration. Sure enough, a blue and white packet of Ducados peeps from the pocket of the man's shirt, the cellophane crackling every time he moves. And he is a restless man. He fiddles with his watch, mops the high dome of his forehead with a scented handkerchief and uses the in-flight safety leaflet to fan himself manically, although it is not hot, not even by my standards. It's late August and it's cool, raining. I decide that my travelling companion must be in thrall to some kind of absent, learned behaviour. We are, after all, still on the tarmac at Dublin airport. I am impatient to be gone. I am aware that any further delay will narrow the gap between acceptable self-containment and the imperative of politeness that will hurtle us all towards strained conversation.

I am not yet experienced enough to know that the seasoned traveller *never* picks the middle seat: it's the aisle or die. But I'm learning.

I'm eighteen, fresh out of school. Highlights for hair have just been invented, except that they're called 'streaks'. I have them. They're only two weeks old, the result of my first, long-lusted-after visit to Dublin's only fashionable hair salon, The Witches' Hut – although I don't think they used the apostrophe back then. I also have a brand new pair of platform sandals in beige suede, a dark brown above-the-knee skirt, a cream jacket (non-creasing) and a blouse with vast, rounded collar tips. I can still recall every detail, down to the bunch of fake cherries pinned jauntily to my right lapel. I've been away from home before, of course – but not like this. This is an Adventure, grown-up stuff. I'm off to Work, to Teach, to Learn Spanish, to Live My Life Doing Things that Require Capital Letters. Adult Things. For a Year. On My Own.

Well, not quite on my own. My accommodation is to be

family-based bed and board, traded for some baby-minding, nappy-changing, housework. But only in the mornings; the afternoons, the evenings, the nights are all mine.

I can hardly wait.

Meanwhile, several thousand miles away, a whole nation is about to embark on an Adult Adventure of its own. As we prepare for take-off, President Nixon declares that John Dean has just completed his investigation into the Watergate break-in, and the White House has been found to be blameless. No White House involvement of any degree or any kind, declares investigating counsel, also White House. Well, that's all right, then. The small matter of a cheque for 25,000 dollars, which has apparently wandered vacantly away from Nixon's re-election campaign, only to find itself in the account of one of the Watergate burglars, is not mentioned.

I'm only trying to learn Spanish, whereas Americans must now begin to struggle with a whole new language, in which the rules keep changing. Deep grammar becomes deep cover and the biggest covert operation of all is to discover where the truth might be hiding. The most powerful, the most respected, the most revered of citizens misspeak themselves, suffer major lapses in memory and run for cover, while five burglars begin the process of unravelling the fabric of the state.

At Madrid, a wall of heat hits me. I navigate the steps down to the tarmac, careful not to fall off my platforms. I'd forgotten about the heat, the glorious, smoke-scented intensity of it. Underneath my feet, the tar is sticky. The terminal building shimmers in the distance. Mr Toupee, two steps in front of me, tugs gently at his hair, then pats it firmly into place. I'd watched as it inched its way forward while he slept, his head nodding and jerking off my shoulder from time to time.

Mr Spaniard, unfortunately, hadn't slept. Nor had he read. He smoked, drank whiskey, called for a steward on three separate occasions. Each time, he fired a volley of abuse in staccato Spanish, his hands gesticulating furiously, so that he seemed possessed of not one, but two angry voices – he did *not* take ice in his whiskey; hadn't he made that clear? He wanted *three aspirinas* for his headache, not two – he had a very *large* headache, *por Dios*. He needed mineral water *con gas* – how long was he supposed to wait for something so simple? A different steward responded to his call each time – can't say I blamed them. Young, dark-eyed, with crisp white shirts and Iberian epaulettes – I didn't mind the variety, not at all. They were endlessly courteous, too. I kept on reading, pretending I didn't understand, couldn't speak any Spanish. My heart sank when my travelling companion barked something at the steward about his destination – Valencia.

As soon as we land, I prepare to make good my escape.

I keep a furtive eye out for both men in the baggage hall. To my amazement, Mr Toupee marches straight through, carrying only a battered leather briefcase. I wonder what business he can possibly have in Madrid – vibrant, cosmopolitan, elegant Madrid. I wonder what his story is.

I spot my Spaniard in the distance and allow him to check in before me. I keep a watchful distance and join the queue for Valencia long after he has marched purposefully away, fanning himself with his boarding pass.

This time, I ask for the aisle seat.

My new family is waiting for me at Valencia airport: Francisco José, Maribel, and Isabel, their tiny, blue-eyed daughter. I am instantly nervous: I hadn't realised she would be so *small*. My baby-sitting experience has been limited to toddlers, positively hulk-like creatures compared to this doll in elf's clothing. I am to learn, however, that the strength of her will is matched only by the power of her lungs – a spectacular combination that leaves all known toddlers and their tantrums in the ha'penny place. Must be that colourful Latin temperament, tuned early and often to withstand the decibel level of family rows, arguments on buses, shouting matches on streets.

My Spaniard is also greeted by his family, a stunning wife and two black-eyed little boys who cling, one to each leg, shouting, 'Papá! Papá!' I am astonished at the instant transformation. The man laughs out loud, hugs his wife, throws his sons in the air, clearly delighting in the happy terror of their whoops. In a heartbeat, he has changed from boorish to bonhomie – a bit like those racing cars that accelerate from nought to ninety in six seconds.

Only then it hits me how the man must be terrified of flying. I could have been kinder, more friendly.

The departing figures of small boys clinging to a loving Papá seem to say that things are not always what they appear to be.

I hope that my jaw hasn't dropped, but I can't be sure. *Piso* translates as 'floor, storey or flat'. But this is nothing like any 'flat' I've ever seen in 1970s Dublin – dingy, grime-encrusted buildings synonymous with poverty and deprivation. This is a vast living area, glossy-magazine kitchen, two bathrooms, three bedrooms and a *pantry* – this is a big house, a proper house; it's simply *on* the flat. I am to visit many more *pisos* over the next twelve months, all of them reflecting, more or less, their owners' relative affluence. I am very taken with the idea of living right in the city centre – Spaniards build *up*, it seems, not *out*. Young people don't seem as hung up on the notion of ownership, either, I've noticed. Renting is just fine by them.

Two weeks on and I've landed my first teaching job. I feel something of a fraud. Most of my pupils are considerably older than their teacher. The Instituto Mangold is a solid, reputable language school, already locking horns with Berlitz and other private institutions in the suddenly burgeoning marketplace of 'English Lessons with Native Speaker'. The whole world, it seems, wants to speak English. I teach from four in the afternoon until ten o'clock at night, three days a week. Six classes, one after the other, quick smoke-breaks snatched in between, amid the mêlée of students leaving and students entering. It's not too bad – but then I have no previous work experience with which to compare it. Two afternoons a week, I give more intensive, more lucrative, one-to-one lessons, preparing their content as I make Isabel's breakfast, change her, bath her and run the daily gauntlet of dressing her. The child is a born naturist.

I struggle every morning with English grammar, too: all those words, phrases, constructions heretofore taken for granted now need to be explained, tied down, imprisoned – my students will accept nothing short of certainty, immutable rules, finite numbers of exceptions. I make out lists of examples to illustrate the perfect tense, the formation of plurals, the use of *El Genitivo Sajón* – the Saxon genitive, something I never even knew existed. I try to reduce the peculiarities of English to a safe, predictable set of sensible regulations. My students don't like surprises.

In the dog-days of September, in Washington, Bob Woodward and Carl Bernstein are busy cooking up surprises of their own. Not so much cooking, perhaps, as *serving* – no amount of braising, boiling or roasting could make these revelations palatable. Spanish magazines, newspapers, TV and radio broadcasts all begin to resound with the same names: Howard Hunt, Gordon Liddy, John Mitchell – I still can hear those names today, only with Spanish intonation. My language-learning has to twist, tango, quickstep to the beat of the first global political scandal I've ever known. My vocabulary explodes. I learn the language of corruption.

Newscasters become more excited, commentators more exercised, journalists more incisive as they all struggle to steal a march on one another in satisfying the public appetite for scandal. This is opera, Greek tragedy, flamenco, even. In Franco's Spain, Watergate is just as flamboyant, as compelling, as arousing as Gypsy dance – and it takes your mind off your troubles at home. Spain watches, at a safe distance, what promises to be the downfall of the world's most powerful leader.

Six weeks before my departure to Ireland for Christmas, I cross the Plaza del Caudillo, plane ticket in hand, delighted at my bargain-basement flight. I feel lucky, so I buy a lottery ticket from the blind man sitting on the path, his crutches beside him. His legs are two blunt stumps – another Civil War veteran. Most of them in their mid-fifties, these veterans are all over the city, maimed, crippled, blinded. It takes me months not to feel an overwhelming horror at their predicament. Then more months to get over the shame of no longer feeling it.

They seem stoical, these silent men, these *mutilados*, resigned to the hand fate has dealt them. Their sightless fingers count out the change for each lottery-ticket buyer, day in, day out. They never, ever, get it wrong.

The newspaper kiosks seem even busier than usual today. I don't pay much attention – I'm already in danger of being late for Immaculada's lesson on the subjunctive, not nearly as perilous a mood in English as it is in Spanish. On my final leg of the *plaza*, I see what all these people are queuing up to buy. The banner headlines scream at me: what had once seemed certain downfall is now nothing of the kind. Nixon has just been re-elected in one of the largest landslides in American political history. He gets sixty per cent of the vote, while Senator George McGovern limps off the stage, into the wings, crushed.

Things are, indeed, not what they seem.

In January, I acquire a boyfriend. He has been hovering for some time, always on the outskirts of the group of us who do everything together. We've gone native, this motley crew of Irish, Scottish, English, with a handful of Valencianos thrown in; just like the Spanish teenagers themselves, we hunt in packs. Eight, nine, ten of us head for the coast every weekend, to the then quiet town of Jávea. One of our number is fortunate enough to own parents who own a villa by the sea. They, of course, are horrified by the outdoors in winter. We are delighted. It is our first winter ever without coal fires, chilblains and head colds. It also means a cheap weekend, where we play loud music, eat an eclectic mix of foods, and laugh and argue long into the night, fuelled by cheap – but excellent – Spanish wine. We pile into three cars every Friday, load up the guitars and the LPs, and spend forty-eight hours setting the world to rights.

The young Valenciano men, at first, can't believe their luck. The age of chaperoning is not yet dead in Spain and there is a belief abroad that foreign girls have looser morals. Their learning curve is steep and fast: thirty years ago, Scottish, English and Irish young women were possessed of a common perspective, a shared emotion far stronger than lust. Fear, we agreed, is the most effective contraceptive of them all.

The three Valenciano members of our group are all medical students. Ricardo, who finally hovers shyly but definitively in my direction, is in third year. Medicine is the ultimate middle-class aspiration: *Nuestro hijo, médico*. Our son, the doctor. As it happens, this is also Ricardo's own choice. His parents keep him on a tight leash – not because he is in any sense a tearaway, but because he is quietly, solidly, committedly anti-Franco. He must pay, by enduring strict financial constraints, for the privilege of disagreeing with his parents.

There is a growing feeling among Ricardo's contemporaries that things must change, that Franco can't live forever, that an alternative must be ready to seize the day for democracy. In the meantime, they watch and wait.

Starved of anything that approaches political commentary on their own troubles, Spaniards continue to wallow in the washing of the White House dirty linen. In February, the Watergate Seven are found guilty of conspiracy, burglary and wire-tapping. On the eve of my nineteenth birthday, the American Senate votes by 77 to 0 to create the Select Committee on Presidential Campaign Activities. Humpty Dumpty isn't falling off his wall yet – just teetering nervously as it begins to collapse underneath him. This time, I don't even need the dictionary. While my students struggle with the past imperfect tense, I am now dreaming and counting in Spanish – sure signs, I'm told, that I'm well on my way to mastering the language.

Other lessons are harder, however. It's Friday and I'm packing a small bag, ready for Jávea. Isabel's grandmother, Mercedes, accosts me. A tiny woman, she is formidable – in direct inverse proportion to her physical size. She terrifies me. In typical, self-absorbed teenager fashion, I've spent months considering nobody's needs but my own. Maribel, it seems, has wearily made enquiries about hiring a baby-sitter for Isabel while she and her husband go to a wedding. I am told, in no uncertain terms by powerful, wiry Mercedes, her glasses glinting, that this behaviour is absolutely unacceptable: *insoportable*. Too bad about the plans, she rails, too bad about the birthday celebrations, do what you contracted to do. Your parents taught you better.

I am mortified. My crime is heedlessness – the preserve of the very young. I have been tried, found guilty, and sentenced forthwith to a life of responsibility and maturity, of duty – *obligación*. There follows an afternoon that Atticus Finch would have approved of: putting on someone else's shoes and walking around in them. I have the grace to apologise, tearfully; my Spanish family has the grace to forgive me.

I change Isabel's clothes and, for once, she doesn't fight me. Then I wheel her to the park. At ten months, she's beginning to take her first, faltering steps – that splayed-leg approach to walking that makes every toddler look like John Wayne. I take both her hands and encourage her towards me. She is uncertain, takes two steps, sways a little, tries again.

I know just how she feels.

April brings Easter and holidays. I have learned to negotiate now, both at home and at work, about things like free time and hourly rates. I travel to Granada – this time, in Spanish company only. I feel almost at the end of a process: I am now as comfortable in Spanish as I am in English, and long enough in the country to see the warts of a society that at first had appeared close to perfect. The Alhambra is thrilling, filled with the dark presence of the Moors and the blinding light of water.

I stand at Tarifa, the most southern point of Spain, windswept, exhilarated. If I reach my hand out, I can just touch the coast of Africa. This is living, I think. My universe has expanded to such an extent that I can barely remember who I was in Dublin. There is that tangible sense of being grown up, of the limitless possibilities of life, of future. It is one of those perfect moments: a heady mix of insight, euphoria and minor-key wisdom. Thirty years later, that moment still is as vivid as it was on a stunning, blue, April afternoon.

When I get back to the car, my bag has been stolen. Although we've all pooled resources for this trip, the other three are strapped-for-cash students. One supplied the car, another the house we were staying in, another most of the food. My role is that of bursar. Now we cut short the trip and head back to Valencia, picking up pesetas off the floor of the car to pay for petrol on the return journey. Nobody shouts, nobody blames, nobody asks why I was stupid enough to leave a bag in the car in the first place. In the land of Franquista repression and a brutal Guardia Civil, such theft is astonishingly rare, but nobody cares to remember that now.

The long journey home is a silent one. I feel an excruciating sense of failure. Somehow, our group never quite recovers. Exams, deadlines, extra classes take over and we meet only sporadically. Ricardo forgives me, of course, but very soon he comes under pressure of a new and more refined kind. He confesses, finally, that his parents are giving him a hard time over the Irish girlfriend they've never met.

For the first time in my life, I feel the weight of class, the uptight, buttoned-down methods of preserving privilege. I learn what it is not to live up to the expectations of others. I am struck, too, at how repression filters all the way down the system. Total obedience to El Caudillo means total obedience to Mum and Dad. For the first time in eight months, I miss my home – my Irish home.

Isabel no longer fights me in the mornings. I have learned to devise all sorts of games to divert her attention from the process of getting dressed. I like being with her; her needs are simple, direct, easily met. My bruised, rather than broken, heart means added energy in the classroom too. We play games there as well, and listen to records on the ancient turntable unearthed from the school's 'audio-visual' cupboard. Pop songs, mostly, that the younger students want to learn.

I teach the older ones a new verb – 'to compromise' – and we have fun with that too. *Compromiso* in Spanish has a whole other meaning – that of duty, obligation. It is one that I have already learned. That leads us on to other false cognates, false friends which promise what they do not deliver. *Constipado*, for example: the common head cold. Or *oposiciónes*: competitive state exams to enter the civil service. We discuss the gaps inherent in communication, the nuances of language, misunderstandings that arise out of social expectations and cultural differences.

We may not have all the words, but we make do with gesture, guessing, even sketching. Students start coming out with full sentences – it's as though some sort of critical mass has suddenly been achieved overnight. They even argue in English. I have hit my stride and begin to think that this *might* just be the way I'd like to earn my living.

All that summer, Nixon hurtles towards his inevitable downfall. But he doesn't give in without a fight. In June, John Dean tells the Watergate investigators that he discussed the cover-up with the President on at least thirty-five separate occasions. He speaks for seven hours, outlining the comprehensive programme of political espionage engaged in by the White House – with full Presidential knowledge.

I decide to sit the exam for the teachers' qualification in the Escuela Oficial de Idiomas in Madrid, in July. That piece of paper is very highly prized: it entitles its owner to teach English in the state language schools all over Spain. It's keeping my options open – a way of earning a real living should I decide to stay on. Only a very limited number of these coveted diplomas are issued. I have been warned that competition is stiff.

Two hundred or so of us line up before the off. I eye up the opposition. Mostly Spanish, mostly already qualified teachers, judging by their conversations. I figure I might have an advantage – particularly in the translation stakes. The dozen or so native English-speakers draw close to each other in the square outside the exam hall. Although we've never met each other before, it suddenly feels very much like a case of us against them.

I have to stay in Madrid overnight; results will be posted the following day. The plane ticket, the exam fee, the stay in the hostel all cripple my meagre resources. For forty-eight hours, I eat nothing but oranges, bought on the cheap in a small supermarket beside my hostel near the Puerta del Sol. The heat is a killer.

The results are posted at midday. I fail. So do all the other native speakers. One of our number is on the fourth attempt. He shrugs and figures if he keeps on trying for long enough, they'll let him in. I decide I don't want it that much, peel another orange and get on the bus to the airport.

Nixon moves the goalposts. Claiming Executive privilege, he refuses to testify before the Senate Committee. He also refuses to hand over any documents or tapes. The Senate Committee responds with a subpoena, which Nixon ignores. In August, the Senate makes an unprecedented move that has Spanish newspaper headlines blazing again: the investigators take legal action against their own President. August is indeed a wicked month.

By the time Spiro Agnew has resigned in October, and

Nixon's personal tax returns are under investigation, I'm back in Dublin. I've decided to take up my college place in Trinity, following the lucrative six weeks I've had as a temp in London.

My return to the English-speaking world was a strange one: language suddenly seemed blunt, without colour or texture. No flamboyance, no flamenco. I felt as though someone had cut my voice in half: I could no longer use my hands to emphasise, dismiss, convince. I was reminded time and again of my bolshie Spaniard on the outward journey – how I'd failed then to read the terror in his hand gestures, seeing only aggression.

I missed my Spanish pupils, too, and my Spanish family, particularly Isabel and her new baby brother. Thirty years later, all that connection is still intact: Isabel is married, with children of her own. Somehow the age gap between us now is a lot less than it was then.

I still followed all the newspaper and television reports, but somehow Watergate had lost its gloss. It was no longer exotic, no longer a challenge to dive for the dictionary in order to follow the global soap opera I'd been watching almost on a daily basis for over a year. Now it was just a tawdry, long-drawn-out battle of wills with occasional highlights, such as Nixon claiming, 'I am not a crook.' By that stage, he was well on the way to impeachment.

And the inevitable happened in Spain, too. At the end of a nauseatingly prolonged death – or life – Franco finally loosened his grip on the country after more than three decades. We got the news in the middle of a Spanish language class in Trinity College, we and our native-speaker teacher huddling over a transistor radio. There were tears, joy, celebration – and we started learning the language of change.

Spain had, finally, embarked on an Adult Adventure of its own.

And I was glad to be home.

# LOUISE EAST

# THE EXTRAORDINARY TALE OF HOW I NEARLY DIED THREE TIMES IN ONE WEEK

Over the years, I've written for *The Irish Times* about a ragbag of different travels, from Christmas in a Guatemalan orphanage to being rescued by the Flying Doctors in the Australian outback, but there's one story I've never put into print, one that's possibly the most astonishing of them all. It's not that it's secret; I've told it on quiet nights at the pub and at dinner parties when all that's left are cake crumbs and empty glasses. It's the story I pull out when backpacker credentials are being compared and I need to impress; it's my forty-five pound carp, my eyeball-to-eyeball encounter with a yeti. Now that I've decided to write about it, I realise that a small amount of fudging, polishing and juggling was performed every time the tale was told – an unconscious sleight of hand to make it quicker, more dramatic, more logical.

Usually, for instance, I describe the events that follow as taking place over the course of three days, yet I've just rooted out the sketchy diary I kept at the time and see it was nearer a week. At some point, I must have gathered three days of that week into one bunch, and in time, I forgot the elision too. Time has taken its toll as well; this happened in June 1996, almost seven years to the day before I start to write, and many of the finer details (the names, the distances, the timings) are blurred. But what has never been smudged is the true wonder of the story. Nor have I forgotten the sensation of living through something strange, something almost untellable. This then, is the extraordinary tale of how I nearly died three times in one week.

It took place in Colombia, which will surprise no one who has been there, or who has read *One Hundred Years of Solitude*. A huge fan of García Márquez, I had refused to expect the Colombia of his books; nothing, I thought, could be as vivid, spiritual, bizarre and harsh as that fictional world. I was wrong; Colombia's magic was quite real, its realism, quite magical. Although my nails were dug into my palms when I arrived, my head full of drug wars and terrorism, I stayed much longer than I had anticipated, never quite finding a good reason to leave. Four months later, despite an invitation to stay on in a near idyllic beach house inhabited by a motley crew of travellers – Colombians, Kogui Indians, two monkeys and a parrot – I realised I was tired of dividing myself between 'here' and 'home', tired of saying goodbye, tired of moving on. It was time to go home, but I had just one last port of call, a national park on the Caribbean coast, called Tayrona – a place that in its remote inaccessibility had become a kind of traveller El Dorado.

Former home to the Tayrona people, it combines hundreds of acres of thick jungle with a stunning coastline of rocks, like dinosaur eggs laid on golden yellow beaches. By that stage, I had taken on the independent traveller's neurotic search for virgin territory, and the best thing about Tayrona was its aura of impenetrability. No proper roads ran through the jungle; after the entrance gate some forty minutes off the main coast road, there was only a track, which took an hour by mule (if you were feeling flush) and nearer two otherwise. Accommodation was limited to camping, and amenities to a small café, a freshwater tap and some rough toilets. I was travelling with Ana, an Argentinian friend from the beach house, who was small and shaven-headed, a street performer who would never use ten words if twenty would do.

We pitched her small green tent under some palm trees near the water and settled into a feckless routine of swimming, reading, writing and painting, snoozing through the afternoons and making lazy plans to get home. Every day we discussed the idea of walking to Pueblito, an abandoned village some two hours inland, and every day we opted for more lotus-eating, and tomorrow. Eventually, with our supplies running low, talk of a huge, abundant avocado tree gave us energy, and we set off late in the morning but full of good intentions. There was no marked trail as such, just a wandering clear space in the otherwise dense jungle, then a snaking path made of those massive egg-shaped rocks. Rolled into place a long, long time ago, they gave the Tayrona of Pueblito a kind of remote security system; no one who did not know the sequence of jumps could approach – or leave – the village at speed.

In my mind's eye, I have always seen that day as luridly sunny and blue-skied, but two blurred photos I found with my diary show it to be overcast and heavy with brilliant white cloud. Although indistinct, the photos also show skeins of vine like spiders' webs, glinting streams and a distant waterfall like a smudge of chalk, while in my diary, I noted blue-tailed lizards and a long, wavering trail of ants, each carrying a tiny fragment of leaf. Pueblito itself was haunting, a place far from the sea winds and thick with an air of something interrupted: abandoned tumbledown buildings half reclaimed by the jungle, giant turquoise butterflies, a circle of avocados, rotting and oozing under a laden tree. I was glad to leave.

What happened next happened quickly and without drama. Sudden stomach cramps (a routine part of life) caused me to fall behind, and, hurrying to catch up, I absent-mindedly strayed off the path. Quickly, the ground became steep and the vegetation more insistent; a path can be a fairly dangerous thing, as it lets you forget what lies on either side. As I bounced downhill, still on my feet but not entirely in control of them, a Hollywood cast of snakes flashed through my mind, hooded, fanged and ready to strike. When a dart of pain went through one hand, it felt oddly inevitable, not shocking at all. Yet looking down at the tree trunk I had grabbed, it was not a slow coil of warm skin I saw, but a glistening hedgehog of white spines seamed onto the tree along one side. The spines were about nine inches long, the whole thing no bigger than a foot across, but I couldn't tell whether it was plant or insect, a pupa of some strange moth or a cactus dressed up in a Philip Treacy hat. All I knew was that it hurt like hell, and that I had fallen well behind the last of Pueblito's visitors.

I wasn't unduly worried though; stings happen, bites too. Shaking my hand and muttering curses to the trees, I retraced my steps and found the path again. Over the next ten minutes, the pain grew truly immense, and my cursing became correspondingly loud and angry, a mixture of bad Spanish and dirty English. When that pain started to travel slowly but unmistakably up my arm in a line approximating the faint blue of an artery, I started to panic. It was not the pain that was terrifying – it was the dull, dead paralysis it left in its wake; I could not move the fingers of my left hand, couldn't feel my own fingernails digging into my forearm. I began to run instead of walk, jumping from rock to rock and cradling my left arm with my right, while shouting for help.

No answer came, but something else did; a tingling in my

other arm, then the same creeping paralysis, and soon I had two arms crooked like ram's horns, without feeling or movement in either. When my feet started to tingle and lose feeling too, I sat down by a stream and wondered whether to go on. I remember clearly marvelling at the way life turns out, that I, who had always imagined myself dying in a nursing home in Rathmines, bored and fractious, chasing missing jigsaw pieces around a board, would instead meet my end here, on my own, surrounded by deep, impenetrable green. I couldn't do it; I got up and staggered on.

Daylight was starting to fade and although I knew the intermittent roars were packs of howler monkeys crashing through the trees, rather than tigers, they emphasised the ridiculous wildness on which I had intruded. I remember repeating the names of my family to keep myself calm. And I remember two Indians, probably Koguis from their all-white dress, who paused and looked at me, their faces smooth and blank, before continuing on their way, without comprehension. What I don't remember is exactly how I got myself back to camp, some two hours from where I was stung, only that I stumbled in, talking in Spanglish of a 'white thing that ate me', then collapsed into a hammock.

It was clear to everyone, even myself through the dark fog of my own panic, that arriving back among people had solved nothing other than the dilemma of whether to die alone or not. The only road was hours away through the jungle; the hospital in Santa Marta further away still, and even there, an easy antidote was unlikely. Thanks to Sting and his Amazon obsession, every good teenager of the 1980s knew the one about the four zillion undiscovered plants and insects in the jungles of South America. I had been stung by one of them. As I lay there, I distinctly heard the precise tones of a Swiss nurse camping nearby saying, 'It is extremely unlikely they will have a cure for this, even if we do get her there in time.'

It is at this point that things enter the realm of the fantastical; a hiatus in which coincidence, Fate and the miraculous decided to join the gathering. From out of the muzzy twilight walked a tall, thin medicine man leading a donkey laden with bags, plants, bottles and boxes. At the beach house, I had heard about these medicine men who walk from one end of the coast to the other and back. The villagers know they can rely on an appearance twice a year, and hoard up complaints, minor injuries and grievances for his arrival. He came and stood over me, listening to my description (nothing more than 'white, spines, bite') then returned with a bottle of liquid in which leaves were suspended. He poured some on my hand, and gave me the bottle to drink – it was bitter, backed with alcohol, unidentifiable. He lit a match and held it to the puffy sting. His eyes were very bloodshot, his skin very dark, and he smiled as he muttered an incantation. He could have been slightly drunk.

Taking both of my hands, he levered me upright, saying in Spanish, 'Dance with me, dance with me.' I was annoyed, I remember, irritated by his laughter, by his air of carelessness.

In all, the treatment took less than five minutes, then he turned back to his donkey with the words, 'You will have no feeling in the hand for twenty-four hours, then it will be fine.' He wouldn't hear of payment; it was hard to get him even to accept thanks as he continued down the beach, his pale trousers glowing in the dark.

It happened exactly as he said; over the next day, feeling gradually returned to my hands and feet. By the next evening, I was fine.

There are several different possible interpretations of what happened that day. It could be that he saved my life, that without his antidote and sorcery, I would have slowly ebbed away from the tents, the jungle and all thoughts of Rathmines's nursing homes. It's also possible I would have recovered anyway, that my rapidly increasing paralysis was caused by hyperventilation through panic, the bite of those white spines, nothing more than a nasty sting. I have always shied away from too rigorously analysing what happened, because it seems too blessedly magical to pigeonhole. It was a moment when life had the logic of a Grimm's fairy tale, and I was not interested in forcing it to behave otherwise. Working out the name and effect of the plant would require a return to the jungle and a battery of tests, and in the days that followed, hospital tests were the last thing on my mind.

After a few days of recovery, I caught a bus back to Santa Marta, from where I planned to catch a flight to the island of San Andrés, a peculiar duty-free island off the coast of Nicaragua, through which cheap flights to and from Colombia are routed. From Guatemala City I had an open ticket back to Ireland, a place that seemed impossibly distant, exotic and remote by then. I read on the bus (*Don Quixote*, my diary tells me), blessed with a window seat and a road that was fairly straight and well-paved. It should have been yet another routine trip, but as we came into a bend, our bus suddenly did a slow, almost graceful, diagonal waltz (oil on the road? brakes? who knows?) to meet its counterpart coming from Santa Marta. There was a jarring thud, a loud crunch, a slowing down of the moment, and for me, a flash of indignation; 'Well, that's just typical.'

We couldn't have been more lucky; all along the road were the fossils of other, more lethal crashes. Ours was little more than a game of over sized dodgems and none of the passengers or the driver was anything other than bruised and alarmed. An emergency window was smashed and, one by one, lugging bags and baskets and the inevitable chickens, we climbed down the wheel onto the road to wait for rescue. I sat on my rucksack, and continued reading.

When finally we arrived in Santa Marta, I felt the same sense of indignant inevitability (oh, the eternal indignation of the European traveller) when I heard no flights had left for San Andrés in over two weeks. Why, I can't recall – strikes perhaps, or maybe the weather. Jumping into a taxi, I went straight to the airport to find chaos: people camped all over the floor, families cooking up dinner, and long queues at every counter. I also found a rumour, whispering around the hall – a flight was about to leave. I'm ashamed to say I used everything I could to get on that flight. I cried, claimed I had been bitten by a snake, threatened the airline with the fuss resulting from a dead 'whitey' at their ticket desk, and all of a sudden, a seat was found. But I had to hurry. Which is how I came to leave Colombia, sprinting, with a guard, an airline rep and two customs officials, attempting to give me a hasty body search, for company.

When we reached the hot tarmac, the steps had already been curled up, but I was gestured to the front of the plane, to a tiny ladder poking out of the cockpit. The only seat not listed on the travel agents' screens was, of course, the jump seat in the cockpit. As I scrambled in, the pilot, co-pilot and navigator all swung round in their seats to give their full attention to this fine curiosity, a red-faced gringa who spoke Spanish like a navvy. The navigator, I remember, wanted to know if 7 Eccles Street, home of Leopold Bloom, was still standing.

We spent the flight chatting lazily, the blue sky above us, the blue sea below, and all around us, a reassuring arsenal of dials, levers, buttons and lights. I felt cosseted and secure, as though these three men, with their talk of wives and children, the books they loved, their views on the drug war, were my three escorts, charged with delivering me home, safe and sound. As we started our descent into San Andrés, they grew serious, their gaze suddenly intent. As it should be, I felt; such was my own interest in the swinging dials and the slow sureness of our descent, I scarcely noticed the cloud billowing round us or the buffeting turbulence.

Only in the last minute, as we broke through the sullen cloud did I see why they were so silent and tense. The rain was almost horizontal, the palm trees bent to the ground by a tormented and furious wind. The runway looked as wet and choppy as the sea beyond it. Later, I learnt we had flown into the tail end of Hurricane Alma, with little or no warning. The crew, expecting the usual sunlit runway and light breezes, were ill-prepared for the swirling chaos that greeted us. Yet a plane is a more implacable force than you might expect, a good match for strong winds and rain, and with both pilots leaning forward a little and the engines roaring, we touched down, jumped, skipped, then touched home again. But as we bounded along the runway, at what seemed like phenomenal speed, the three-bar brake between the pilots' seats suddenly slipped out of position with a sickening clunk. The navigator leapt across the cockpit, both pilots twisted in their seats, and all three leaned on that brake, achingly slowly pushing it back into place. We shimmied, we skidded, we slid, and finally, seconds later, we halted. The nose of the plane was over the end of the runway, and at the end of the runway, was the sea.

Within a week of stepping down from that cockpit, I was back at home in Ireland, shucked from my rucksack and folded back into clean clothes, family and the routine. I had seen neither family nor friends for ten months, and in the days before e-mail, I had heard little either. One friend had managed to conceive, be pregnant and have a baby while I was gone. I had my own stories to tell too, but, like many a returned wanderer, quickly learnt that there are only so many travel stories you can tell. Somewhere, not long after the drive back from the airport, I simply stopped telling the story of my return journey, with all its vivid colour and spooky coincidences. It was too lurid a tale for a Dublin summer, too long an answer to a simple question, and I realised I felt slightly embarrassed at my own good luck. When I told it again, years later, around suburban kitchen tables or in the gardens of cheap *pensioni*, it felt like a story that had happened to someone else, a show-reel featuring a different version of myself.

Now I think my reluctance to dwell on that week is more

than simple embarrassment or expedience. In part, it's a kind of uncomprehending gratitude, a sense of wonder, a feeling of looking into a whirling vortex of questions, then backing away with none asked. Yet it's also a rejection of all that: in the midst of the quotidian, our minds shy away from the extreme, unable or unwilling to tackle the what-ifs, and the why-mes. With the benefit of hindsight, I can see that this rackety week of disaster and good luck stoked a belief in the inevitability of the unexpected, an unstable but nourishing fuel that is as useful at home as it is away. It certainly didn't stop me travelling again: one of the greatest gifts we are given in life is that of being safe, but it seems to me, the only way to celebrate it is to plunge into the unknown again, a little bit smarter, a little more stubborn, and always with an ear open for a good story.

# JEAN BUTLER

## A BED CALLED HOME

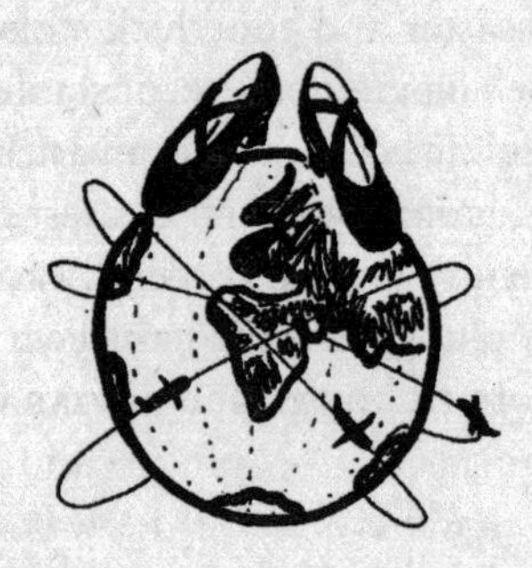

It was to happen again and again, this incredible urge to pack my suitcase, call a taxi, say goodbye to friends and family, and board a plane. It was an unsettling reminder of how I had spent the last twelve years of my life, on the road, in strange hotels, apartments, theatres, dressing rooms and bars. I had longed for the day when I had a bed called home.

I remember the first time I felt it, this feeling that I had somewhere else to be. Three months had passed since I returned home to Dublin after the close of my own dance show, a show that had kept me in London and New York for the best part of the previous year. I was wandering through my barely furnished house looking for something, but not knowing exactly what. On hands and knees at the back of the closet, I found myself rummaging under several bin bags destined for Oxfam. In one determined effort, my hand latched onto and dragged out my now-dusty suitcase. I sat back on the floor, the suitcase worn and crumpled in a heap before me. It seemed to stare, dumbfounded, as if disturbed from a long sleep. 'Where are we going?' it asked. I swallowed hard and breathed deeply. The closet smelled of fresh paint. 'Nowhere,' I heard my voice say. 'We're going nowhere.'

My mother says I packed my bags at seventeen and never came back. Although true, it was not, as she might sometimes think, a grand plan devised secretly with great ambition to flee home and spread my wings. It was something that just happened, through dance and a curious independence marked by a burning desire to experience all that an alternative life had to offer.

It wasn't entirely my fault. As a child, I had been taken by my parents to the circus, where I marvelled wide-eyed at the clowns and the lion-tamers, the gymnasts and horse-whisperers, pulling on my pink candy floss, utterly hypnotised. Later that evening, on the way home in the car, fingers sticky with salt and sugar, I announced that I would be in the circus when I grew up. I would see the world, performing feats of magic with my horse, Snowball, live in a travelling caravan, and marry the ringmaster. I would wear a lavender satin leotard, fishnet tights and matching shoes with diamond-studded heels. My parents laughed, and knowing they could never afford a horse, packed me off to Irish dancing classes as an ill-fated compromise. Dance was to become my three-ring circus, my escape from New York and life as I knew it.

My first tour as a dancer was with the Chieftains, Ireland's greatest cultural export at the time. My very first concert, which turned out to be an audition in Carnegie Hall on St Patrick's night, was the start of a new era. The very next day, the chief Chieftain, Paddy Moloney, called me up and asked me to come on the road with the band – thirty-six cities in forty-seven days. Without hesitation, I packed my bags and was off, touring with six strange men, each one old enough to be my father. My parents dropped me at the Royal Riahga Hotel on 57th and 7th, where I boarded the Chieftains' Ford

Transit van and sat quietly in the back seat closest to the window. I waved goodbye and watched as the city disappeared behind us, my feet tapping gently and excitedly. I was now a professional dancer. I was going to see the world.

I discovered almost instantly that life on the road was a curious, mostly nocturnal, existence. I worked at night and travelled during the day. And I loved it. All of it – the crowds, the theatres, the sound checks, the snazzy hotels, the band and the stars that came out to play. Richard Harris, Roger Daltry, the Pogues, Mick Jagger, Mel Gibson, and several other muzo and acting friends who joined us on stage for a ditty or two. The first month flew by in a tremendous haze of hotels, concerts and after-show parties. Quietly I felt I'd arrived.

By the second month, I realised I'd arrived alone. At night, my circus of reels and jigs united in harmonious performance; by day it dispersed into individual solo performances. The Chieftains never sat together on planes and always requested hotel rooms on separate floors. Thirty years on the road had taught them this invaluable lesson in privacy, but this was my first tour and I longed for a playmate. Loneliness weighed down my suitcase like a brick, solid and impenetrable. I missed my family. I missed my friends. I wondered how the Chieftains could tour months on end, year in and year out, without the intimacies of loved ones and comforts of home. It was almost instinctual what happened that morning at the airport at the end of the never-ending tour. I stood next to the band's six-foot-four fiddler – my buddy, Seán Keane – in a queue at the check-in desk. We were tired beyond exhaustion, standing in our sleep, waiting for the moment we could board yet another plane and close our eyes until it was time for the Ford Transit to take us to another hotel, another theatre, another concert. I don't know why I did it. I don't even know how it began. But as I leaned against Sean, something in me made me wrap my arms around him, chest height, and hold tight. He jolted initially, as if startled, then he let out a roar as he draped his arms around me. It was the first hug either of us had had for two months. I can still hear his laugh and see the smile in his eyes.

Rule number one: never go too long without physical contact. This is top of the list on my personal survival guide for jobbing dancers. There were many more rules to come – some learned out of necessity, some out of experience. Never take what you can't carry, as no one else is going to carry it for you. Never trust hotel alarm calls, especially for a 5 a.m. leave time. Always take a book of matches from the hotel room and write down your room number the minute you check in; this way you'll remember where you'll be sleeping that night. Always use the safety lock on the door because the 'Do Not Disturb' sign doesn't make the slightest difference. And beware the minibar.

My years with the Chieftains took me far and wide, travelling through the States, Canada, Europe and Japan. I used to save the printed itineraries as a reminder of where I had been. But as time went on, one tour dissolved into the next and the details were lost in a fast-flowing stream of cities and countries. I have been around the world and back, and now all I can remember are snippets of time frozen by particular sensory experiences. Madrid on a drizzly Sunday morning, shops closed and restaurants scarce, the clang of the cathedral bells breaking the silence of the ancient town. An inedible bowl of French onion soup tasting of murky dishwater in a concrete block of a hotel surrounded by oil mines in the desolate town of Fort McMurry, a hundred miles south of the Northwest Territory. Osaka and the smell of raw fish hitting the tappenyaki, flesh crackling like splinters of wood in an open fire. The scorching heat of my first Californian sun burning my face at the roof-top pool of the hotel, Burgess Meredith lounging under a pink umbrella to my right. Driving through the Rocky Mountains from Banff to Calgary, a funny ball of anxiety filling my stomach as the sheer muscle and authority of the snow-tipped peaks flanked the narrow road we sped along.

Fear also accompanied me on my travels in those first years on the road. Days off between gigs were a rarity; downtime essentials like laundry and a proper meal were welcome diversions. New Yorkers tend to believe that nowhere outside their city is as dangerous and I was no exception. My guard dropped. I thought a walk to the nearest sushi bar in Kansas City would be a welcome break from road food and aeroplane slop. The evening sun was just disappearing over the flat empty sky as I left the hotel entrance behind me and walked south on Main Street. The concierge had said to head straight for about twenty minutes or so, past a railway track, and toward the lights of the mall. It was a balmy mosquito-filled night, without even the slightest breeze to cool the sun-baked, tar-covered street.

I walked through the town, over the railway tracks and found myself in a deserted stretch of unwelcoming road. A pleasant-looking blond-haired and fair-skinned man, about my age or a bit older, appeared from behind a telephone booth. We struck up polite, though cautious, conversation. He was heading my way. He too was going to the mall. I could follow him. And so I did. But forty-five minutes later, my pulse rose ever so slightly as I found myself with this stranger on the outskirts of a barren, disused industrial estate. Out of the corner of my eye, the twinkling lights of the mall now shone, full and promising, in the direction opposite to where he was heading. Instinctively, my voice now wavering with nerves, I relayed that people were waiting for me in the restaurant and that I might go on ahead. My pace accelerated at the same time as something grabbed my arm.

'No. It's this way. I'm sure,' said the stranger.

My heart froze and my legs began to shake. As he steered me away, a little voice inside my head said, *Wait*. Wait until he's not ready. Then *run*.

And so I did.

When I arrived at the mall my head hurt and my lungs ached. Trembling, I sat down at the sushi bar and ordered two pieces of yellowtail and a bottle of sake. The food sat in front of me, limp and unappetising. I could not eat. I could not talk. I could not move. I stayed there for twenty minutes and said a few Hail Marys in thanks for what could have happened. Who would have thought? Kansas City. Dorothy. Toto. The Wizard of Oz. This was supposed to be a safe place. I wryly remembered the Wicked Witch, and realised nowhere was ever safe if you were a woman on your own. I would get a cab. I would go back to the hotel, lock my door, and order room service.

I paid the bill, turned to leave and stopped dead in my tracks. Outside the restaurant there was a green wrought-iron bench and on that bench sat the stranger who had grabbed my arm only a half an hour before. He smiled now, sickly, with a crooked grin.

I walked away quickly and calmly until I found help. The security guards dropped me at the hotel reception and waited till I was safely inside. No charges could be pressed, but they had my detailed description of the man. I went to bed that night with his face filed in the dark corner of my mind.

Things like that happened on the road, but usually not twice. I carried on touring with the Chieftains for several years, and although the novelty never wore off, I found myself becoming accustomed to a routine of travel, theatre, gig, bed. I eventually became numb to the outside world. I lost touch with friends, missed/forgot family birthdays, and found it harder and harder to return home. It wasn't the 'home' bit that bothered me. It was the lack of purpose that came with it, after I unpacked my bags and laundered my clothes. My life, as I defined it, seemed to be elsewhere, and insignificant to those around me. I felt misplaced amongst their normal existence of exams, promotions, new jobs, and relationships. All I had were a few highlights from a world they couldn't imagine, or share. It hit me hard: the realisation that life went on without me. Time passed, continued, ebbed and flowed in unstoppable terms and regardless of personal experience or witness. At home, I was a stranger to myself, and, on the road, a stranger to everyone else. I longed to belong, but didn't know where.

It was on my second trip to Japan that something shifted in my consciousness, making things clear. It wasn't anything anybody said or did. It was an experience that made me realise that belonging was a choice, not a feeling. And I had the power to choose. I was standing at the pedestrian lights at Tokyo's famous Shibuya Station, waiting to cross the enormous intersection where five roads converge into a sort of Japanese Times Square. I perched my toes over the curb, balancing on the sidewalk like a bird on a wire, waiting for the lights to change. I looked up at the foreign asymmetrical billboards and futuristic skyscrapers and felt a pressure building behind me, in front and to the side. Across the street, a seemingly infinite number of small dark-haired people began to congregate in a sharp black triangular formation. The pressure behind me, now at breaking point, pressed against me. I lost my balance, one foot landing on the road at the precise moment the lights changed. The opposing triangular formation dispersed and moved forwards towards me, as I was swept almost by force into the middle of the intersection. I stopped and felt as if I were on the break of a wave. All around me, hundreds of Japanese men and women and children scurried hurriedly, quietly and uniformly across the street from five different directions. I looked up at the sky, raised my arms, and slowly walked on the spot, turning around and around as the pedestrian traffic washed over me. I was tempted to join the mass of people, step into line, blend in. But I didn't. I waited and watched until I was alone again in the middle of the intersection, and moved off only when the cars advanced upon me.

That was one of the last tours I did with the Chieftains. I went back to university in England and chose a different type of life, one of seeming normality – studies, student parties and productions. I revelled in the freedom of my student days and cherished the friendships and experiences I collected. But always, somewhere at the core of my being, I felt on the outside looking in, as if my existence there were transient and I was on a holiday of sorts. My mind wandered often and far. At night, as I closed my books and settled under the duvet, I dreamt of my three-ring circus and awoke wondering where it would take me next ...

# ROSITA BOLAND

## BURMA, BURMA

Burma, Burma. I always thought of it as a duality – a country whose name seemed to repeat itself automatically, like a faint but clear echo in my head, resounding down the years. Burma, Burma.

I can't recall when I first heard the name Burma, but like some conch shell, our home always housed the evidence of an outside world. From the radio on the fridge, news bulletins punctuated the day in the kitchen. The RTÉ television news was a nightly ritual, which I often ended up watching by default from early childhood, since at that time, in Clare, we had only one channel. We took *The Irish Times* and the *Irish Press* every day; the *Sunday Press*, and the London-based *Observer* and *Sunday Times* at the weekend; and every week, *The Clare Champion*. The newspapers were left lying around and I sometimes scanned their pages after I'd read what to me were the only really interesting parts: the cartoons and the television schedule.

By osmosis, bits and pieces of world news must have sunk

in. I understood virtually nothing of what I read, saw, or heard, but it did register clearly with me as a child that the world was vast, unstable, complex and exotic. I did retain names of places. Indochina. Rhodesia. Cambodia. Iran. Vietnam. China. India. East Pakistan. Ceylon. And, at some point, Burma. A litany of the elsewhere, which lodged somewhere in me.

December 2002, near Kanchanaburi, Thailand. I sat by the window of a branch-line train, looking out at thick green landscape, lush and dramatic. There were strange-looking mountains in the distance – like stone hills. The sky was a clear, hard, hot blue. My passport was back in Bangkok, at the Cambodian Embassy, and I was on a day trip while waiting for my visa to be processed. I had picked the trip at random, knowing almost nothing about Kanchanaburi until that day.

This piece of track we were on was part of the few remaining miles of the Thai–Burmese railway, which was built by prisoners of war in the Second World War to connect the previously unlinked countries by rail. Some sixteen thousand POWs died building this railway, most of them in 1943, doing in sixteen months what had originally been scheduled by the Japanese to take five years. Many thousands of local people who worked as labourers also died, their exact numbers unrecorded. The railway line has long been dismantled; no trains now cross into Burma.

Earlier we had walked over the infamous and now-rickety but still-used bridge on the River Kwai, looking down through the uneven planks at slits of the opaque river. There are floating restaurants on the river now, shops full of souvenir tat, and on the bridge itself, countless tourists with cameras, hustling each other to get the best shots. I sat on the train a couple of hours later, looking out the window, thinking of the forced labour of sixty years previously, and the irony of how little there was left to show for it, apart from the acres of war cemetery at Kanchanaburi, collective national memories, a misleading film, and a few miles of railway track through a mesmerically beautiful landscape.

'Burma! Burma!' The words were full of an odd combination of both urgency and glee, repeatedly shouted close to my startled ear. It was our guide. He hung out the window and gestured beyond the odd stone hills, towards an expanse of teak trees with their huge leaves; towards an invisible border, less than twenty kilometres away. I had had no idea we were so close to the border. Transfixed, I stared into the distance until my eyes hurt and the greenness swam, breaking up into fragments and glittering like emeralds. I found myself thinking: I will always remember this moment. In that precise instant, I decided to go to Burma.

Three months later, the Air Mandalay flight I was on into Rangoon landed so hard on the runway that everyone on board was temporarily winded. For my first few minutes on Burmese soil, I gulped uneasily for breath and looked out at the relentless darkness of an Asian night.

The pilot came on the tannoy as the plane finally came to a stop. 'I must apologise for the hard landing,' said the laconic Australian voice. 'But the runway at Yangon is very short and I didn't want to miss it.'

In the taxi on the way into Rangoon, I registered only that it was still intensely hot, there was almost no street lighting, and that even from a just-landed perspective, I felt I had absolutely no grasp of the country I had arrived in. It was so dark I could hardly see the driver, let alone anything beyond the windows of our battered car. He was busy telling me the black-market dollar–kyat exchange rate when he stopped and gestured to the left. 'Madame, look.' I looked.

High on the city's skyline rose an immense golden stupa, bigger than anything around it, gleaming even under the harsh floodlights that picked it out of the darkness. It shone with the unmistakable soft brightness of pure gold, blazing in the darkness. When I went there next day, I learned that the stupa is made of sixty tons of solid gold, added to over the centuries and constantly regilded. It is topped by a gold canopy, decorated with thousands of diamonds and rubies, extraordinary Aladdin-like details you can see by looking though a telescope. In daylight it has the effect of making everything around it seem slightly insubstantial by comparison, so pure is the refracted golden light, and so potent the atmosphere of devotion; it is Buddhist Burma's most sacred site. 'Shwedagon Paya, very famous, very sacred,' the taxi-driver announced proudly, and went back to his black-market calculations.

At the simple Three Seasons guesthouse near Mahabandoola Road, my room had strings of jasmine flowers hanging from the door handle. There was no window. That first night, the rooms with windows were already occupied. From childhood, I have slept with curtains wide open, and I felt disorientated by the lack of a window. It was very hot. I left the light on and did not sleep well. There were several mirrors in the room, and every time I woke, dazed and disconcerted by unexpected reflections, I thought there was someone else in the room.

When I finally got up at 7 a.m., there was the surprise of more fresh jasmine flowers on my door handle outside, each white blossom carefully threaded and knotted at a precise distance from the other; a string of scented pearls. Later, when I thought of those flowers and that first morning, they seemed like a promise for the days that lay ahead in Burma – unexpected, exotic, and ephemeral.

My first sight of Inle Lake in the Shan State, some six hundred kilometres as the crow flies from Rangoon, was from the air. After months in Indochina, tired of travelling overland on ancient, unpredictable buses on pitted, unpredictable roads, I flew from Rangoon to Heho. On internal flights, Air Mandalay does not bother with the niceties of in-flight safety announcements. Only once before had I been on a flight similarly lacking these reassuring incantations – flying over glaciers and through ten thousand metre mountains from Skardu in Baltistan to Islamabad with a Pakistani airline, where a prayer to Allah for a safe landing replaced the usual aviation routine announcements. I guess it made sense; if we crashed in those mountains round K2, not even the most punctilious safety instructions could have saved us. The lack of safety announcement on Air Mandalay reminded me of that other flight and unnerved me a little.

By the time I saw Inle Lake, I was more or less hallucinating about breezes and cool air. Back in Rangoon, it was hitting forty degrees Celsius, a debilitating, humid heat that was sucking energy even from the Burmese people, who were used to it. It would get hotter still, and by the time I reached the plains of Bagan, two weeks later, it was so hot I sometimes worried about running out of water while exploring remote temples by bicycle, even though I never set off without at least three litres every morning.

But at Inle in early March, it was still cool. From the air, the long, narrow lake lay shimmering in the dry landscape like a dream. Inle Lake is twenty-two kilometres long and eleven kilometres at its widest point. For generations, Burmese people have come here, both to escape the heat of the cities and to visit the statues of Phaung Daw U Paya on the lake, one of Burma's most famous Buddhist sites.

Inle has an international fame beyond being a destination of retreat in the hot season, or for containing a place of veneration. At Inle, the skilled Intha boatmen use a unique, one-legged method of rowing to propel their skiff-like vessels across the utterly calm lake. They use only one oar. They stand on the stern, using one leg as a support, and wrap their other leg round an oar, thus becoming a sort of graceful human rudder. The height lets them see where the mercurial fish darken the water, so they can then drop their cone-like, bamboo-supported nets in one swift movement. It also lets them navigate easily through the hyacinths that tangle the lake, and around the many reclaimed pieces of land, which are used as floating gardens for vegetables and the masses of pink and white flowers that are heaped up everywhere at shrines.

With Deb, a smart, droll, clued-in American woman and the only other Westerner aboard the flight from Rangoon, I hired boats out of Nyaungshwe two days running. As a foreigner, you must take a boatman with you on the lake; you cannot go alone. The first day, our boatman was a boatwoman, a beautiful laughing woman who stopped the dugout canoe at one point to make us each necklaces from white water lilies, splitting the green stalks expertly and tying them at the back of the neck so that the flower hung down at our throats like a magnificent pendant.

For an afternoon, we slid through the tranquil shallow backwaters of the jungle close to Nyaungshwe, overhung by banyan trees. My hair lifted from under my hat in the small breezes that rippled the water. The thick, exhausting heat of Rangoon seemed a lifetime's distance away. Our boatwoman took us to the arcane-looking shrine that stood on a floating island amid a tangle of weed and trees. A nat shrine, she told us – the lake's most important nat shrine. The banyan tree that had grown around it, and hidden it from sight for decades, had recently rotted, and the wooden hut-like structure within which the shrine stood was now exposed, the legs of the hut vanishing into the water. It was about twenty metres away. From the dugout, there was no way of looking at it more closely, nor would it have been appropriate to do so.

It was the first time I had seen a nat shrine in Burma. Nat, or spirit worship, predates Buddhism in Burma. There is a belief that nats – spirits – have influence over places, and thus to protect these places, spirit houses have to be built to contain them, and must be tended to regularly. The big old shrine under the banyan tree that we were looking at was to protect the general area; other smaller spirit houses are created within private homes.

The following day, Deb and I went out on Inle Lake proper, with the boatwoman's older brother and his friend. There were wooden chairs in the boat, and red umbrellas stored beneath them, which we used as protection against the sun. By 8 a.m., when we set off, the sunlight was already so strong that the lake water was burning a fierce reflected white that hurt my eyes even through my sunglasses.

We passed the Intha boatmen, preoccupied with their fishing nets; we passed the floating vegetable gardens and houses on stilts; we passed the shouting children who played in boats outside their island homes, jumping as lightly and easily from one boat to another as if they were passing between the back gardens of a street in a town.

Somewhere in the middle of the lake, a solitary pillar arrowed high out of the blazing white water, topped by what looked like a golden phoenix. Our boatmen gave it a wide berth and respectful glances. Their English did not run to the words for an explanation. Puzzled, we looked back at the pillar. A mooring post? The deepest point of the shallow lake?

In the afternoon, we stopped at the Phaung Daw U Paya, the Shan State's most religious site. Why is it that, over the centuries, some places of worship become more famous than others? At the Phaung Daw U Paya, there are on display five statues, thought to be of Buddha images, each between two and four feet high. Nobody knows how ancient they are, possibly eight hundred years old. And nobody knows what the images represent, because, over the centuries, they have been covered in inches of gold leaf, placed there by male devotees. Women must give their gold leaf to a man, who will rub it onto one of the five statues, thus attaining merit for the person who supplied it. The gold leaf comes in square packets of varying sizes; in Mandalay, I had bought a packet of ten exquisitely wrapped, two-inch-square pieces for the equivalent of a dollar.

The images at Phaung Daw U Paya now resemble gold snowmen, their original shapes long lost under the layers of gold leaf. Until recently, once a year, the five statues were carried to all the monasteries in the villages around the lake by ceremonial barge. The extraordinary, elaborately decorated barge is moored in a floating covered dock beside the temple. It too gleams with gold. Some fifteen years ago, or twenty, but no more than thirty and definitely within living memory, the barge capsized, tangled in that year's unusually thick growth of hyacinths. The shallow lake swallowed the five images, returning only four of them to the horrified crew, who searched in vain for hours for the fifth and smallest statue.

When they returned to Phaung Daw U Paya, the fifth statue was where it always stood, covered in hyacinth roots. Since then, it has never left the temple, and only four of the images now traverse the lake. The pillar with the phoenix-like bird we had seen earlier in the day marks the spot where the barge capsized. When I heard that story, I smiled with unwilling, but certain, disbelief.

A week later, I went on a three-day trek from Kalaw, a small town in the mountains to the east, and a day's travel from Inle Lake. The best-known trekking lodge in the town is the Golden Kalaw Inn, owned by a Burmese man who prefers Westerners to call him Mr Eddie, and who leads treks to surrounding villages when enough people show up at his lodge. Mr Eddie is a wiry, slightly nervy man with a perpetually preoccupied expression and an innate sense of grace. When he laughed, which he did at unexpected intervals, it was impossible not to laugh too.

There were three of us on Mr Eddie's trek, which cost the ludicrously small sum of five dollars a day, including all our food. The other two were Peter, a self-effacing, diffident Canadian who had been living in Bangkok for seven years, and Seuw, a prickly, unlikable Malaysian woman who sulked for the entire three days. Seuw was on her second visa extension and had been in Burma for almost three months, most of that time going to places well off the beaten track. This trek, she kept telling us, was 'too touristy'. On the second day out, she discovered it was actually Peter's fourth visit to Burma, and that he had been in places she had not got to. She retreated into a bitter silence. Me – in Burma for a mere three weeks, and travelling only to the better-known places – she had no time for at all, especially when she heard I had 'cheated' by flying to Heho instead of taking the two-day bus journey.

The first evening of the trek, Peter, Seuw and I slept in a thatched bamboo hut at a spot known simply as the Viewpoint Resthouse, which overlooked mountains and terraces of tea-bushes – a gloriously beautiful place. The following day, we trekked to Myin Htalk village, where we were to spend the second night, in the house of friends of Mr Eddie's.

To my shame, I cannot now recall the names of the gracious man and woman of the house, nor of their three laughing children – the oldest, a girl with mischievous eyes, and her two small brothers – whom we played with before dinner, and after breakfast next day. Their house was on stilts at the side of a hill, made entirely of teak, since that was the cheapest and most easily available local material. There was no glass in the windows; at night, wooden shutters closed over the window-spaces. In the main room, a triangular shelf for the spirit house was set into a corner. When we arrived, the little curtain across the shelf was open. I stared into this dim space, wild with curiosity to see at close quarters what I had read about in the impersonal clipped prose of my guidebook. There were odd little figures made of something I did not recognise, standing in small bowls of water. 'Water spirits,' Mr Eddie said, looking over my shoulder. White threads were tied around the water spirit bowls. There were faded pictures propped up at the back, as well as the end of a candle and pieces of fruit. The spirit house was there to protect the main house and all in it. When I looked again, a little later, the curtain had been drawn across it.

That night, myself, Peter, Seuw, Mr Eddie and Mr Joe Joe, his trekking friend from Kalaw who was also overnighting in Myin Htalk, were all to sleep together dormitory-like in a row on bamboo mats on the teak floor of the main room. The children slept in a room off the kitchen and the parents had their own room, off the main room. The woman of the house brought mats and rugs. I shook out my silk bag and climbed into it with my clothes on.

Despite all the exercise that day, I could not sleep. I lay on my side and watched the man and woman of the house, sitting and talking by the fire in the kitchen with Mr Eddie and Mr Joe Joe. The only light in the house came from the fire; the candles had been blown out. After a while, I heard snores coming from both Peter's and Seuw's piles of bedding. I turned round and stared into the darkness of the far side of the room, where the spirit house stood, not far from where I lay, hidden in the darkness. Then everyone else went to bed, but still I could not sleep. I watched the last embers of the fire die out and listened to the snores that filled the room.

When I first saw it, I thought I was imagining things. I shut my eyes for a moment and opened them again. It was still there. A bluish-white light, completely unlike the soft yellow gleam of candlelight, was flickering around the spirit house. It moved a little bit on either side of it, but kept returning to the spot where I knew the spirit house stood. There is no electricity in the village of Myin Htalk. I did not know whether I was scared or interested. In the end, I decided I was interested.

Then I heard the noises. Once the fire had gone out in the kitchen, pans left on the floor started rattling. There were loud squeals, and thumping, scuttling, scuffling sounds, some of them not far from where we lay. They were not made by mice.

Everyone else snored on. I sat upright in the thick darkness, my heart pounding. I am terrified of rats; even the thought of them makes me weak with fear. Too frightened to care what caustic Seuw would think of me should she wake, I leapt out of my silk bag, grabbed a rug and my torch, and bolted for the door and the veranda outside.

In a chair on the veranda, I tried to compose myself. My torch burned a rod of light through the solidly black night. The woman of the house saw it through a crack in the wooden planks of their room and came out with a candle to see what was wrong. Too mortified to explain, but determined I was not going back into that scuffling room again, I asked for Mr Eddie, whom she had said was awake.

When he came out, I explained about my fear of rats. And that I was going to stay up and read until dawn on the veranda. He listened solemnly, and then smiled. 'Yes, the rats here are bad,' he said simply. 'One jumped out of the spirit house onto my face just now. It woke me up! So don't worry; everyone is afraid of something. For you, it is the rat. If you want to stay out here, you stay out here, and if you need anything, you call me.'

For someone who hates rats, there is perhaps no more disturbing thought than the notion of one landing on your face in darkness. Mr Eddie had been sleeping alongside me. For the remainder of that night I thought about the light I'd seen coming from the spirit house. Knowing my fears, had it been some arcane warning for me to move, from the spirit nats? There was nowhere else to go that night. I stayed on the veranda until dawn, reading by candlelight, thinking about the nature of fear, and the mysterious blue light I had seen.

At dawn, I heard people stirring and went into the kitchen, where Mr Eddie and Mr Joe Joe were brewing green tea on the smoky fire. Mr Joe Joe asked where I had been in Burma so far. I told them about visiting Inle Lake and asked them if they knew the story of the fifth golden image that had supposedly reappeared from the water.

'Yes, yes, this is true,' Mr Eddie said. 'The water is shallow there, everyone was looking, nobody could have taken it without being noticed. In Burma, these things do happen.'

'Near Pindaya there is a holy monk, now very old, who has been seen in two places at one time,' Mr Joe Joe said matter-of-factly, handing me tea. 'This is true also. Everyone knows it.'

The fire was hot and bright in the still-dim kitchen. I drank the tea, and despite having had no sleep all night, I felt oddly refreshed and ready for the day's trek, a vitality that did not fail me as the day progressed. We were quiet for a while. I thought of monks who appeared in two places at once; of the lost golden Buddha that had materialised out of nowhere; and of the strange blue light I had seen, where it should have been impossible for a light of any colour to appear. Burma, Burma, I thought, where such things can happen.

Rosita Boland's article about Burma appeared in *The Irish Times* of 10 April 2003. It is reprinted here as an appendix to give the reader an idea of the current political situation in that country.

Of all the countries in South East Asia, Burma – or Myanmar as it is now officially called – is the one over which the thickest fog of misinformation hovers. The bare facts are clear: a military junta has ruled the country by force since 1962, and although Aung San Suu Kyi's party, the National League for Democracy, won the 1990 so-called 'Free Elections', her party was infamously never allowed to take power.

Many Western countries have chosen not to trade with Burma, in protest at its abysmal human rights record and there is a well-publicised campaign urging tourists not to visit. The Burmese government, however, actively welcomes tourists, since all foreign tourists not on package-tour visas must change $200 at the airport (you are only permitted to arrive by air) into Foreign Exchange Certificates – one of their ways of attaining precious hard currency.

Package tourists pay in full in advance for their trip, thus the government benefits one-hundred per cent from these visitors, something which anyone considering travelling to Burma should be aware of. For obvious reasons, Burma does not issue visas to journalists; thus at its embassy in Phnom Penh, I stated a different profession on my application form.

Anything to do with money is a complex seesaw in Burma. In February, the kyat was worth 1,200 to one (cash-only) dollar on the black market. At the end of my three weeks there, it was down to 700 and sliding. It was explained to me by local people that at the beginning of March, the government issued statements that the banks (which they control) could collapse. People rushed to withdraw money, but were limited the first week to 200,000 kyat per account, 100,000 the second week and 50,000 the third week. As a result, nobody spending, and not much kyat in circulation, with the idea being to weaken the dollar exchange rate. To control privately accumulated funds, in the recent past, the government has arbitrarily decided overnight to make worthless certain high-denomination notes. For those luckless people who had hoarded money at home in these denominations, they awoke one morning to find their banknotes were literally worth nothing.

There is a huge black market in Burma, the logistics of which confused me at first. School textbooks, for instance, cost 250 kyat at the government rate, but 1,250 at black market rates. I was told this in a shed that served as a village school. Shouldn't it be the other way round? No, the reason being that only twenty per cent of the required number of textbooks are sold by the government, thus if you want your child to have an education, you are forced to pay four times more on the black market for the books they need. Few village people can afford this, and therefore their children go uneducated – and uneducated people are generally less of a threat to any form of authority. It can only be a calculated decision by the junta.

Out walking through rice paddies with a local man in the Shan State, I was told that in this part of Burma the climate is so hot that the farmers traditionally plant rice only once a year, as there is not enough water for a second crop. Earlier that year, the military visited every farmer in the area and instructed them to plant rice twice in 2003, and to use all spare seed to plant the second crop.

The result, he told me, will be that the second crop will fail; there will be no surplus seed left over for planting next year, so it must be bought at great expense from China; and the necessary vegetable crop which should have been planted in place of the second lot of rice will now not exist. Needless agrarian disaster. Why? 'Because the government does not like it when people have enough to eat,' he explained grimly. 'They like to keep us under control.'

And in full control the military is. In Rangoon and Mandalay there are huge hand-painted signs, headed with 'The People's Desire'. Two of them read: 'Oppose all foreign nations interfering in internal affairs of the State', and 'Crush all internal and external destructive elements as the common enemy.'

Soldiers are present in large intimidating numbers everywhere, openly toting machine guns. The army regularly possesses private houses for its own use, and forces entire towns and villages to relocate elsewhere because it wants to move in its troops.

The people of Burma are poor, yet they live in what should be one of the richest countries of South East Asia, since Burma contains extensive ruby and sapphire mines, the biggest teak forests in the world, and the famous Kachin jade mines, a stone highly prized all over the East. But all these natural resources are now owned and controlled by the government and nothing goes back to the people, in the same way that their 'taxes' never convert into roads or hospitals or twenty-four-hour electricity; it simply goes straight into the military kitty.

There are many areas of Burma which are strictly off limits to foreigners. The government does not want them to see people working in forced labour and it certainly does not want them to see the people who are forced to work as human minesweepers on the Thai–Burmese border, a rumour I had heard which several people confirmed to me as true. 'That's why local people here are very happy with independent tourists visiting,' the man who walked with me in the rice paddies explained. 'We feel safer; there is no forced labour here. You can walk into any house here and be welcomed.'

And it was true. I've never been so welcomed in any other country. Children everywhere sat down and helped me learn simple Burmese phrases; restaurateurs tried to refuse tips, saying they were just happy I had eaten there, and when I insisted, I invariably left with mounds of fruit; fellow passengers on buses and pick-up trucks plied me with food and questions; people everywhere gave me gifts – one man came running out of a shop to present me with a tiny jade elephant 'for lucky, for lucky'; and many times, people shut up their shops when I visited to take me to drink tea and talk, with the understanding I used no names or even place-names through which they could possibly be identified.

It's impossible to predict what lies ahead for Burma now, after close on 150 years of turmoil. The junta does seem horribly entrenched. But one man I met said with great conviction: 'A time comes round for everything and our time will come.' Let's hope so.

And in all this, Burma is truly exotic and wildly beautiful, with its landscape of teak forests and the Irrawaddy River; Rangoon's fabulous and immense solid-gold Shwedagon Paya, decorated with thousands of precious gems; its culture of venerating the vast monastic population; the ancient, arcane temples of Bagan; and the ruined royal cities of Mandalay.

There are some backpackers in Burma, but nothing like the numbers elsewhere in Asia. However, I saw a depressingly big number of package tours. To go or not has to be an individual decision. If you do go as an independent tourist, carry cash dollars to exchange for kyat through any private hotel or shop, i.e. not at the government bank; stay only in privately run guesthouses, buy handicraft from local shops not government emporiums, and eat in private restaurants. That way, your money goes directly to the people.

And the people, not the sights, are always what make any journey. Of all the experiences I've had in the last five months, the warmth and hospitality of the Burmese people will shine most brightly in the treasure trove of my memory.

Reprinted courtesy of *The Irish Times*

# TERRY PRONE

## HOW TO SLEEP ON PLANES

When the woman beside me woke me up, she was furious.

'You slept all the way,' she said accusingly.

A bit fogged, I nodded, wondering why me sleeping had her so wrought up.

'You slept before we even *took off,*' she said.

A member of the cabin crew began to hover, I assumed to protect me from this woman if she went bananas altogether in a new version of air-rage: landing-rage.

'I never slept at all,' the woman went on bitterly, joining the procession of people stepping into the aisle.

If she hadn't been so cross, I'd have given her a quick tutorial: How to Sleep on Planes. It's a funny thing, though. Most people who fail to sleep on planes regard their insomnia as a virtuous state. They resent the hell out of those of us who snooze the airmiles away, but consider themselves as somehow more sensitive and fragile for not being able even to doze in flight.

Anyone can sleep on a plane. It just requires a bit of planning and cash.

For starters, you can't afford to rely on one of those miserable little flat cushions the airline gives you. You have to invest in an inflatable pillow. Best is a half-moon-shaped thing called a Hedbed, which inflates handily on only one lungful of air and slides in at the side of your head. Particularly good if you have booked a window seat, the Hedbed is easy to keep in hand luggage because it deflates to nothing. Next in line is a U-shaped pillow with a flat back to it. Least desirable is a U-shaped pillow with an inflatable back to it – this tends to shove the user forward, whereas the flat-backed one allows your head to tip to the side but keeps you anchored against the back of the seat.

Even if you've brought your own pillow, you don't let go of the one the airline supplies, because of an oddity nobody seems eager to correct: aircraft seats have amazingly hard armrests. You could get an ulcerated elbow during a long flight, they're so rock-like in their resistance. However, if you tuck skinny airline pillows down between you and the seat so that the overlap covers the armrest – one on each side – you can hope for a comfortable night.

Elbows are a law unto themselves. Give them a hard armrest or two and they'll wait until you doze and then insert themselves in the fleshy parts of the travellers on either side of you. From your point of view, this is a good thing, not least because other people's fleshy parts tend to be pleasingly warm. From the point of view of the owners of the fleshy parts, though, it has drawbacks, and they are likely to jam your elbow back into your own area with an affronted air.

Cabin-crew members do the same with your knees, if you're in an aisle seat and are a knee-extender. Their gentleness in shoving your knee back into your seat-space diminishes as the flight progresses. If a study were done, it would show that the first time they come through the cabin with their metal trolley, they pat protruding knees in a motherly go-on-home-now way. The second time, they give a brisk nudge. The third time, it becomes the equivalent of a clip over the ear. The fourth time it's as friendly as a smack up the side of the head. The fifth time, they don't bother protecting your recidivist knee, they just whack it with the sharp corner of the trolley and make like they're surprised when you leap upright with a yell of pain.

Keeping your knees to yourself is simple enough. You must, first of all, make damn sure your hand baggage is in the overhead bin, not under the seat in front of you. If it goes under the seat in front of you, the amount of room left for your legs is minimal. Either you stick them on top of the case, in which case they get jammed and your blood circulation ditto, or you slide a leg into the narrow channel on either side, which inevitably leads to at least one knee protruding into the aisle. In addition to getting hand baggage into the overhead bin, and gaining foot space as a result, I also clip an elasticated belt around my knees. It unsnaps at a touch, so if the pilot makes one of those announcements about ditching, I'll be out of there as fast as anyone else will, but it gently reminds my legs not to wander far from home.

I find that watching me clipping a belt around my knees tends to make the stranger in the seat next to me uneasy, but that's a good thing. Uneasy fellow passengers stay silent. Relaxed fellow passengers talk. Even if you manage to fall asleep in the gaps, they make sure to wake you at meal times in the hope of more conversation, not knowing that your Sleep on the Plane Plan requires you to have a snack in the departure lounge, so you won't need to eat on the plane.

In the departure lounge, at the time of the snack, is when to take Melatonin: roughly half an hour before take-off. Melatonin, available from natural food and herbal stores, not only helps put you to sleep on the flight, but also helps reduce jet lag after the flight. (Jet lag happens only if you're flying west to east. You don't get it if you fly north or south. If you fly far enough west, you get confused and exhausted, but not jet-lagged. Being jet-lagged is characterised by two distinct symptoms. The first is a hunger for sleep so profound you'd sell your baby and your mother for it. The second is a distanced wakefulness. You are alert, but – like that song – you see everything from a distance, as if someone had double-glazed you during the flight.)

The key thing to remember before you settle down to sleep is that what they do to you during the flight is desiccate you. You go onto a plane as plumply full of moisture as a fresh grape and you come off it like a raisin. One of the more serious complications of this is the possibility of your congealing blood developing clots. Hillary Clinton got one in her leg as a result of undertaking a great number of flights within a few days during a campaign. Wearing flight socks, those heavily elasticated things every airport sells, not only helps you avoid clot formation, but also helps prevent your feet and ankles from swelling. On the day of a flight, steer clear of coffee, because it's a diuretic and so removes some of your precious internal moisture before you even get on the plane, and drink lots of water.

A water bottle in the pocket of the seat in front of you is invaluable. In advance of any long flight, I open a plastic water bottle, drink about a quarter of the contents and freeze the rest. Drinking some of the water means the rest has room to expand while freezing. Frozen water is easier to transport because it's less likely to leak (or splat if dropped) and it gives you a constant supply of something cool to drink, so that you don't have to annoy the cabin crew for ice.

Enemies of sleep on a flight are many. Starting with the pilot. Most of them, particularly the women, are business-like. They belt up when they've nothing much to offer. The talkative ones are infuriating and can be spotted even before take-off: when the basic sit-down-and-shut-up announcements by the cabin crew are overridden by a cheery captain blithering about cruising altitude and route, it signifies that the captain is a microphone-lover.

Microphone-loving captains interrupt good sleeping time to tell passengers to look out the left-hand side of the plane to view a mountain range or a lake. Some day one of these guys is going to get a critical mass of obedient passengers, who are all going to climb over to the left-hand side, thus endangering the equilibrium of the aircraft. Microphone-lovers also announce births, marriages and retirements at random intervals throughout a long flight. And they're given to announcing the beginning of the start of the commencement of the onset of descent, thus creating, three-quarters of an hour before touch-down, the expectation of imminent landing. What's really worrying about this is *where* they say they're going to land. They talk about landing 'in the Detroit area' or 'the Atlanta area'. The passenger who mutters under their breath: 'You'd better land in the Detroit *airport*, on a goddam *runway*' feels like a control freak in the middle of all this comfortably casual imprecision.

The other enemies of sleep on a plane are passengers, and there are a lot more of them about these days. Ten years ago, on longer flights, once the seat-belt sign had been switched off, savvy fliers would be in the aisle, headed for lines of unoccupied seats, where, by tipping up the armrests, they could provide themselves with a full-length bed for the duration of the trip. These days, every seat is taken, and a lie-down is rare.

If those extra passengers behaved themselves, it would be fine. Instead, they set out to murder sleep. Some of them are aisle-walkers, who avoid clots by walking a marathon in plane-lengths. Some are stretchers. They're the ones who climb over you every few minutes in order to get to that wide space outside the loos, where they can touch their toes and show off their flexibility. Some are finger-rappers. They're the worst. They bring a Walkman everywhere with them, and jig in time to the music it sends through its earphones.

By far the most annoying kind of finger-rapper is the kind who snaps the tin lid of the now-redundant armrest ashtray up and down, up and down, until the cacophony renders all nearby passengers murderous. I once saw one of those murderous passengers wait until the finger-rapper went to the loo, at which point he snuck out of his seat in a speedy slither. He stuck the lid of the over-exercised ashtray in place using a chunk of well-chewed gum before slithering back to his own seat and letting on he'd never left it. It may not have been hygienic, but it was amazingly effective. The rapper, on his return, never realised why the ashtray had stopped co-operating.

Ever since, I carry a few of those Blu-Tack adhesives with me and secure the ashtrays around me with it before any other passenger gets on, at least on those airlines where frequent-flier status allows me to get on ahead of most of the payload. The Blu-Tack trick is useful, not just with Walkman-wearers, but with toddlers, who love the rhythmic clapping of the metal flap. If it never moves at all, they experience no deprivation, whereas if they get started, trying to stop them creates major trauma.

Blu-Tack is one of the essentials to be stuffed in a carry-on. Another is nicotine gum. Nicotine gum is needed for the long flight where you find yourself beside a full-time smoker in extreme withdrawal. Serious smokers, particularly male versions of the breed, convince themselves that by backbone and gritted teeth, they'll get through a long flight. They reject, with contempt, the idea of carrying nicotine gum. Two hours into the flight, they're grey in the face. That's the point at which a fellow passenger offering some gum to chew that just happens to be filled with nicotine becomes a pal for life. The pal does have to pretend to chew some of the gum and also has to wordlessly indicate the sufferings of withdrawal even if the pal has never smoked in her life, but these physical white lies radically reduce the trembling and fidgeting and coughing of the person in the next seat.

The final thing every good plane-sleeper needs is a two-faced watch, which gives you the time at your point of embarkation and the time at the place where you land. Invaluable, these, if you want to avoid irritating relatives or colleagues by telephoning them in the middle of the night. If you want to buy a posh one, many airlines offer them in their duty-free catalogue, and Orvis, the travel people, offer them on their website. My flight watch cost me ten euro in a flea market. It's so big and crudely clear that even jet-lagged eyes can make out the time at a bleary glance.

Why is it so important to have such a watch?

Because it saves you asking the passenger beside you what's the right time and thereby provoking them into telling you that you slept all the way, growl, growl ...

# TINA REILLY

## THINGS *NOT* TO BRING ON HOLIDAY – ONE TODDLER

Last year, yet again convincing ourselves that we'd come back refreshed and invigorated, my husband and I took the kids down to West Cork for a holiday. And we weren't heading down to a cottage or an apartment or anything as ordinary as that – nope – I'd booked us into a hotel. Visions of lazy mornings, followed by even lazier afternoons lolling about in the pool had been dancing about in my head for months. I'd exfoliated, shaved and preened myself in preparation for this fantastic break. And, at first, all went well. Despite the fact that the rain was coming down in sheets, I'd dressed the kids in their new, holiday clothes. Son looked fantastic in his combat shorts and khaki T-shirt, and my two-year-old daughter was the vision of cuteness in her lilac dress and jelly sandals. Husband, who'd decided to drive, had donned his sunglasses in honour of the occasion, and at ten o'clock we set off.

Twenty minutes into the five-hour journey, Husband suddenly remembered that he'd left his togs behind. But there was no way he was going back for them. Hadn't all the kids on the road waved our car on its way? Hadn't we dropped our key off at the neighbours'? 'No,' he said. 'It'd look stupid if we went back now.' Instead, he decided that he'd stop off en route and purchase a pair.

Have you ever tried to buy swimming shorts in late August?

There were none – well, none that Husband would wear. He's not a 'swimming trunk' kinda guy and despite me trying to convince him that *maybe* he could be, he remained adamant. 'I'll only wear shorts,' he kept saying.

As the car ate up the miles and the number of shops thinned out, I became completely fixated on his lack of swimming attire. Nightmarish images of me minding two kids in a swimming pool began to surface. Every sports shop we passed, I begged him to stop and check them out. Would he? Nope. A minor scuffle broke out.

Then Son got in on the act. 'But who'll mind me in the pool if Mammy is looking after the baby?' he whined.

'Good point.' I nodded.

Husband gripped the steering wheel ever tighter and said nothing.

'Are we there yet?' Son asked.

'No.' I handed him a drink. 'Another little while.'

'I don't want to go on lollidays,' Little Daughter piped up. 'I want to stay at home.'

I laughed nervously. When Little Daughter says she doesn't want to do something, it's generally a forewarning of disaster. 'Of course you want to go,' I cajoled. 'It'll be fun.'

'I don't like lollidays.'

'But you've never really been on one before,' I said, still in my patient parent mode. 'Wait until you see the pool.'

'I don't like pools.'

'Well,' I said, gritting my teeth. 'Daddy can mind you so, seeing as he has no togs.'

'Oh, for God's sake,' Husband muttered irritably. 'Stop going on about it.'

'I'm not going on about anything,' I said.

He gripped the steering wheel tighter again.

'Are we there yet?'

'No.' I handed out some biscuits. 'Another little while.'

'I don't like lollidays.'

I ignored Little Daughter, who was glaring at me from her car seat.

'I have to go to the toilet,' Son said. Then the dreaded after-statement. 'Number two.'

Husband looked back at Son. 'Are you sure you need to go?'

'Yeah.' Son looked baffled at the question.

We pulled up outside a quiet-looking pub. Husband switched the engine off and looked expectantly at me.

'What?'

'You bring him in.'

I gawped at him. 'I'm not bringing him in – sure he'll want to go into the men's.'

'No, he won't. He'll go in with you.'

'He's a *boy*,' I said.

'Yep, yep, I am,' Son said.

There was a silence. Husband stared out the window.

'You're just afraid of bringing him in and everyone looking at you!'

Husband laughed slightly. 'That's stupid. He's just too young to go into the men's.'

'You're afraid of going in there and buying nothing!'

'Don't be ridiculous!'

'You're the one being ridiculous if you think an eight-year-old boy wants to go into women's toilets!'

'I don't like lollidays!'

'I'm beginning to feel like that myself,' I griped, folding my arms and staring fixedly out the window.

There was silence for a bit.

'I think it's coming,' Son said calmly.

Husband sighed wearily and opened his door. 'Right, come on.' A pious look at me, which I ignored.

The two were gone for a long time. When they came back, Husband had his arms full of crisps and Coke and peanuts. He dumped them into the back seat without a word.

'Feel a bit peckish, did you?' I giggled.

'Well, I had to buy something – the toilets are right at the back of the place. They were all staring at us.'

'I want some crisps.' Little Daughter was trying to grab a packet from the car seat.

'Do you like holidays?' I asked, holding a packet out to her.

She narrowed her eyes. 'I just want crisps.'

'Do you like holidays?'

'I like holidays,' Son said. 'I *love* holidays!'

I handed the packet to him.

Little Daughter started to scream. 'They're mine! I want them!'

'Do you like holidays?'

A huge scream. Then a very bad-tempered *yes* was spat at me.

I handed her some crisps.

'I want those ones!' She pointed to the packet her brother was eating.

'Fine.' I calmly took the half-empty packet from my son and handed it to her. Son's eyes lit up when he received yet another full packet.

'Ha, ha,' Little Daughter said. 'I have these ones!'

Husband and I shared a laugh while Son whispered loudly, 'She's silly, isn't she, Mammy!'

'He's touching my seat!'

'I am not.'

'Mammy, he's on my side!'

'I am not!'

'He's looking out my window!'

'Mammy, I'm not.'

And on and on and on.

As we neared Cork, the sun began to peep out. Stupidly I began to think that it might actually be a good sign. It was like a big welcome banner in the sky. 'Hey,' it said to me. 'This is where you should be. This will be a great holiday!'

Of course Cork is not West Cork, as any seasoned traveller will tell you. Firstly, there is at least another ninety minutes' travel time ahead – longer if you're stopping off every few shops to check out swimwear – and ninety minutes' travel time in Ireland is like going into a different weather system.

It was pouring with rain when we reached our destination. In fact, it was so bad we had to stay in the car for fifteen minutes until it abated. Then Husband and I yanked open our doors and grabbed a child each and legged it up to the hotel.

The family room consisted of a double bed, a single bed and a travel cot. There was a television in the corner, and tea and coffee-making facilities on a low table. Son wanted to try out everything. He plugged in the kettle, minus the water. He marvelled at the table lamps. He flicked on the TV and was delighted to discover that it was fitted with Sky Digital.

'This is brilliant!' he pronounced, making himself comfortable on the double bed and flicking about madly to see if he could find the Man United channel. 'Why can't we get Sky at home?'

Husband and I declined to answer.

Daughter, meanwhile, was examining the travel cot. 'I don't like that,' she said. 'I don't like this room. I don't like lollidays.'

I rubbed my hands over my face. Took a few deep breaths and immediately felt dizzy. I tried to tune out by picking up the hotel manual. I soon discovered that the children's meals were being served in the dining hall at that very moment. The idea of the children's meals was to feed the kids and get them out of the way so that the adults could eat together later on. As husband and I hadn't had a meal alone in what felt like decades, I decided that that is what we would do.

'Who wants dinner?' I said in my best cajoling voice.

'I do,' Husband said.

I shook my head and pointed to the manual.

'Ohhh.' Husband now had *his* cajoling voice on. 'Who wants yum yum dinner?'

No one answered.

'Chips,' I said. 'I bet you'd like chips, wouldn't you?'

Son shook his head. 'I want to watch TV.'

I took the remote control from him. 'You could watch that at home,' I said crossly.

'No I can't,' Son pouted. 'You and Dad won't get Sky!'

'Look,' Husband said. 'You and your sister are going for dinner now. There'll be no arguments. Right' – he picked up Little Daughter – 'let's go.'

It took us ages to find the dining hall and when we got there dinner was in full swing. Kids were piling burgers onto their plates and some had massive mounds of beans. Husband whispered to me about the waste of food and how like the Americans we'd got. Son broke away from us and immediately began piling burgers onto his plate. Little Daughter screamed that she didn't want a dinner.

Many burgers later, Son was raring to head off to the children's club, so we found someone and he happily went off with them. Husband and I looked fondly after him. He was soooo adaptable.

'Now,' I said to Little Daughter, whose new lilac dress was smeared with force-fed beans. 'Wouldn't you like to play with loads of nice toys?'

'I don't *like* nice toys!'

'Well, horrible toys then,' Husband said a tad irritably.

Daughter wrinkled up her pert nose and batted her eyes. 'No.'

We ignored her. We found the crèche and handed her over.

'She'll be fine,' the girl assured us. 'Don't worry.'

Husband and I tried not to run all the way to the restaurant.

My mind was busily trying to get it through to my body that finally, finally, Husband and I were on our own. We didn't have to be constantly telling someone to 'eat up' or threatening non-eating behaviour with a taking away of dessert privileges.

Some lovely waitress had just put a delicious basket of fresh bread on our table when a shriek broke the adult calm of the restaurant.

The sound chilled my bones. It was as if someone had caught their fingers in the kitchen mincer.

The shriek grew louder, and Husband and I went into immediate denial. We began talking to each other in cheery voices while the rest of the punters gazed all about them wondering where the crying was coming from.

A dishevelled twenty-something entered the dining hall with a red-faced, tear-streaked, heaving bundle of lilac. 'Mammmyyy!'

I jumped up, mortified, and the breadbasket tumbled to the floor. While Husband tried to rescue it, I relieved Twenty-Something of my sobbing child.

'I don't like the crash!' my daughter screamed. 'Bold Mammy! Bold Daddy!'

People smiled in sympathy at me.

I smiled in a sort of drowning hopeless way back at them.

The nice waitress appeared at our table. 'Would you like a high chair for her?'

I nodded, thinking very un-motherly thoughts to myself.

A high chair was duly bought over. Little Daughter was given some bread, which she devoured. We decided not to eat any of the bread ourselves and doled it out to her as we ate our meal. Only Little Daughter wanted soup, and spuds, and whatever we were having. Husband ended up feeding her, while I ended up urging her to eat.

Our dinners grew cold as we piled attention on her to show the whole restaurant that we weren't really a bold mammy and daddy.

Night fell. The kids' club ended and Son arrived back to us full of stories about other youngsters he'd met. Then he informed us that he wanted to sleep in the double bed.

'I want the double bed too,' Little Daughter said.

'No.' I rolled my eyes. 'This is *your* bed.' I pointed to the travel cot. 'See, isn't it nice?'

She looked at me as though I was bonkers. 'No.'

'There's a nice sheet in it,' I said, trying not to sound too desperate. 'Look, teddies on it.'

Little Daughter peered in at it. 'Nice sheet,' she concurred.

We got the kids into their pyjamas, played a few mindless 'I spy' games, and finally informed them that it was time for bed. Son, despite my protestations, jumped into the double bed and snuggled down. Little Daughter screamed as we put her into the travel cot.

We turned off the television – the idea being to let them go to sleep before we turned it back on again. We'd planned to order a few drinks from the bar and whisper as they slept.

Only they didn't sleep.

Little daughter screamed for about an hour until we took her out of the travel cot. Son flicked the telly back on. Husband looked in despair at me and asked, 'Who wants a drink from the bar?'

Drinks over, we attempted to put them down again. It was now after midnight and Son was ready to conk out. His eyes grew sleepy as we put him into the single bed and tucked him up. Little Daughter was tired too, so we waited until she was just asleep before placing her ever so gently, and ever so slowly into the travel cot.

'NNOOOOOO!'

I jumped.

Husband hissed some sort of nasty curse.

Little Daughter stood up and attempted to climb out.

'Go asleep!' I snapped, my patience gone. 'You ruined our dinner, now you're going to ruin the night!'

Husband patted me on the back, took Little Daughter out and proceeded to walk about the room crooning songs to her.

Little Daughter gave me what I could only imagine was a smile of triumph before snuggling into his arms.

Eventually she seemed to fall asleep. I was half-asleep myself.

Husband stood over the cot and braced himself. Gently, as if he was handling some highly toxic nuclear material, he lowered her into it.

'NNOOOOOOO!'

'OH FOR GOD'S SAKE!' I pulled the duvet up around my ears.

Husband was about to take her out again. 'Don't do that,' I shouted over the noise of my daughter shouting. 'She's making a fool out of us!'

'I have to.' Husband grabbed her up. 'What will the people on this floor think? They won't be able to sleep at all!'

'I don't care about other people,' I almost sobbed. 'I just want some peace!'

Husband put his arm around me. 'I know, but just look at her – isn't she cute?'

Little Daughter smiled up at us. 'I want double bed.'

'And you won't cry if you come in here?' I said.

'No.'

So into the bed she came.

'I have no room!'

Husband sighed deeply.

I pretended to be asleep.

'I HAVE NO ROOM!'

Husband's patience snapped. 'Well, you'll have loads in your cot, won't you?' he said, picking her up and planting her in it.

Hell with sirens on broke loose.

It was now close to three in the morning.

I attempted to remedy the situation. I put my hand into the cot. 'You hold onto me as you fall asleep,' I whispered. 'And I'll dream nice dreams all about ice-cream and you can share them.'

Little Daughter stopped howling to consider. 'Strawberry ice-cream?'

'Uh-huh.'

'I don't like that.'

'Any ice-cream you want then,' I whispered.

'Chocolate.'

'Fine.'

She lay down. I shoved my hand in, almost falling out of the bed to do so.

In the morning, my arm was so stiff, I couldn't swim in the pool.

Husband did though, in his madly overpriced designer swimwear that he'd purchased from the hotel shop. It had cost about half our holiday budget.

This then was the pattern of our summer break. Little Daughter flatly refusing to go to the crèche, us having to feed her at the table. After four days, she wouldn't sit at the table, so we had to forfeit our meals in the hotel dining room and have them in our room or else visit restaurants that were frequented by very few people, in the hope that they wouldn't mind a protesting toddler. In West Cork, such places are thin on the ground. At night, there was screaming and shouting, and by the end of the two weeks, Husband and I were like two zombies.

Fantasies of being at home, with the kids tucked safely in bed while I lolled across the sofa watching *Fair City* obsessed me for three days before we took our leave.

Husband drove at breakneck speed all the way back to Kildare.

Little Daughter and Son were promptly despatched to bed. Husband and I sat down together in the kitchen. It was eerily quiet and big.

Shaking his head, he said, 'D'you realise this is the first break we've had since we went on our break?'

Family holidays – they make you appreciate being back home.

# CIARA DWYER

## MOROCCO

I knew nothing about Morocco. And when I say nothing, I mean nothing. If you had asked me to point it out on a map of the world, I would have answered like a vague nineteenth-century Polynesian woman who had not heard of the invention of maps and told you that it was 'far away'. Perhaps it was near Timbuktu, or beside that Bermuda Triangle. Which continent was it on? I had no notion, but being clueless was not a problem. I trusted the smiling blonde girl in Budget Travel who showed me the brochure. She had drummed her French manicured fingers into her computer keyboard, looked at her screen, then my face, and said, 'Morocco'. It fitted the bill.

I wanted somewhere that was cheap, had sunshine, and a bit of culture. I had emphasised the word 'bit'. My demand for a morsel of culture had cropped up after the previous year's holiday, which I had spent on the hell hole that is Ios – a Greek island that has been taken over by the boozing Irish and English. For a full fortnight, I did not come across any

Greeks, unless you counted the grey-haired bus-driver with the bracelet and the goats. I had accidentally bumped into him on my first day, when I had the bright idea of walking to the beach. I got lost and ended up in a nudist enclave full of uninhibited German girls who bounced with their beach balls and flaunted their blue tattoos, which snaked around their hips, where a bikini might have been tied, had they been wearing any. I had never been big on doing the museum thing, but after a few days in Ios, where the English lads bragged about their conquests – 'I jabbed her' – and others boasted about their bowel movements, which they had left floating in the sea, I decided that I wanted a culture that had nothing to do with yobs or booze.

'I want to go to Italy,' I had told the travel agent, and listening to my demands, she quoted prices. Whereupon I nearly fainted, and so Morocco was plan B. It was as clinical and practical as that. It had nothing to do with the allure of the Arab world, the magic of the mosques and the medinas. It was cheap, it was sunny and, in short, it was not Ios. Perfect.

Nobody ever told me that it was in Africa. And as for the whole Islamic culture thing, I was a dunce. But in hindsight, that was probably the best way to be. Morocco was one great big culture shock. And I fell in love with it all – the people, the men (yes, they are very beautiful), the culture and the customs. Ten years on, and I am still in love with the country. I love it, hate it and love it all over again. It has changed me. Like the writer Ruth Prawer Jhabvala and India, the homeland of her husband, I now recognise the stages in my Moroccan cycle.

When I am there, I feel utterly at home. I embrace the simple ways of life, the delightfully lethargic pace, and I vow that I am going to stay there, forever. It's the little things that I love. The way the man with the kind eyes in the corner shop, Ahmed, has become my buddy. We chat and he asks me why I haven't married yet. And I ask him the same thing.

Neither of us has an answer and we laugh about it. I tell him if I hit a certain age, and there is nothing doing, he can give me a baby. He serves the customers in between our conversation, and then waves goodbye as he pulls down the shutters and heads off for his long lunch at midday.

A week later, I am complaining of its primitive backward ways. The poverty depresses me and I cannot look at the young girls with heavy make-up – they are almost always prostitutes – without my eyes filling up and feeling both sad and sick at the thought of what they are driven to do. The sight of the poverty grinds you down. As I walk to the beach, there are a lot of beggars. Many are deformed and wave their stumps of arms and legs as you pass by in the hope that you will become sympathetic and give them some money. One legless man hobbles about and pushes himself on a flat board on wheels. He doesn't brandish his disability, but he is as heartbreaking as the rest of the beggars. One woman sits under a tree, with her baby in her arms. But she has her dignity. She doesn't harass you; she doesn't beg. She sits with her eyes downcast, focusing on her infant. And as you give her money and she raises her head, it is the look in her eyes that kills you. There is a mix of gratitude and desperation. Today your few dirhams will feed her child. How can you be a happy tourist concentrating on tanning after that?

I have French and so I can talk to many Moroccans. I listen to tales of corruption, of people who have fallen on hard times, and gaunt-faced fathers, who tell me about the nights when they have not enough money to feed their children. And I want to weep. I sit in my room and feel guilty for being so lucky. Here am I, like so many Western women, worrying about the size of my ass in a bikini, joining WeightWatchers and the like, and scolding myself for eating too much. And in Morocco, less than four hours from Dublin, there are people who don't have to try to lose weight. Instead, they struggle to stretch their dirhams to feed their families.

Morocco has long lost its tourist gloss for me. When I have

overdosed on tales of hardship, and lain on the beach for too long, watching the young Moroccan boys offer their bodies to elderly German men, I feel sick and want to go home. The young Moroccans are ruthless, flaunting their skinny chests and flattering fat old men, as they rub the massage oil into their bodies. But it works both ways: the Germans know that they have power – money – and so they will pay for their Moroccan pleasures. Over the years, I have got to know Morocco, warts and all.

To rob Patrick Kavanagh's line – I have looked through a chink too wide – and when that happens, it is no longer my lovely Morocco and I want to go home. The poverty, the deprivation, the people scrambling to eke out a living, are all too much for my soul. There is no social welfare in Morocco, no dole, and the very idea of rent subsidy is laughable. Unemployment is a huge problem. You will talk to university graduates who cannot get a job as a waiter, let alone something for which they are qualified. But they are all willing to work. You will often see men and women sitting at the edge of roads, with their buckets and tools. The men will wait all day, hoping someone will pick them up and avail of their cheap labour; and the women are ready to clean and cook and do whatever domestic chore they can to get a few dirhams. When I witness this, I get angry and sad and start to count the days until I go home. But once back in Dublin, I miss Morocco. In many ways I think that it is a better place than Ireland. And then I dream of going back. Morocco is not like other countries. It gets under your skin.

But let me begin at the beginning. For me, a country is its people. And the Moroccans are a lovely race; like the Irish or the Italians, they are warm and friendly and like to chat. It is not simply a question of them inviting you to their homes for some couscous – and indeed they will do that – it is the small things they do, the random gestures of kindness.

Take the night flight to Morocco; we had just left Dublin airport and a baby began to cry. You could hear the tuts and feel the tension in the air – what sort of parents would be irresponsible enough to bring a baby on a long flight? Did they have no consideration for the other passengers, who were all set on sleeping? The infant's wail pierced the gentle hum of the plane. Everyone was getting tetchy, especially the man who was sitting in beside the baby. And then the Moroccan air steward took the baby in his arms, smiled at him and played with him until he was utterly pacified. It was a simple thing to do and probably broke with airline protocol, but it showed warmth and it worked. At times like that, you wish all the world could be as warm as the Moroccans. They are a tactile race.

I remember the first morning I woke up in Morocco. There was a strange noise, like a cow mooing. I had not noticed a farm on the way in to the hotel the night before. I discovered later that it was the muezzin in the mosque, calling all Muslims to prayer. This early-morning call, I was told, included the line, 'It is better to pray than sleep.' (Now, that was debatable.) But the sun was shining and it was no great chore to get up and face the day. I left the hotel and headed for the beach. A frail old man shuffled past me and said, 'Good morning.' Charmed, I returned his greeting with a smile. What a wonderful country it was. And then he talked some more. 'And the pussy is good?' I was shocked. And such a sweet old man too. He looked like somebody's grandad. But this was probably the greatest introduction I could ever have to Morocco.

One minute, the men are on their mats, facing east, as they say their prayers, and the next, they are nipping off to brothels or picking up girls on the street. The country is a mass of contradictions. And so I learnt the art of survival in Morocco. If you are a woman alone, you will be harassed. It doesn't matter if you look like a nun, or indeed are one, they will try it on. They will hiss at you, as if you are a cat; they will make such strong eye contact with you that they are in danger of walking into poles or tripping. And then there are the truly persistent ones who will continue to walk beside you, hoping that you will crack with a snarl or a smile – anything, as long as you react. The worst insult is to ignore them.

I developed my own strategy to avoid these men. A simple procedure. I never left the hotel without sunglasses, so they could not make eye contact. I listened to a Walkman, so not one hiss would I hear. And I would wait until I got to the beach before I put on skimpy sun-tops. As well as making sense, this was a mark of respect for their culture. If I dressed conservatively, perhaps they would behave towards me in that way. This was my hope. But there wasn't a chance of it working. If you are alone, they assume you must be lonely and looking for company. 'I only want to talk to you,' one man shouted at me as I ignored him. And maybe that was all he wanted. But there were enough Moroccan men with gamey looks in their eyes that taught me otherwise.

I could divide Moroccan men into two groups: the ones who harass you on the street; and those who are my buddies. I come across this second group as I go about my day. They are the waiters who work in restaurants, the sweet teenagers who take the money for the sunbeds on the beach, and the hotel receptionists who show you photos of their families. This is the real Morocco. They do not see you as a mere tourist and they include you in their day-to-day lives, as you get on with your holiday. I have had a receptionist in Marrakech call me back as I was heading out for the night. He ordered me back to my room and to collect my fleece as it was cold. They are sweet people and a breed apart from those who hiss and call on the street.

Moroccan men sometimes get a bad press, as though they are all extreme fundamentalists. Morocco may not be as strict as Saudi Arabia, but the roles for men and women are still clear-cut. Traditionally men work while women stay home to cook and care for the children. As the roles are defined, life does seem less complicated here than at home, where more and more women have joined the workforce and kids are dumped in crèches. But society in Morocco is gradually changing. I have had meals cooked for me by Muslim husbands, while I have sat and chatted to their wives, so it is far from the Stone Age. I have watched a father go over his daughter's homework with her. So the roles are not that rigid. The extended family is very important in Morocco and families help each other out, by minding each other's children and generally being supportive.

It was inevitable that a nation so fond of talking would end up using mobiles. Now the women take them out of the folds of their kaftans, some sending text messages to say hello, or phoning their spouses, but ending the call before they answer, as an economical way of saying hello – I am thinking of you, without actually talking.

It is unfair to paint Morocco as a nation of predatory men. Those types exist all right, but so does a way of life that has long disappeared from Ireland. Morocco is not for everybody. You may not be looking for a simple lifestyle, but if you are, it is there to see. My mother says that it reminds her of Ireland in the 1950s. It can often look like a slice out of a Kavanagh poem – 'the bicycles go by in twos and threes'. People don't have much, so they make do with what they've got and take care of those few things. They get their shoes repaired and clothes mended, and there is a quaint respectability that comes from having very little but wanting to put your best foot forward.

The simple way of life that first charmed me is still there. As the men walk down dusty roads with the hoods of their djellabas up, pointing at the dusk, they look like something out of the Old Testament. And life is distilled to a few basic elements – love, family, children and the continuity of life. Here, children are not regarded as nuisances; at night, families go for a stroll and toddlers laugh as their fathers whoosh them onto their shoulders and wives smile on. Old people are not just cherished, they are revered. They are honoured for having endured the long years of their lives. And like children, they enjoy a special place within Moroccan society. I have been in trains when an elderly person has joined the carriage, and all the Moroccans, both men and women, have made a fuss of them. Thankfully the DART invisible stare has not travelled this distance. If Moroccans eat in a train carriage, they share whatever they have with everyone else.

There are simple traditions that keep the sense of community alive. The women visit the hammams (steam baths) together and wash and talk and relax. The men do the same. Men are as good at chatting as the women. They will sit for hours on end in cafés, all huddled around a pot of mint tea, and they will talk and watch the world go by. Nor are they afraid to show their affection for each other. It is quite common to see heterosexual men walk hand in hand, arm in arm.

Morocco may be a poor country and the people may not have much, but they are exceedingly generous and hospitable. When you visit somebody's home, you become part of the family, as everyone eats from the same plate – the tradition being that everyone is equal at the table.

On my first trip to Morocco, I met some girls at the hammam. They invited me to their home for dinner the next day. Now, each time I am in Morocco, I visit them. The head of the house is a widow and she works hard to support her family. But on her one day off, she invites me to her house for dinner. The meals are always scrumptious, elaborate dishes, which she has spent all day preparing. And after the meal is over, this dear woman plumps up the cushions behind me and orders me to lie down, to let the food settle in my stomach. She has no English or French and I have about four phrases in Arabic, but we communicate through smiles and hugs.

I visit another family when I am in Morocco. Each time we have the same argument – why did I book a hotel? Next time I am to stay with them, they tell me. When I am there, they put on BBC World on the television, especially for me, and on the table they thoughtfully put a knife and fork in my place, in case I do not want to eat with my hands. Nothing is too much trouble. We wander the souks together. They teach me how to make the glorious harrira soup, and I play with the children of the house. They have even looked after me when I have had a dodgy stomach.

When you go to Morocco, you must find your own version of it. Stray from the tourist centres and talk to the people. I have belly-danced in Fez. I have befriended toothy tramps and I have squatted over their hole in the ground. I have returned to Dublin with my feet painted with henna, the colour of kippers, and found it difficult to get used to eating again from my own plate with a knife and fork. And I didn't think it would happen, but I even missed the hissing men.

I have travelled to other countries, but nowhere comes close. Morocco has its faults, and its problems are endless, but for all that, the country has become like an old lover of mine and it will always have a special part in my heart.

# GAYE SHORTLAND

## from *HARMATTAN*

***Author's note:*** I lived in Africa for sixteen years, spending much of my time with the nomadic Tuareg, legendary warriors and rulers of the Sahara, whose way of life is now in danger of extinction as droughts decimate their great herds of camels and goats. I fell hopelessly in love with the whole culture, eventually marrying into the tribe and producing three children along the way. My novel, *Harmattan*, is based on part of that experience. Ellen, the Irish protagonist of *Harmattan*, is therefore a thinly disguised version of me.

In this extract, she has travelled with some Tuareg friends into the desert in search of her lost lover Amodi, but when they finally reach his family encampment, there is no sign of him.

'Ellen,' said Haruna indicating Muhane with a movement of his head. 'I'm going to wash that girl.'

And wash her he did, with the proficiency of one who has watched children being washed thoroughly and economically from a single bucket or calabash of water every day of his childhood on the green moist plateau of Jos in Nigeria.

The result was spectacular. Her skin changed from dusty beige to gold, her stiff scraggy halo of dusty hair sprang into gleaming black curls and a truly gorgeous little girl emerged, enthusiastically surveying herself in my hand mirror. Haruna and I went to the market and bought her a pair of blue rubber sandals, a small green and gold striped top and a bit of plain royal blue cotton for a wrapper. She was unrecognisable.

I pondered on how odd it was that Yassine should make no attempt to wash her. But that was the way of the desert – children ran naked and wild, often in the bitter cold, adorned only with a few blue beads and a few leather-encased charms, until some mysterious alarm bell sounded – puberty, I suppose – and suddenly they were kitted out in clothes and headdresses and sandals and jewellery, with braided hair and oiled skin. Was it economy or what? Or a superstition? The Evil Eye, maybe, would be attracted if any attention was lavished on them. Who knows, we might be blamed yet if any accident or disease befell Muhane.

Tiny little Raechitu, in her beads and charms and blue dye, we left as she was. . . .

Staying in In-Gall was proving expensive. Troops of men came by all the time, either to survey us or visit the women. They sprawled all over the place, spindly legs propped on bony knees, and had to be fed and given tea. Haruna was constantly being sent to the market (on my money) and given instructions about cooking. We needed to leave before the money gave out altogether but I had to wait for the natural moment – too soon would be offensive.

Courtship was, in fact, rampant though muted, with the men also having a go at me. I didn't know how to square it all off with the fact that Yassine was just newly widowed but, after all, it would soon be a priority for her to find a new provider. In truth, I still hadn't perceived anything that could be called grief but, then again, there could be any amount of pain hidden beneath that mask of serenity. And living hand to mouth, fearing for the very survival of one's children, would take the edge off any grief. But I wondered why she was not living with her kinsfolk or Yusuf's parents and what the alliance between her and A'isha was all about.

A'isha begged from me constantly and I ended up giving her two of the few wrappers I had with me. She, in return, sent Ilyas to the market – again, on my money – to buy plastic, coloured thread, from which she wove a bunch of intricately patterned bracelets in the inevitable blue and black, with touches of white and red and green. I sat and watched her nimble supple fingers, fascinated by her skill.

'You must come back for the Cure Salée the Salt Cure,' she begged, halting in her weaving, her face alive with excitement. 'Every year all the Tamajegh people gather, with the Arabs and the Wodaabe and others – from all over Niger! Many, many, many people! They bring their animals to lick salt and it is a time of great festivity, with drumming and singing and dancing and courtship. You must come!'

In-Gall was obviously an ideal place for an unattached Tuareg woman to be – I had been intrigued to notice that even now the unmarried A'isha didn't always sleep alone.

'But come at any time – we are always here,' she whispered urgently. 'Always in In-Gall. Any time you come back, you will find us here. Any time.'

'But what if you marry again?' I asked. 'A man from the desert?'

'No, no,' she said vehemently. 'If you come, you will find us here. In In-Gall.'

Was she hunting for a husband from among the townsmen? I took the plunge. 'Are you trying to marry a rich man, A'isha?' I said jokingly. 'Maybe a merchant, a Hausa alhaji who has been to Mecca?'

'Never, never!' she cried, shaking a finger vigorously. 'The Hausa men marry four wives! Our men marry only one! I could never live with another woman! I could not have patience with that!'

And I was reminded of the extraordinary fact that Tuareg men, though entitled as Muslims to the prescribed four wives, generally shun polygamy, favouring a brand of monogamy that is emphatically serial but monogamy nevertheless.

A thought struck me. 'Did you want to leave your last husband, A'isha? Or was it he who wanted to divorce you?'

'*Kai*! I left him.' She said no more, busying herself again with her bracelet-making.

I didn't doubt her. Very often, it was the women who walked out – literally – on a marriage, another indication of the high status of the women in this matriarchal society. Traditionally, inheritance and succession were passed through the mother's side, giving women a power and respect rare in African society and unique in the Muslim world. When the French first came, they took the Tuareg women to be as promiscuous as mythical South Sea Islanders, so free and independent were their manners.

I was losing count of the days we had stayed, uneasily aware that we were settling in as if it were home. A little daily routine was being established. Every morning dawned with a bit of brigandage – Haruna and Ilyas had taken to grabbing passing goats and pulling them into our hut, where, with Haruna holding them by the head, Ilyas milked them into a big purple plastic cup. We drank the warm, sweet, foaming milk, feeling very clever and guilty. Then visitors began to arrive and we generally held court throughout the day, falling asleep on our mats in the sweltering heat of midday, waking to drag the mats outside and wait for sunset, the coolness of evening and the stars. Sometimes we went to the market in the mornings or to spend the day in other households. In the late afternoons, I took to wandering around with the children in the cool of the gardens under the shade of the date palms; we bought the huge tomatoes and melons grown there and ate them as we walked.

Ataka, of course, was plying his trade, producing rings and necklaces for anyone who could come up with a piece of silver or gold. And A'isha was constantly begging me to forget Tazerza and stay in In-Gall. While all this was going on, I felt like a diver poised on a high-board.

We had to move on.

We were loading up the obligatory gifts of sacks of millet in the market, getting ready to leave, when I saw the old man, Yusuf's father, approaching on a donkey at a trot. He was dressed in cheap white cotton, rather than the formal black or indigo. Above the white veil of his tagilmoust, his eyes were wary.

We confronted each other – snake-catcher and snake – which was which? He asked to speak to me privately.

In the gloom of a nearby tin-roofed shack, he gently reprimanded me in a mixture of clumsy Hausa, Tamajegh and sign language, for giving his son's money to Yassine. She was a beautiful young woman; she would marry again quickly; she was no good and didn't care about him and his wife. She had already refused to live with them even before Yusuf had died. But where were he and Yusuf's mother to find money to live? Yusuf used to take care of them – they had no other son – what would happen to them now?

I cursed myself for getting it so wrong – he was right, of course – Yassine had resources; he had not. Then I did the only thing I could – I lied and said I would speak to Yusuf's *maigida* and would return to In-Gall as soon as I could and I would bring some money for them. I suppose I meant it at the time. But, in fact, I never went back to In-Gall.

We were practically on our way when I saw the small procession approaching: Yassine, the children and some boys bearing a trunk, a mat, a *bidon* for water. A'isha brought up the rear with a face like thunder. Yassine and the children were coming with us to Tazerza, to visit her sister, who lived in neighbouring Tassara.

I tried to talk her out of it, as did A'isha vehemently. We

wouldn't be coming back through In-Gall so she might be stranded. But she was adamant – she was coming with us.

So then we had to add another two sacks of grain to the roof-rack – for the sister. Jesus. We'd be lucky if we didn't snap an axle with this load – eight sacks of grain and the extra passengers with their gear, besides me, Haruna, Ilyas, Amodi, when we found him, and our own gear.

So we set out, heading along the sandy road to the north-east at first, as if we were returning to Agadez. Then we circled north, cutting across the track that led to Teguidda-n-Tessoumt, and headed west, speeding along the harsh dry flatlands. To the south was Tchin Tabaraden and ahead of us, Tazerza, with its goatskin tents in their dry-season resting-places. There, an arm's length away, was Amodi. I had my joy in my sights now and it could not escape me.

At night, we slept on mats on the level sand and one night, as we lay beneath a glaring stupendous moon, a party of Tuareg appeared like apparitions risen out of the sand, speaking in quiet murmurs. Women emerged from the group and insisted on rigging up a bed for me with carved wooden posts they took from the back of their camels. Tightly woven leather and straw mats were laid on top and dyed leather pillows.

They had come east from the Azaouagh area and had passed through the dry-season camp of Ilyas's people. Was Sideka there? Yes. Had they been anywhere near Amodi's encampment? No. But, yes, they had news of him. Yes, he was well. Yes, he was there.

But Amodi was not there when we arrived. My pride forbade me even to ask about him, so I spent the first morning in an agony of suspense, sitting at the door of a goatskin tent smiling at the world, furious with Haruna and Ilyas that they didn't have the wit to ask about him and tell me where he was, thinking at any moment to have a sudden sight of him striding eagerly over the sand. I was also afraid to ask – afraid of what I might hear.

Eventually his mother, Tsalert, a fine-boned tiny elderly-looking woman with a lovely face, casually remarked that he was at a household 'away to the north' but 'he was coming'. I pretended indifference while feverishly wondering: how far, how long? But what was the point in asking? They only understood distances in terms of time, and time in the desert was an ever-flexible and fluid commodity. They would despise signs of impatience – think it comic and ridiculous.

I smiled at Tsalert, praying that she would tell me more but she did not.

I loved Tsalert. Because of him. And wanted her to love me. But she never really acknowledged any special relationship between us, despite the fact that I always showered her with presents – thick rolls of soft black cloth, strings of beads, Maria Theresa silver coins to have jewellery made from and, of course, the all-important sacks of grain. She needed all the support I could give her. She had been divorced from Amodi's father many years before, and had gone away to Tassara in the north, leaving her ten-year-old son behind. Since then, she had married several times but there had been no other surviving children. When her last husband died, leaving her destitute, Amodi had gone and brought her back to Tazerza. It was an unhappy situation – Amodi's father was dead and Tsalert had to live side by side with Maryam his widow.

Amodi felt fiercely protective of her and I would have done the world and all for her if she had responded to me a bit more. But she remained slightly aloof. Perhaps it was the universal policy of 'if I pretend it isn't there, maybe it will go away'. My own mother back in Ireland stuck to much the same policy.

They slaughtered two goats on our arrival. I always felt half-guilty, knowing how precious each animal was now after the droughts. But it was a matter of pride for them – hospitality being a great virtue. It was strange – whenever I tried to come up with a word to describe that trait of theirs I could only come up with the Irish word *flaithiúlacht*, which means the virtue of being hospitable and open-handed, a concept springing from our own feudal system. We still use the word in Ireland as if there were no English equivalent that expresses the notion, and there are other words – *grámhar*, for instance, which means loving, warm, demonstrative, in the same larger-than-life sense.

The Tuareg have some special words for strange concepts: a word for 'hunger for meat' is one of them. My arrival gave them the opportunity to satisfy that hunger, living, as they did, on a spartan diet of millet with milk.

I watched the hapless goat being held, neck to the ground, the clean slit across the throat executed with an accompanying prayer – and indeed they would starve rather than eat an animal which was slaughtered without the requisite prayer – the brief jerking of the body as the eyes glazed over, life departing visibly, spilling like the blood in the sand. And as always, it amazed me how quick and clean it was. As was the rest of the process. I had always imagined skinning would be like a gory scalping in Hollywood westerns but, instead, the skin was stripped from the hanging carcass in a clean and bloodless way – for all the world like a jump suit being unzipped and stripped off, leaving the naked body.

We ate the tender meat, shredded and oiled and seasoned in a large wooden bowl, passing the wooden spoon from one person to the other.

Three days passed with no sign or news of Amodi. I hung between painful tension and the joy of knowing that, if I had to sit on my mat for a month, sooner or later I would be in his physical presence ... I sat on my mat and waited and watched.

The women sat there, dark eyes glinting, draped in indigo-steeped, soft black cotton, their babies suckling at firm brown breasts. Placid, good-humoured, they chewed tobacco, drank sweet tea and chased for lice in each other's glossy blue-black hair. As always, I was repelled by the animality of it all. Fascinated by it. Envied them that.

'Ellen!' they cried. 'Stay here with us and drink camel's milk until you become a beautiful woman! Big!' They made circles with their arms to show how big. They spoke to me in clumsy Hausa and often made remarks in Tamajegh, which they assumed I didn't understand, unaware that I knew enough to follow conversations. They rubbed indigo dye into the insides of my arms, marvelling at how luminous it looked on my pale skin. 'Beautiful!' they said. I was pleased that at least in one small way they granted that I surpassed them – I could make indigo glow better.

One laughing young woman, Djanetta, was particularly energetic in courting my friendship. She had been away visiting when I visited before. Djanetta fell more than a little short of the Tuareg ideal of beauty – her teeth were large and her lips too generous, so her constant expression was a huge toothy grin in a face full of lively warmth. Her voice was shrill and nasal. She struck me, oddly, as the type who might be a nun back home. Like Yassine, she was a tiny woman – it seemed as if Tuareg girls were genetically programmed to grow outwards instead of upwards in their teens, while the boys strode on to become tall and sinewy.

Little as Djanetta was, her breasts and buttocks stuck out aggressively. In the desert, I mused, it seemed that a childbearer had to have the capacity to store fat – like a camel – the buttocks being the hump.

Yet the desert was full of contradictions that constantly confounded me. The women of the neighbouring tribe, the Peuhl, stalked stork-like through the landscape with graceful elongated frames, bearing their enormous calabashes of milk on their heads. Aquiline faces delicately tattooed, hair gathered into a huge top-knot on the forehead, each ear pierced a dozen times around the edge with huge hoops of some light metal like tin, wearing short little bodices which left the lower half of their breasts bare and short skirts of woven striped cloth – they were fantastic figures against a surreal landscape, like something out of the post-nuclear world of Mad Max. And lean, very lean.

I could but marvel at this miracle of ethnic survival, these two separate cultures living side by side over the centuries, never intermingling. And, for me, there was a flip side even to this miracle – the thought that it was yet another symptom of a self-absorption I found threatening.

Djanetta smeared blue dye liberally on me at every opportunity. 'Beautiful!' she cried, slapping one supple finger on her palm and flicking it through a loose fist. And she pulled two dark blue bracelets from her arms and put them on mine. Crude circles of glass, they glowed marvellously in the sun.

The old men fretted at the way my hair hung about my face 'like a madwoman'. Finally, when Abu Bakr, Amodi's uncle and head of the extended family group, began to fuss about my hair, I agreed to go through the lengthy process of plaiting. So Zaynabu, Amodi's little half-sister padded off to get some hair-gel from another tent. A year before, she would have scampered like a young gazelle but now she was about twelve and at that age they would be getting her to eat up and become fat and beautiful. She was already very beautiful, very like Amodi, with full lips, almond-shaped eyes, delicate brows and a perfect luminous oval face.

Lying on my side, supported by a leather pillow under my armpit, I tried to make the best of an embarrassing situation. I'd had this experience inflicted on me before and I hadn't liked it then either.

Yassine, still with us, was elected to do my hair. She smathered a copious amount of the blue hair-gel they used onto her palms and began to smear it vigorously on my hair. I hated the gooey gel for starters and then there was the effort of concealing the fact that I didn't have the suppleness or muscular tone to keep poised in that position for a long period of time without strain. Nor did it help that I knew enough of the language to understand when Zaynabu's mother, Maryam (a handsome heavy-boned woman not at all like her little sylph of a daughter) muttered, 'Ears on her head!' – meaning that my ears stuck out at more than the accepted angle.

They tut-tutted over the red-brown colour of my hair.

'El-len!' Maryam cried in her drawling tone. They always cried my name out shrilly as if I were deaf. 'There is a trader who comes sometimes – a Hausaman – and he has a hair-dye – black-black – if he comes, we will buy some for you! It will make your hair very very black – beautiful!'

I raised a feeble grin. Fuck their black hair. It irritated the hell out of me that they could see no beauty or merit in anything that was strange or different.

Yassine was working away busily, using various little blunt knives to twist sections of my hair into knots and pin them out of the way. She flashed a scrap of broken mirror before me a few times and I saw that, as ever, she had chosen a style where an intricate structure of tiny plaits projected low onto my forehead and ran down the sides of my face. I thought it made me look like a pig – but of course they loved that chubby look.

'Good!' smiled Abu Bakr when the process was at last finished, running his gnarled hands with pleasure over the intricate result. I was uncomfortable and self-conscious – it felt tight about my head and, sure enough, it made my ears stick out more than usual. I smiled.

I tied my dark-blue headscarf around it, covering it up, and felt better.

It was all absorbing and wonderful but it was difficult. If I had been with Amodi, soul and body singing with the joy of his presence, it would have been so much easier. But I was heartsore, anxiety and longing and impatience eating away at me. It was hard to be gracious, it was hard to be fun, to give all passers-by their money's worth entertainment-wise, when

I felt like lying down and dying with the nervous strain of waiting and wondering.

And, of course, there was sweet damn all privacy. I was on show at all times, to all people. The kids formed a constant border of grinning faces to my every activity. And if I just sat, they sat and stared. I was used to this exposure to an extent even in Zaria, where I constantly wore dark glasses to the market or wherever, so that I didn't have to make eye contact with all the staring eyes. And where, even in my own house, I literally had to lock myself up in my bedroom to get a moment alone – and then they'd be knocking at the door, knocking at the window – they just had no concept of private space. The local Nigerians in Zaria were better – they had some concepts of privacy, from the colonial experience of working as servants but primarily from their own culture where, for instance, rich alhajis kept their wives in a form of liberal purdah. It was the difference between living in mud architecture and living in leather tents.

What I needed was a great black veil like the Tuareg women – turn the back, pull the veil down over the face and spread it wide and that signalled a claiming of space, a little nodule of privacy around the woman. But I didn't have a veil, they couldn't interpret my subtle signals and I didn't know theirs, and they stared without mercy.

***Author's note:*** Ellen does soon find her Amodi but her great love for him is only the starting point in a struggle to come to terms with his culture, which at times seems utterly alien.

# NENA BHANDARI

# ENDURING INDIA

Please let us get an upgrade. Please let us get an upgrade. It was the eve of our trip to India and I was beginning to panic about travelling in economy for the nine-hour flight. I admit it, I'm a princess who likes to travel in comfort and style. Surprisingly the thought that I would be spending a week travelling on the back of a motorbike with my boyfriend of four years, together with over eighty other riders, on roads where over eighty thousand people die each year, hardly crossed my mind. This small matter had been put aside in a part of my brain and would only resurface when necessary. At that moment, there were pressing issues to worry about – like deep vein thrombosis and my sartorial elegance, or lack of it, on the forthcoming trip.

Scott, my partner in crime, had decided to unpack all my holiday wear from my fabulously large Louis Vuitton case and then repack the most unfashionable clothes in a hideous red rucksack. My sexy silk dresses and cashmere shawls were lying in a heap on the floor. The scoundrel had substituted my

Prada shoes and bags for a pair of Birkenstocks (which, apparently, are very trendy, if you're into that sort of thing), black chunky leather boots and a first-aid kit containing no useful narcotics whatsoever. There were tens of packets of Dioralyte and Imodium but not even one single Valium. The thought of having Delhi belly and being dressed like a confused student at an anti-globalisation rally caused me to hyperventilate.

I couldn't believe now that this trip was all my idea. On my twenty-first birthday, my parents had given me two (first-class) tickets to India. I was utterly horrified at the thought of going to a third world country, so I begged them to change the tickets to New York, which they kindly did. In return, I promised that I would go to their homeland by the time I was thirty, even though I knew my lack of interest in this faraway country was unlikely to change. India was my parents' home – not mine. My parents had moved to Ireland from India more than five years before I was born in the comforting surroundings of the Rotunda Hospital. I had had the luxury of private education in south Dublin. All my friends were Irish and I felt no different from them. At school, I still had to make it to assembly every morning at eight fifty, unlike the Jewish students who had an extra ten minutes in bed, and on Christmas mornings I would wake up as excited as David Murphy next door.

How was I supposed to know that time would go by so quickly and that my parents would remember the promise made almost nine years ago? I knew the reason they wanted me to go to India was for me to get to know my relatives, but when I made the promise there was no mention of meeting or staying with any of them. So when it came round to organising the trip, to be on the safe side, I devised a plan whereby it would be impossible for me to meet or stay with any uncle, auntie or cousin in Delhi or the Punjab. After checking an atlas and surfing the web, I enrolled Scott and myself on a charity motorbike trip with a strict schedule in the south of India.

In return for raising money for the Rainbow Trust, which cares for children with life-threatening or terminal illnesses, and the Pain and Palliative Care Society, which improves the quality of life of patients with terminal cancer, we would be given the pleasure of riding the 'tested, trusted, timeless' Royal Enfield Bullet.

About six months before the trip was to take place, after a night of debauchery at the Morrison, followed by some serious fun at Lillie's, I had put the idea to Scott. The only fact that I had remembered from the website of the English organisers (Enduro India) was that the first few nights were to be spent in a five-star hotel in Calicut. Scott needed no convincing, and as he had recently bought a scooter, he thought that the impending trip would motivate him to get his motorbike licence. He was always the more adventurous one of the two of us and usually it was he who came up with the ideas to provide respite from the drudgery of our jobs as lawyers.

After paying the one-thousand-pound-sterling registration fee and having various nights out in the name of charity, which involved our friends putting ten pounds in a charity pot for every drink consumed, it was too late to back down. Before we knew it, we had handed over the required six thousand pounds, half of which was made up from donations from our drunken friends and proud parents, and the remainder from our own pockets.

On the morning of our departure, with our open-face Momo Design helmets in tow, my La Perla bra and knickers snug under my clothes, and Scott's newly acquired motorbike licence tucked in his pocket, we flew from Dublin to London to meet up with the other people who would be accompanying us on our journey to Calicut and for the rest of the trip through the southern states of Kerala and Tamil Nadu. It was only in the taxi on the way to Dublin airport that it suddenly hit me. The others wouldn't be normal like us. No doubt, they would be leather-clad, heavily tattooed and bearded Hell's Angels who listened to Meat Loaf. Our freaky holiday colleagues probably spent weekends in large groups, on long excursions on their Harleys, even in freezing cold weather – all in the name of recreation.

Thankfully Scott was not motorbike mad; he was happy with his scooter. I, on the other hand, hated his scooter and, much to Scott's chagrin, constantly referred to it as a moped. I refused to ride anywhere on it – helmets are a no-no when I spend an hour every morning struggling with a hair straightener in an attempt to create a silky mane, appropriate for dealing with pinstripe-clad, high-powered clients seeking legal advice.

When we met our fellow bikers, I was relieved. There were a few beards and tattoos but nothing too scary. In fact, everyone seemed pretty normal, apart from their dire fashion sense. Most of the bikers were English but there were a few Germans and Americans, and Scott and I were part of a small Irish contingent made up of five people. As I expected, there weren't that many women and any there were were hard to distinguish from the men.

Within a few hours of arriving at the luxurious Taj Hotel, it soon became apparent that bikers, regardless of their sex or nationality, like to drink copious amounts of alcohol. They downed bottles of Kingfisher, the glycerin-tasting beer, like their lives depended on it. But maybe that was just their way of dealing with the looming trip. Maybe, like me, they were trying to ignore the fact that this was going to be one of the most dangerous trips they had ever undertaken.

For the first two days, everyone was taken out in small groups to get used to riding their allocated 350cc Bullets on the Indian roads. Our first excursion was along the coastal road to Kappad Beach, twenty kilometres from the haven of our hotel. As soon as we left the hotel, I was homesick. I wanted to be back home, not on a motorbike with Scott, who was a fair-weather rider and not that experienced. I should have just promised my parents that I would go to any third world country and not specifically India. We could have been lying on a beach in a beautiful resort in St Lucia if I hadn't been so stupid.

The stench of dung and fish drying in the sun, together with the sight of various overturned lorries, made me feel physically sick. I was sweating in the thirty-five degree heat, and my inner thighs and bum were already feeling sore. I watched the roads for potholes, and each time we approached one, I held onto Scott tightly, but my bum still suffered. I was in such pain that I hardly noticed the cows sitting in the middle of the road or the goats in the auto-rickshaws. My suffering wasn't strong enough, however, to lessen my fear of the chaotic traffic. Lorries, buses and rickshaws hurtled towards us, face on. I was sure that my life would flash before me at any moment. I didn't dare take my hands from Scott's waist to return the friendly waves to the local people who greeted us along the route.

The evening before we were to set off on our first of seven full days of riding, I began seriously to worry for our lives. The convoy of eighty-eight bikers, seven doctors, six mechanics, three ambulances, four jeeps, four journalists, two film crews and a ten-tonne truck to carry all our luggage was blessed by a clergyman. It felt like we were going to war, with the distinct possibility that we would not return with all our limbs intact. We might not even return at all. Our only allies were our comrades on the trip; apart from that, everyone and everything on the Indian roads was a threat.

I was not alone in my feelings of apprehension and anxiety. I knew from the looks in the other riders' eyes that they also had their reservations and were just as nervous as I was. How could they not be? The minister who was accompanying us was probably there only to read the last rites to some unfortunate rider who hadn't abided by the government handbook on driving in India, which states that adherence to road rules often causes fatalities, rather than the reverse. We were all at risk.

There was constant pressure by the organisers that we should wear our protective armour; they kept reminding us to expect the unexpected. I felt uncomfortable and looked like a dwarf in my new, ill-fitting Kevlar-lined combats and denim jacket. The others had come in their well-worn leathers. To make matters worse, there were rumours that ambulances were to be located at three of the many dangerous hairpin bends on our route on the second day.

The huge elephants and banging of drums to see us off at six in the morning filled me with even more terror. Before I could get on the back of our bike, adorned with garlands of marigolds, I had to get rid of the lump in my throat. I was overcome with all kinds of emotion – sadness, regret and, most of all, fear. I was so scared that when one of the many photographers from the national papers approached me to take a photo, I couldn't put on my usual VIP smile.

I was very tempted to ride in one of the jeeps, which most of the women would resort to during the trip, complaining of aching backsides. However, the memory of the dignified patients and selfless doctors and nurses at the Pain and Palliative Care Society's hospital, which we had visited the day before, reminded me why I was there. I understood the difference that one person can make, giving others hope when it really mattered. Initially I had felt humbled and embarrassed that my idea of doing my bit for charity was to throw some change into a collection box. But now I was motivated to do the right thing. Shakily, I clambered onto the bike and we set off on the eight-hour journey from Calicut to Masinagudi.

It didn't take long for frustration to set in. Because of the scorching heat, we had to stop every forty kilometres for water. I just wanted to reach the next hotel as quickly as possible and in one piece. We had been warned to expect the most basic accommodation so that we wouldn't be disappointed, but I didn't care. I just wanted to be somewhere away from the blaring horns and fumes, some place to give my aching bum a break.

I also wanted to give my hands a rest from all the waving because about two hours into our journey I was so fed up panicking each time Scott took his left hand off the handlebars to wave at the friendly passers by, that I took over this diplomatic duty. I felt like a Bollywood star greeting my fans, most of whom were children with coconut-oiled hair and black kohl-lined eyes, smiling broadly and running alongside our bike, shouting, 'Hi! Hi!' The men in their vests and dhotis (a loose white loincloth) always smiled and waved, but to get more than a shy, awkward grin from a woman was rare. But because I was a woman, I was privileged to receive excited salutations from these mysterious ladies, who kept their faces hidden behind their vibrantly coloured saris.

When we arrived at our destination, the very basic Jungle Hut, the bombshell was dropped. Our first full day of riding was merely a warm-up. A bloody warm-up! The nine hours' riding planned for the next day, from Masinagudi to Palghat, would be a lot more taxing. My aching bum throbbed in protest at the very thought.

After another 6 a.m. start, we set off on the second leg of our trip. Within ten kilometres of leaving the hotel, we hit the much-talked-about hairpin bends. All thirty-six of them. Notwithstanding the fact that we passed the ambulances dealing with various casualties, by hairpin seventeen, I was quite comfortable leaning in line with Scott's body as soon as I felt him hit first gear. After completing all hairpins unscathed, I felt a sense of relief. Scott and I were the only Paddies who had remained on our bike. We couldn't fall off now.

By mid-morning, I had made up my mind that no matter how uncomfortable I felt in my unstylish biker gear, I would continue to wear it. A total of ten people had already fallen off. Luckily all of them were wearing 'lids', as they called their helmets, so they didn't sustain any head injuries, but those who weren't wearing any other protective clothing had their skin ripped off, leaving behind deep uneven grazes, caused by gravel scouring their raw, pink flesh.

For most of the afternoon we rode on the winding roads of the Western Ghats mountain range, and through wildlife reserves that are home to tigers, monkeys, deer and elephants. Soon I was turning left and right on the back of the bike, straining to catch a glimpse of some animal before it ran to shelter. The snake slithering into the dry, barren grass as it crossed our path; the smell of the huge mounds of elephant dung; and the screeching of monkeys overhead – all were constant reminders that I should appreciate that it is not every day you can turn 360 degrees and be totally engulfed by nature. I was so much more at ease, I could even let myself get excited about the prospect of travelling on the restricted Kundah Road.

The organisers had been trying for months to obtain permission from the Indian government for the group to travel this route, and it was granted only hours before we were due to reach it. As a rule, no foreign nationals are allowed to travel on the road, and it does not appear on most maps. This was not, as everyone thought, a result of there being a large hydroelectric plant that the government felt was at high risk from terrorist attack. It was because of the elusive bandit, Veerapan, and his gang of thirty men, who scour the Kundah Road for victims to kidnap and torture. (Fortunately I wasn't given this information at the time.)

All the riders congregated at a checkpoint at the start of Kundah Road, and with an escort of policemen armed with AK47s, we descended the hundreds of hairpin bends to the base of the plant. A concrete monstrosity, it destroyed the beautiful scenery of the lush tea plantations, but I was too preoccupied with the juxtaposed feelings of an intense, refreshing sense of freedom and an aching behind to really notice. But I became truly energised when the clean, fresh air hit my face, and with my arms outstretched, we whizzed down the zigzagging road.

Our last hour, with no water stops, was spent on a national highway, with signs everywhere warning that it was one of the most dangerous roads in India. I was so tired after nine continuous hours of riding that my eyes were threatening to close. Even so, I didn't realise how utterly drained I was until we reached the next hotel and I dismounted. I couldn't stand upright and my legs shook under me. I was sweating, dizzy and my body ached all over. All I wanted was a Kingfisher (the beer I'd sniffed at earlier) and some sleep. And, strange as it may seem, I wanted the morning to arrive quickly, so that I could be back on the bike again.

After another early start on day three, we wound through the tea plantations along the mountainous roads and started our eight-hour journey to Kodaikanal. Throughout the day, it became apparent that there were two types of people on this trip – the bikers who wanted to race ahead to reach our next destination as soon as possible, and those who wanted to take in as much as possible of India and her people. I found myself in the latter group, though I too had initially wanted to push on to the comfort of the next hotel, to give the waiter a baksheesh to make me a sneaky cocktail while I sunned myself. But now I was curious about the country I had refused to acknowledge for most of my life. This country of poverty, dirt, smells and, most of all, the worst-dressed IT geeks imaginable.

Again, everywhere we looked, we were surrounded by nature. At every bend, I wondered how this place could get any more beautiful, but it did. There were lakes full of water lilies, a solitary tree laden with purple blossom amidst the short tea plants, or a magnificent view of a mountain crest lined with trees and looking like a dinosaur greeting us.

We stopped at every opportunity, and in silence we

appreciated the breathtaking vistas. Apart from the odd Bullet put-putting past, the tranquillity was overwhelming. We were a million miles away from our hectic lives in Dublin 4. Even my bum was beginning to be at peace.

I found it increasingly difficult to comprehend the hardcore bikers who had no interest in discovering India. Few stopped to look at the scattered villages or to have lunch, for fear of getting the much-talked-about Delhi belly. One of the guys had even brought enough corned beef to last him the whole trip. But when I went with Scott and a couple of the more adventurous bikers to a small village off our map, we enjoyed a filling lunch served on banana leaves, and I was left with an experience that made me realise something I should have realised a long time ago.

The village had come to a standstill because of us alien visitors. Scott and Jo, a young man from London, looked in the window of the local school. You would have thought they were Ronan Keating and Justin bloody Timberlake by the reaction they got. The classroom full of thirteen-year-olds went mad. They clambered to the window, screeching and putting their hands through the iron bars just to touch the men, who were now wearing their shades and trying to act as if they weren't fazed by this crazy adoration. But when I approached the window, the pupils' expressions said it all: 'Bugger off! We're not getting excited about you – you're one of us. We want to see the white people.'

All my life, I was Irish. My parents may have been Indian, but I was Irish. I preferred Tayto crisps to samosas and Bailey's to Chai. I spoke with an Irish accent and could hardly put two sentences together in Hindi. The colour of my skin had never been an issue. I had never thought about it until now (except when I went on holiday and tanned so easily without going red). When people asked me where I was from, India did not even enter my mind. I was a coconut-brown on the outside and white on the inside. And although there wasn't a drop of Irish blood flowing through my veins, I was Irish.

Yet I was Indian too.

Before our arrival in India, I would never have believed that I would have anything in common with people from a country so enveloped in ancient traditions. I had previously been subjected to a very small part of its culture when my parents had control of my social life. They would drag me to fellow Indians' houses for dinner and make me listen to a crooning Asha Bhosle in the car on the way. But that was the extent of it. They gave up trying to teach me anything about India or its culture when I was fifteen.

Now, when the local lads asked us our 'good names' or which country we were from, I knew not to answer and to let Scott speak. The women in the villages and towns we visited rarely spoke to strangers of the opposite sex. If I had been white, I would have spoken to the Indian men, like the other women on the trip, but I found I just couldn't do it. I felt I was letting the Indian women down. I felt more like an ambassador for the non-resident Indians all over the world. Having lived in the West all my life, I didn't want the Indians to know that I had turned my back on their mystifying country and had neglected their culture.

When we arrived in Kodaikanal, I inspected my bum and found two blisters. I hadn't been aware of them throughout the day because there was too much to concentrate on and my *derrière* hadn't been a priority. But I wasn't going to allow them to develop into a nasty rash like the other women had, so I made Scott buy a pillow to attach to the seat for the next day's journey.

What a godsend! We rode the eight-hour trip from Kodaikanal to Munnar oblivious to all the bumps on the mountainous roads. It was like travelling first class in the motorbike world. I could tell when Scott was fixing the pillow to the seat with gaffer tape that the other bikers were secretly envious. Uncharacteristically, I didn't care if it looked stupid, or if it wasn't something that a real biker would do. I was comfortable and I didn't want anything to get in the way of our last three days of enduring India.

Munnar to Thekkady was a short four-hour journey through picture-postcard scenery of beautiful spice plantations. When we arrived at Thekkady, I was surprised to find that the town appeared to have a larger gay population than Sitges during the summer. Everywhere we looked, we could see men being openly affectionate to each other, holding hands and walking arm and arm. It was great to see such liberalism in the world's largest democracy. However, since I had arrived in India, I had not seen one heterosexual couple display any affection in public. In fact, I had noticed disapproving looks when Scott put his arm around me, so I had made him stop. All the guidebooks say that India is a country of contrasts and contradictions but this was very strange. I couldn't understand how advanced they could be in their attitude towards homosexuality, yet not so liberal when it came to heterosexual relationships. When I mentioned it to one of the organisers, however, she explained that these men were not gay; they were just very tactile. Her shock at my ignorance was unmistakable. She double-checked that my parents were from India and then expressed her disbelief that I knew so little about this inspiring country. Embarrassed, I looked down at my plate of rice and sambar and mumbled that I was born in Ireland and never had the opportunity to visit before.

Our penultimate day of riding through intriguing village after village to Angamaly took much less time than the expected eight hours, even after getting a punctured tyre about fifty 'clicks' (kilometres) from our hotel and miles away from the last village. We thought we were destined to spend hours waiting for help in the sweltering heat without any water, but thanks to one of the nifty Enfield mechanics, it didn't take us long to find ourselves back on the bike again. The angel appeared miraculously from nowhere and in seconds had removed his back tyre, and replaced our banjaxed one with it. As standing in the heat was doing us no good, he insisted that we carry on and he would look for a place to fix the useless tyre. Only in India would you find such generosity.

I had noticed when we were at the Taj Hotel that the staff had been particularly helpful, but I had put this down to good training and an incentive to earn tips. But everywhere we went, the local people were just as eager to please. When we were lost, people would go out of their way to lead us to the right road. We got countless invitations to strangers' homes for dinner and Chai – offers we unfortunately had to turn down because of our tight schedule.

Our last day finally arrived. By this stage, over twenty-five people had had spills (one poor lad was knocked over by an ambulance in our convoy) but Scott and I were still unscathed, with only ten hours of riding ahead of us. However, these ten hours would be the most difficult and dangerous of the whole trip.

Although we weren't travelling through the amazing scenery I had grown accustomed to, the journey was no less exciting. We were riding through large towns full of colour and character, but the roads were abysmal and often treacherous. The traffic of the last few days had done nothing to prepare us for this. We felt like characters in a computer game trying to dodge the oncoming tanks.

Every hour in the larger Indian towns and cities is rush hour. From the moment we hit Thrissur in the early morning until we were four clicks away from the Taj, the traffic was relentless. My eyes watered and I desperately tried to breathe as little as possible – no air at all seemed better than inhaling the choking diesel fumes. And all the while, Scott kept his finger on the horn. There is no such thing as a wing mirror or a rear-view mirror in India, so the only way to let another driver know you are on the road is to deafen them with loud incessant blasts. A vehicle without a functioning horn is a death sentence for passengers.

I was astonished that after nearly a week in India, it was only now that I realised the caste system was still so prevalent. The trucks and lorries were the Brahmins, the priests, blessed with their deafening horns and evil faces. The Kshatriya, the warriors, were the buses, armed with too many passengers. The Vaishya, the merchants, were the cars, with their enviable, fancy air conditioning, and the bicycles and pedestrians were the Sudra, the peasants, quietly content, knowing that they could be indirectly the cause of great suffering. On countless occasions, we found ourselves turning sharply to avoid the many cyclists and amblers who appeared from nowhere. Scott always put our own lives at risk rather than theirs – although physically weaker, they wielded more power than us.

We were the Dalits – the untouchables, the most menial caste at the bottom of the chain. Even the cows ranked higher than us.

On our travels we narrowly escaped a very dangerous encounter with a bus and an unusually healthy-looking palomino-coloured cow with fluffy ears. Instead of crashing into the sacred animal and causing the enormous cow population of India to decrease by one, and deciding that heading straight for the front of the bus wasn't a good option either, Scott veered to the side of the road, swerving on gravel and narrowly avoiding a twenty-foot drop. The shame of injuring or, worse still, killing a cow would have been too much to bear.

We may have been Dalits, but we were riding the king of motorbikes. I learnt that the Royal Enfield Bullet is still built today using the same technology as when they were first launched in India in the 1950s. Just when you find your confidence levels are beginning to rise, a built-in safety device reminds you exactly who is the boss. But, despite its unreliability, everybody loves the Bullet. It has a certain *je ne sais quoi* and demands respect.

Our penultimate stop was at a Toyota showroom, where

our convoy (minus a few injured parties) congregated for the finale: being escorted by the local police along the cordoned-off road, lined with people, which led to the hotel. It was strange to think that I wasn't excited about the prospect of being able to have a lie-in or sit by the pool the next day.

As I mounted the back of our bike, I knew that this would probably be one of the last times I ever rode as a pillion passenger. The next time I got on a motorbike, I wanted to be able to ride it solo.

We waved at the local people for the last time as we entered the gates of the Taj. But I was only a little sad that my trip of a lifetime had come to an end. I was overwhelmed with a sense of accomplishment, relief and, above all, excitement.

Scott and I had completed a risky and challenging journey in the name of charity, without sustaining any injuries. I had experienced the exciting sensation of speeding along on the back of a bike through the most amazing locations, with my arms outstretched, palms facing the heavens, the wind in my face. And now I was about to embark on a new journey – a prospect that also excited me – the journey of discovering my roots was about to begin.

# DERVLA MURPHY

## LETTER TO NIAMH

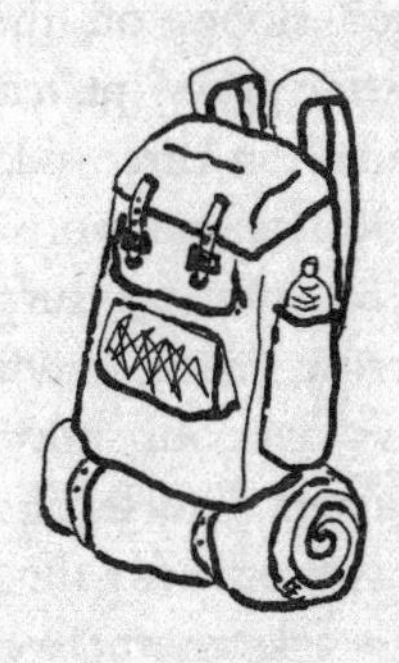

*In January 1997, Dervla Murphy travelled to Rwanda, intending to trek alone through its beautiful mountain region. Instead, she found a country in chaos following the genocide of the Tutsi minority three years before. Unable to travel because of the conditions, Dervla spent the next several months talking to ordinary Rwandans about the horror of the previous years, and about their uncertain future. She wrote this letter to her friend, Niamh, whilst in Bukavu refugee camp.*

BUKAVU, 26 APRIL

Dear Niamh,
You asked for my opinion and here it is: I don't think you'd enjoy working in a Rwandan refugee camp. The one I have just visited is, by regional standards, minute – population 29,000. Many came from the French Operation Turquoise camp, closed on 21 August '94. Others came from Cyangugu prefecture, just across the Kivu Province border near Bukavu.

Their arrival wasn't emergency-creating; as they were expected, the UNHCR's infrastructure was already in place.

From Bukavu a rough track (one of Zaire's main motor roads) climbs a series of precipitous hills, densely forested: bamboo, pines, bluegums, indigenous trees aglow at this season with red and yellow blossoms. At first, one is looking down banana-blanketed slopes into a narrow valley of the Ruiszi river; the forested slopes on the far bank are in Rwanda. Then comes a wide grassy plateau – broken but not rugged country, surrounded on three sides by the Mitumba mountains, rising to 8,000 feet and more.

Twenty miles from Bukavu we turned onto an even rougher track – very narrow, gently undulating – and passed a couple of small villages where our shiny luxury vehicle was observed without friendliness. This fertile region is not over-populated, yet the local welcome for the refugees was, shall we say, mixed ... There is a large impoverished village close to the camp and 'incidents' (sometimes fatal) are not uncommon.

From a high ridge-top, one first sees the edge of the distant camp: huge hospital-tents on an opposite ridge, beyond a wide green valley, and the glinting tin roof of the food-store shed – the only permanent building. The synthetic UN blue of the roof tarpaulins seems a harsh intrusion on an otherwise unspoiled landscape.

Soon we were on the scene of a minor crisis: near the camp entrance, the track had collapsed into a deep culvert. Our vehicle could find a way round easily enough but the giant World Food Programme trucks, due to arrive next day, could not. The camp leaders were panicking at the prospect of food rations running out. A UNHCR expat road engineer and his local team had been requested to come immediately, and stones were being carried to the chasm by corvée labour from the camp. I asked why these young men couldn't also carry food-sacks from the trucks to the store and was told that that would involve 'an unacceptable security risk'. There are a lot of very hungry Zaireans out there but no one regularly drives 1,200 miles from Mombasa, transporting a carefully balanced diet, to sustain them.

The strictly guarded gate of rusty tin was opened by a beaming askari. He welcomed me warmly; elderly expat visitors are treated as possible sources of extra funding. The staff's neat compound holds a hamlet of tents, each measuring eight feet by eight and minimally furnished, standing a few yards apart on the level ridge-top. Marigolds and miniature cacti grow between the white-painted stones marking the edges of little paths. The loo and showers are in portacabins, far down a steep slope overlooking the main camp on its wide valley floor. The dining-room-cum-kitchen is not a room but a lean-to. Many square yards of canvas awning, attached to the top of the high compound wall, are supported by bluegum poles. Beneath, on the earthen floor, benches serve as chairs on either side of a long trestle-table. A generator provides light and keeps the fridge going – most of the time. An excellent Hutu cook, once employed in a Kigali luxury hotel, transforms basic foods into delicious meals. Now the expat staff is down to three – contented folk who, relishing the simple life, rarely visit Bukavu.

Jeejee appointed himself my guide. A volunteer worker in his forties, idealistic and compassionate, he has spent almost a year teaching in the camp school and is adored by his pupils. Scores converged on him, cheering and laughing, as we walked for miles through various 'zones'. I won't even try to describe the surrounding landscape: never have I been anywhere lovelier.

One associates refugee camps with overcrowding and squalor but here the zones are well spread out, some on the valley floor, others on steep hillsides or high ridge-tops approached by lung-testing footpaths. Most mud-brick huts (nine metres by six) stand in small plots where maize and/or vegetables may be grown. A minimum of ten people must occupy each hut, even if a family numbers fewer. A 'bloc' is a group of nine huts under a *responsable*. A zone comprises twenty blocs under a controller. The camp 'chief' is the equivalent of the burgomaster of a Rwandan commune, who in this small camp is in fact an ex-burgomaster. We passed clinics, schools, churches, shops, shebeens, a 'hair-stylist' – all in mud huts – and dressmakers and tailors working by the wayside. On the highest hill, American evangelicals have built a red-brick church: large, circular, brash. This permanent structure infuriates those who argue that the whole camp should look 'temporary'.

The orderliness of this 'town' both impressed and chilled me. I've read about these places being modelled on Rwanda's communes – many refugees living with the same neighbours as before and taking orders from the same (genocidal) local authorities. This camp certainly contradicts the standard image of a great flood of panic-stricken wretches fleeing into a strange land where they suffer as uprooted people. It felt like a disciplined segment of Rwandan society successfully transplanted, at vast cost to the international community. Yet it didn't seem to me a relaxed or contented segment. The small children clinging to Jeejee, and to me as his friend, were cheerful enough though filthy and malnourished; everyone else looked morose. And on all my walks with Jeejee (he discouraged me from walking alone), I saw numerous frightening faces – with killers' eyes. I've seen similar faces elsewhere: in Croatia, in South Africa, in Northern Ireland. Not surprisingly, the camp contains a horrific number of men with such faces. Yet Jeejee remarked that it is reputed to be the calmest, safest (for expats) and most tension-free of all Zaire's camps; otherwise I wouldn't have been invited to visit it.

After the culvert had been repaired, I watched a food-distribution. Again, all very orderly: people queuing with their ID cards, every name being entered in a ledger – so-and-so received such-and-such on 25 April. This immensely long queue was submissive, subdued – too silent. The four men in charge were hard-faced, powerful figures who habitually fiddle the books. It's unlikely that the camp supports 29,000, as expats tacitly admit. Most Hutu refugee 'community leaders' inflate numbers, then sell the surplus rations and buy guns. Since the collapse of the USSR, cheap guns have been showered on Africa. The significance of that grisly economic fact is not sufficiently recognised.

I toured the rows of enormous hospital tents with Muriel, a nurse attached to this camp since its establishment, and proud of its medical facilities – as well she might be. Last week, I visited Bukavu's main hospital and was shattered by its lack of facilities: at present it is a hospital in name only. Medically, the refugees are privileged people, cared for by their own Hutu refugee doctors, surgeons, radiographers, physiotherapists. Zaireans, hearing about this super-hospital, naturally hope it will treat them too, at least in cases of serious illness. But unless they can pull powerful strings they are denied access, their children allowed to die at the hospital gate. This perhaps is inevitable; the UNHCR and its satellite aid agencies cannot be expected to cater for all local medical emergencies. But, equally inevitably, the local people ask, 'Why does the UN think Rwandan refugees are so much more deserving of help than we are?'

One morning, I sat watching the sunrise in a little thatched 'summer-house' on the edge of the expats' compound – their verandah-substitute. Here an askari joined me; Jean is one of the few refugees who speak fluent English and we had talked before. He comes from Kibuye, a town on the Rwandan shore of Lake Kivu where some of the worst genocidal atrocities took place. In June 1993, he graduated from a Kinshasa college as a hydraulics engineer but now has no hope of getting a suitable job, unless the UN needs someone with his qualifications. I asked why he wouldn't go home to a country desperately short of every sort of graduate. His reply revealed that he believes the camp leaders' reports about all the returnees being killed by vengeful RPA soldiers.

In every camp, this intimidating 'warning' campaign is relentlessly maintained.

The camp's 'English Literature' students expressed a wish to meet me. These seventeen middle-class refugees (eleven men, six women, all professionals over thirty) have evidently accepted that even if the ex-FAR troops one day 're-take' Rwanda, the English language – though hated by most Francophones – will be useful in the twenty-first century. (English is the first European language of Tutsi returnees from Uganda.) On four evenings a week, they meet to practise their spoken English in a tent furnished only with twenty camp-chairs – and lit that evening by a kerosene lamp, the generator being off sick. None looked like a refugee; all were well dressed – the women elegant in a Gallic way – and obviously from affluent backgrounds.

Following Jeejee's introduction, everyone clapped loudly, crowded around to shake my hand and welcomed me with genuine friendliness. However, when I tried to switch the conversation from my travels to Rwandas's tribulations, the atmosphere became somewhat strained, though *la politesse* prevailed to the end.

My referring to the killer militia as the '*interahamwe*' (in Kinyarwanda, 'those who work together') caused great offence. It is, everyone told me, 'a derogatory and abusive term'. They protested even more strongly against the word 'genocide'. What happened in Rwanda in '94 was a war, they asserted, with killings on both sides. 'Genocide' should never be used unless proven to the satisfaction of an international tribunal. If proof exists, they asked, why have the leaders not been punished? I could see how, two years after the 'war', the ineptitude of the UN's Arusha Tribunal has emboldened the guilty, making them feel the 'culture of impunity' will always protect them.

It was disconcerting, almost unreal, to be associating with people whom one knew to have been responsible, as commune leaders, for helping to implement the genocide.

They appeared normal, affable, intelligently interested in me as I had been presented to them: an Irish travel writer. 'Normality' was the most sinister aspect of the sort of people I met that evening. Doctors, school principals, lawyers, university lecturers – the authority figures who gave their imprimatur to the attempted extermination of all Tutsi. Tutsi who were often their patients, their pupils, their clients, their academic colleagues, sometimes even their relatives by marriage.

An emotive word, genocide – too often wrongly used nowadays. In '94, confusion persisted for some time, while the massacres were taking place, about whether or not they could be defined as genocide. Naturally Rwanda's 'interim' government put a lot of thought into fudging the issue, but by now, few deny that genocide happened. Plus the slaughtering of some 30,000 'moderate Hutu' – certain politicians, and their supporters, who wished to see the Arusha Accords being made the basis for 'a new Rwanda' which would have disempowered the *génocidaires*.

I left the camp asking myself, 'Why does the UNHCR, in collaboration with various NGOs, continue to collude with the *génocidaires*, docilely playing their game? At a cost of two million US dollars *per diem* ...' This is a political rather than a humanitarian crisis. Two million refugees became victims of the *génocidaires*, having been intimidated into leaving their homes by leaders who were looking ahead. As one (Jean-Bosco Barayagwiza) boasted publicly, 'Even if the RPF has won a military victory, it will not have the power. It has only the bullets, we have the population.' Barayagwiza now lives in luxury in Goma, running one of the camps.

As early as August '94, the UNHCR knew they were nurturing evil people. An official spokesman, Ray Williamson, admitted this. In November '94 a UN report stated, 'Former soldiers and militiamen have total control of the camps', and General Dallaire of UNAMIR II was willing to try to separate the militias from their victims; he had no doubt these would then return home. However, he was opposed by the UNHCR commissioners, and by several major NGOs and denied the necessary mandate. His proposed operation might have involved the deaths of some UN troops, and that institution fears the effects of body-bags being seen coming home (to wherever) on CNN. William Shawcross, writing about the genocide, has angrily observed: 'So often today, humanitarianism is a figleaf for political inaction.' The UN is efficient only at disguising its own moral flaccidity by 'doing good' in a way that soothes uninformed, TV-prodded Western consciences.

It's unlikely you'd feel happy and fulfilled working amongst these refugees. But don't get me wrong. I'm not, post genocide, anti-Hutu, pro-Tutsi. That would be ridiculous, banal. Past Tutsi behaviour was outrageous, brutal, consistently demeaning of the Hutu. Although nothing justifies genocide, that past (both distant and recent) does explain why the organisers succeeded so dreadfully. Also, Rwanda's peasants were and are peculiarly vulnerable to having their inherited antagonisms manipulated. The structure of their society – in pre-colonial times, during the Belgian protectorate, since independence – has been tightly authoritarian in a way atypical of Africa. That counted for much, after 6 April 1994. When told to kill, the peasants killed. When Authority sanctioned the slaughter of their neighbours, tens of thousands of them slaughtered their neighbours, accepting that their own survival demanded the extermination of Tutsi – not sparing the children, this time, as they did in 1959. Repeatedly they were reminded that thousands of those children had recently returned to Rwanda wearing RPA uniforms.

Everywhere aid workers are supposed to be politically neutral, helping all those in need with no questions asked. But maybe it's time to revise that code? Have we not seen enough of where its abuse leads? In this respect, too, my camp visit was disquieting. The three expats are admirable: innovative, resilient, dedicated – not escapists, like some of the younger generation of aid workers, or cynical passengers on the NGO gravy train. Yet they are actively supporting a morally indefensible operation. Perhaps in such situations most aid workers become ghettoised, their lives for the moment centred on the physical welfare of their charges, their horizons restricted to 'humanitarian' considerations. Obviously those three have a good relationship with the camp leaders; they seem to have no difficulty accepting the 'war' explanation – maybe they need to believe in it, for their own peace of mind? Or maybe they are genuinely ignorant of the backround to this 'humanitarian' crisis. It is extremely complicated. I certainly wouldn't understand any of it had Rachel and Andrew not been living and working in Rwanda in 1995. If solely dependent on media interpretations, I'd probably have pushed the tragedy aside as one more distant horror beyond my comprehension.

On 9 May, I go home to Ireland, sustained by the prospect of returning to Kivu Province in November. My friends will certainly assume that this wish to revisit Bukavu is entirely Rose-inspired, another sympton of my personality change. A reasonable assumption, but false. Kivu Province pulls me as a traveller – forget grandmaternal urges. Rwanda, too, sounds like good trekking country; I may also spend some time there. But I hope to see you before then.

Your old friend,
Dervla

# OLUTOYIN PAMELA AKINJOBI

## AFRICAN EXPERIENCES

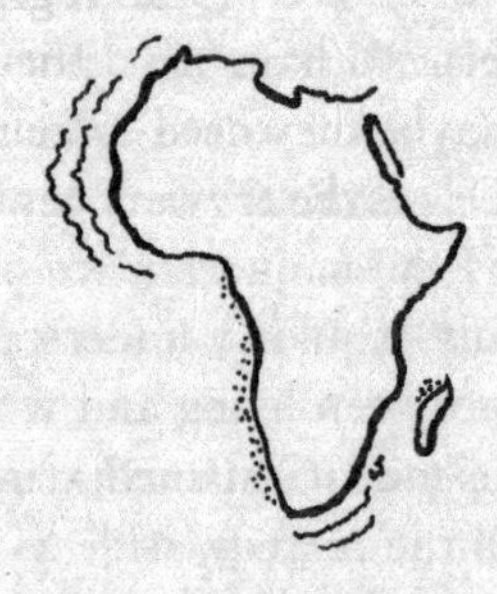

All over the world, strange and unusual things happen to people every day. But it was only after moving to Ireland, from Nigeria, that I realised just how odd some of my friends' and neighbours' experiences really were. The following stories are all true.

Sherifat had lost three children one after the other. They had all died mysteriously between six and eighteen months after birth. Sherifat was heartbroken, and people had started to point accusing fingers at her, saying she was some kind of witch and responsible for her children's deaths. She wanted more than anything to have healthy children, and couldn't cope with any more deaths, so she decided to do her utmost to find a solution.

Sherifat went around the village asking for advice on how she could prevent the deaths of future children. Sherifat didn't believe in orthodox medicine, only in the traditions that had been passed down to her, and also in the local herbalists in her village. One native herbalist told her to kill a chicken and use it to make a sacrifice in the middle of the night to evade a curse that had been placed on her. Another told her to walk naked in the middle of the night carrying a newborn baby's placenta to a river in her village (it was a general belief in the village that the goddess of that river was kind to women who had problems having children). Another herbalist told her to pray by her mother's grave at midnight for seven days. All this Sherifat did, but when she had another baby, he died before he was six months old.

Sherifat lost all hope and almost went insane. On the day this last baby was to be buried, a herbalist she had never seen before approached her and promised her that her children would stay alive if she did what he said. Sherifat listened to him, wondering if he was yet another charlatan. He explained to her that to make her dreams of having a healthy child come true, he would have to cut off the index finger of the dead baby and burn his left hand before he was buried. Sherifat thought it was morbid and very strange but she had nothing to lose as the baby was already dead. She would have tried anything at that stage. So the deed was done and the baby was buried.

A year later, Sherifat had another baby. It was a boy who looked exactly like the last baby she had lost. He was born with his index finger missing and his left hand scarred from burns. Today, twenty years on, the boy still lives with Sherifat in her village.

Something very strange also happened to Patricia, a neighbour's friend. Patricia lived and worked in Port Harcourt in the mid-western part of Nigeria. She had been posted there for a year to do her NYSC (National Youth Service Corps) – a programme designed many years ago for recent college and university graduates so that they can serve their country for a year before they are absorbed into the work system. Though Patricia enjoyed her job, she missed her family terribly. Her parents and her only sister lived in Lagos and she couldn't wait to go back and join them after her youth service. From time to time, she arranged for her younger sister, who was still in the university, to pay her visits. They were very close and meant a lot to each other.

One day, Patricia woke up from a bad dream in the middle of the night. She shook with fright as she realised she had been crying in her sleep. She tried to recall the dream but all she could remember was that something terrible had happened to her sister. She prayed for her family and just to make sure everyone was okay, she phoned her home in Lagos and spoke to her parents and sister. Relieved to find them all well, she went back to bed.

A few months later, Patricia sent her sister a plane ticket so she could come to Patricia's birthday party. Patricia's sister bought a new dress for the party. She specifically chose blue because it was Patricia's favourite colour and she wanted to surprise her with it. On Patricia's birthday, her sister put on the special dress, bid her parents goodbye and left for the airport. At the birthday garden party, Patricia's friends were all bubbling with fun and dancing when her sister finally arrived. Patricia gave her sister a plate of food and took her into her bedroom so they could be on their own for a while before they joined the others.

As they caught up on each other's news, Patricia's phone rang. She excused herself and went into the living room to pick it up. Her parents were on the line telling her between sobs that her sister had died in a car accident. Patricia was shocked. Her sister was there with her in Port Harcourt, eating a plate of party food in her bedroom, and she told them so. Confusion set in and Patricia's parents thought she had gone completely mad. They said they were at the accident scene watching their other daughter's body being removed from the wreck. She had been dead for a few hours, trapped in the taxi that was meant to take her to the airport. To convince herself, Patricia asked them to describe what her sister was wearing. As they did, Patricia screamed that it was impossible because she was there in her room wearing the very same blue dress. Patricia ran into her bedroom to find her sister so that she could tell her parents that a horrible mistake had been made. But the room was empty – the plate her sister had been eating from was sitting on a stool.

Patricia screamed, slumped and lost consciousness. In the hospital, she learnt her sister really had died in Lagos on her way to the airport. To this day, no one can explain the mystery surrounding Patricia's sister's trip to Port Harcourt.

I thought this was really odd until I met Faith and heard her story. Faith had been married to her husband for three years. They had two lovely children, a boy and a girl. Faith had never met any of her husband's relations; all she knew about them was what her husband had told her and the few pictures he had shown her. Faith's husband had explained to her that his parents and relations lived in another part of the country and he couldn't visit them until after his contract job had finished in three years' time. Faith had pleaded with him a number of times to take her and the children to meet his family, but every time she begged him, he promised her he would grant her request as soon as he could. Towards the end of his contract, Faith reminded him of his promise. He reluctantly agreed and they started to make plans to go to visit his family. Faith was really excited and everyone in her neighbourhood knew she was making plans to travel to meet her parents-in-law. She went on a special shopping spree to buy new clothes for herself and the children so they would look smart when meeting their new family.

The spirit of excitement was in the air and to give her support, Faith asked her neighbour and close friend, Amina, to come with her to meet the in-laws. Amina also made preparations and bought a nice souvenir for her friend's in-laws.

The day came at last and they all began the long-awaited

trip. The journey was long and hectic, all squeezed into one small car, and they were glad to stretch their aching legs when they eventually arrived in the village. As they made their way on foot through the village, they spotted a woman seated outside a house. Faith's husband recognised her, and explained it would not be nice for him to walk past the woman's house without saying hello to her but that he didn't want to be late for his family. He pointed to the third house down the road and told his wife, Amina and the children to go ahead of him and tell his parents he had dropped by to greet one of their neighbours. Amina and Faith hurried ahead with the children to the house. The aged couple who lived there looked at all of them with great curiosity when Faith said they had come to visit, but welcomed them into their home. They were all offered seats and, as they sat down, Faith noticed some pictures on the wall. One of them was of Faith's husband and this made them feel more at home. Faith explained their mission and introduced herself, her children and Amina, and told them that their son had stopped to say hello to the woman who lived a few doors away from them. For a few moments, everything stood still, and then the old couple struggled to their feet and ran out the door to call for help. Within the blink of an eye, the house was filled with all sorts of people who looked at Faith, Amina and the two children strangely. No one moved close to them. Faith, Amina and the children were scared. They listened as the crowd whispered to each other that they were not real, they were ghosts.

In the end, an elderly man bravely approached them and asked them to repeat their mission. Faith was worried about her husband and wondered what was keeping him. Pointing at a picture on the wall, she explained to the crowd that she was the wife of the man in the picture and they had all come together to visit because he wanted her to meet his family. Amina opened her mouth in horror as the elderly man explained to them that the man in the picture had been dead for years, and to convince them even more, showed them all pictures of his burial.

Faith's husband never joined them in the house and when the woman down the road was asked, she said she had not seen him. No one set eyes on him ever again. The children he had before he died, and Faith and her children now all live together in the village with his aged parents.

Africa is indeed a land of strange experiences.

# HO WEI SIM

# THE CHOSEN PATH

When I was a child, my uncle told me about the life of Buddha. To me, it was just another story, among the many I had heard. I learnt that he was born a prince in the western Terai region of Nepal. He lived a privileged and sheltered life, until one day, leaving the palace boundaries, he witnessed disease, old age and death. It was the first time he had seen suffering. Touched deeply by the experience, he left his family and lavish lifestyle in a search for answers. After many years, he found enlightenment.

Apart from that, I associated Nepal only with Everest, Sherpa guides and brave Gurkha soldiers. I knew little else. But the lure of Nepal was irresistible, and, a few years ago, my husband, Donal, and I found ourselves looking out through an aeroplane window at an ancient city sprawled across the wide expanse of a high dusty plateau.

Fresh off the plane, we were dying to explore Kathmandu. We were only a few yards away from our little hotel when, out of the blue, a Nepalese man walked up to us and smeared

red powder all over my face. Then he strode away, throwing a good-natured smile over his shoulder before disappearing. The powder clung to my skin and my T-shirt, bringing me years back to a primary school classroom in a little town in Malaysia where I was born – I was a seven-year-old girl adding water to powdered paint in my palette.

Donal and I were gobsmacked. What was going on? A man cycled by and suddenly a flying missile was thrown in our direction. Donal dodged neatly. A plastic bag of blue water smashed at his feet.

Looking up, we saw faces peering down at us from the flat rooftops of low buildings. Wised up at last, Donal and I skirted close to the edge of the road, watching out for an ambush from the air. Another tourist beside us darted out suddenly. A missile came flying, exploding just a few feet away. It missed him but covered us with a fine spray of yellow.

Donal and I crouched momentarily at a narrow crossroads. We would have to make a dash for it. The other side of the road was only a tantalising twenty feet away.

'Now!' Donal whispered, as he took off. I followed.

Another missile connected, this time smack on top of my head. I spluttered. Before I could even think, a Nepalese man stepped forward. Clasping his palms in an apologetic gesture as if to say 'pardon me', he smeared green powder all over my face, and then skipped away. Vermilion and green streaks ran down my clothes. I hadn't thought my tropical-print T-shirt could have been any more colourful. I was left with the image of his smile – open, honest and true.

Donal, relatively unscathed in our adventures, couldn't stop laughing. This was, as we learnt later, Holi, or the Festival of Colours, in Kathmandu.

We were here for ten days to trek the Annapurna trail. The day before, we'd closed the door on an empty apartment in Singapore. Virtually all our belongings, everything we had accumulated over our years in Singapore – me, eleven, Donal, seven – had been packed up and were on their own travels across the high seas, making their way to Ireland.

When I remember our time wandering through Kathmandu, snapshots come back to me: narrow streets; a dense city of flat-roofed buildings; looking up to see long, narrow balconies running along the edge of the upper floors of buildings framed by dark old wood, a little child peering back at us. Later we were to witness the cremation of a child who had fallen from such a balcony, her mother sobbing while the pyre was lit, a little arm sticking out from under wood and flowers.

In the shops, beautifully embroidered cushion covers and rugs were hung in doorways and stacked on the floor in piles. I imagined young women bent over them in dark huts, working by candlelight, chatting and laughing. How many hours were spent creating these things of beauty, later sold for the price of a meal? I remember the many little bars and pubs opened to cater for tourists like us, pizzas and Blue Note jazz on offer. Many had been set up by tourists who could not bring themselves to leave this place. And how was it that the Nepalese tolerated us travellers – drawn here, searching, not knowing what we were looking for? The second-hand bookstores dotting the city were filled with books by Lobsang Rampa, and about spirituality. And yet in the midst of all this yearning are the Nepalese themselves, ever smiling, ever humble, calm and centred. How tolerant they were of our crude attempts to 'find' ourselves in their backyard.

A few days later, we sat sipping Mustang tea in the first of many tea houses dotting the trail up to Annapurna. The tea had been slowly brewed over a fire, oily and thick and peppery. We had flown from Kathmandu to Pokhara and made our way to the beginning of the trail by bus. And there, beside a small plot of wheat ripening in the sun and a tinkling mountain stream, I began a letter to my unborn children, who were not even two twinkles in Donal's eyes, to tell them why we were leaving Singapore – this strange twist of fate that would take them from growing up in dense high rise to fields of green. And as I wrote, I remembered watching from the windows of the bus from Pokhara that morning small groups of Nepalese children of three or four years, walking unaccompanied in single file beside the road. I could not imagine children in Singapore being trusted, or even needing, to make their own way anywhere. I could only recall the tantrums on the underground MRT train, a child clinging tightly to the Filipino maid, mother and child locked in misalignment.

And so we made our way slowly in our ascent towards Mount Annapurna and Mount Machhapuchhare. The first two days were hard. Any notion that we were going for a pleasant jaunt in the hills quickly died. Luckily, we didn't have to carry our own backpack. We had a porter, a young lad of fifteen or sixteen. He had his own bag strapped across his forehead. We thought guiltily of the cans of spam and sardines in the bottom of our backpack, which our Singaporean travel agent had urged us to bring. The food there is inedible, he had stressed. And although we were relatively free from the burden of luggage, save for pure guilt, climbing what seemed at times to be a wall of steps was almost unbearable when muscles seized and your heart was bursting.

Gradually a pattern emerged. We would rise before dawn, brush our teeth with freezing water, and spend the morning trekking. We climbed many a precipice, some with a sheer drop on both sides. Often we came across mule packs carrying heavy loads, hearing the bells tied around their necks before they came in sight. By lunch-time, we would arrive at the next village and there we would stay, at the lodge of our choice, till the following morning. And because it was too cold to stay in the rooms, all of us travellers would sit around a table in the reception-cum-dining-room, chatting and trying to keep warm. Some were on the way up – newcomers like us. Others were on their way down and were keen to share their stories. Some had been on the longer Annapurna trail, a thirty-day trek, culminating in the treacherous Thorung La pass. We came across the same faces as we repeated this routine successively over the next few villages. In this way, we got to know some people quite well.

Our Singapore agent had been so wrong about the food. We relaxed in the afternoons over a stream of *muumuus* (dumplings) and pizza (made, I suspect, from a Naan base), while I continued my letter to my unborn children, trying to find words to explain our yearning for a more natural way of living than we had experienced in Singapore.

In this very pleasant way, we got to Deurali. This was the last village on the trail before Machhapuchhare Base Camp (MBC) and, finally, Annapurna Base Camp (ABC). We stayed at a lodge at the end of the cluster of lodges, first in line for MBC.

The heat nibbling at my feet was delicious. They lounged luxuriously in the envelope of hot air beneath the rectangular table, with a host of other pairs of feet gathered in a circle, like delegates at a conference, basking in collective enjoyment. A wool blanket tacked to the side of the table sealed in the warmth from the gas lamp. The lamp stood in a deep recess in the centre, around which our feet happily congregated.

Outside, the elements raged. The wind rattled at the doors and windows, reminding us that the lodge was little more than a shack at the edge of a very high mountain.

The door flung open and a handsome young Sherpa swept in. Outside was the rest of his expedition, all mountaineers, professionals. In comparison, we were little more than hill-walkers out on a Sunday hike. They camped outdoors and cooked over portable kerosene stoves, while we stayed in lodges and ate tuna macaroni. The peak of Annapurna was their destination, not simply its base camp. He shouted rapidly and urgently above the roar of the wind to our innkeeper. She went into the kitchen quickly and emerged with a couple of wooden sticks. Our guide explained that someone from the expedition had fallen and broken his leg. The young Sherpa thanked her and swept out again.

The innkeeper was a strong sensible woman of about thirty. It had been a shock to discover that she was about our age, as she looked ten years older. Her skin was stretched tight against the frame of her face. It shone with a kind of ruddy goodness. In a strange way, although she was plain, she was also beautiful. She had four children, who were at boarding school in Pokhara, and she missed them. Her movements were slow and calm. She was dignified and content, despite what was clearly an austere and demanding existence. The previous morning, as she did every other morning, she'd walked all the way from Deurali to the main highway for her supplies, a trek that had taken us five days to cover.

She smiled as she set before us the latest in what was turning out to be a culinary tour of the Himalayas. At last this was the infamous *dhaal baat*, lentil curry and rice, which was supposed to be the ultimate example of the terrible food we were going to have to put up with. On the contrary, although it was a bit mushy, it was really quite tasty. It was warming and just what we needed.

The *dhaal baat* had taken our minds momentarily away from the terrible conditions outside. I looked out the window. Although it was only three o'clock in the afternoon, the sky was dark and clouds, dense with snow, gathered around us. Any notion of continuing our trek the next morning was receding rapidly with the horizon.

I returned to my letter-writing. How could I capture, in a few lines, our life in Singapore, memories of encounters and impressions formed over more than a decade? We had been happy and had good jobs. Partnership had been mentioned. Life was safe; that wasn't to be underestimated and yet it left us with the feeling that we could very easily envisage our existence over the next two or three decades – and we didn't like what we saw. Car, condo, credit card, cash, and country club. The five Cs. This was the Singapore dream. But wasn't there more to see, to do and to achieve in life?

The wind died down. It grew very still outside. The sun came out and covered everything with a brilliant sheen. All the same, we sat huddled around the table, glad of the warmth from the gas lamp below. There were two Korean girls, a couple of men from Brazil, a Dutch guy, an American couple, an Israeli, and a loud, funny fellow from Manchester.

And there was another Malaysian in the company. As strange as life can be, Vittal was from my home town in Klang, which I had left thirteen years previously. We had actually known each other vaguely, both of us active in chess circles. He was in the neighbouring boys' school. And to add to our surprise, we were struck when a couple of Nepalese men produced a chessboard and started a game. Rather illogically I hadn't expected the Nepalese to be keen on chess. But why wouldn't they be? It was not long before Vittal and I sat down to a game. And as I contemplated my pieces, I was transported momentarily to another world in Klang – hot, dusty, and so far removed from this lodge high in the mountains.

The sky darkened again. Then, as Vittal took my queen with his knight, a Nepalese man ran in. He shouted excitedly. The innkeeper ran to the door, shouting 'Avalanche!' She tried to bar the door but instead of staying put, a number of us mindless tourists rushed out, almost trampling each other in the process, before she could do anything. My fellow travellers, once civil and well-mannered, had turned into an unruly mob. 'I've got to see this!' someone yelled, expressing the collective thought. Cameras flashed.

I have to confess that Donal and I would have been among the errant ones if we'd had the chance. But like the others who remained inside, we rushed to the windows.

At the window, I could barely take in what I was seeing. A snowdrift was rolling down the cliff above us, like a huge mist descending heavily and quickly. I braced myself for impact. Then everything went white.

When the blur of whiteness cleared, we were surprised and, in some perverse way, disappointed to find that we were okay. The lodge opposite us, which had seemed destined for certain destruction, had also escaped unscathed, apart from being hemmed in by a lot of snow. People from all the lodges streamed out and stood staring at the mountain peaks above us. Cameras flashed again. Our fantasies had not been fulfilled. But our naïve reception of this first avalanche was to change rapidly over the next twenty-four hours.

Night went by uneventfully. As usual, we made our way back to our rooms only when we were ready to go straight to sleep. It was freezing. We got undressed as quickly as we could, before crawling into our sleeping bags – our eyes, noses and mouths barely peeping out of the snug cocoon of comfort. As we blew out the candle, the steam from our breath whirled in the cold air.

We woke to find the whole countryside covered in snow. The latrines had frozen over. There was no water even to brush our teeth. There had been three avalanches during the night, which, rather incredibly, we had slept through.

We were snowed in. Outside, wind and snow reigned. There was no question now of going up to MBC. Visibility was poor and avalanches were happening even more frequently. Nobody came up from the village below, and although our lodge was the first one from MBC, we hardly expected anyone to come down. There was nothing else for it but to stay put and find solace in food. We ordered a pizza and more *muumuus*, while I continued my letter. 'There is more to life than Singapore,' I wrote.

The door banged open. Some desperate fool had decided to risk the elements and come down from MBC, after all. He hurried in and shut the door against the wind. 'I just missed being hit by an avalanche,' he panted.

Moments later, the door banged open again and a young

Israeli couple burst in. The girl slumped to the floor, crying. They had been hit by an avalanche; snow sat on the creases of their jackets and on their backpacks. 'We thought we were going to die,' she sobbed. 'Now I believe in God!'

The mood in the lodge was now in contrast to the carnival-like rapture with which we had received the first avalanche. We sat quietly around the table, waiting.

Suddenly we heard a loud crack. By now, we knew what it meant. I was sitting next to the window. For a few seconds, there was an awful silence. I looked up and saw the snow rolling down the cliff towards the cluster of lodges, towards us. I was transfixed, fascinated in spite of my fear. The avalanche hit the lodge in front of us. A huge snow drift followed and continued unabated towards our lodge. Donal and I braced ourselves for the windows to shatter right into us. There was an explosion of white.

It would be trite to say that my life flashed before my eyes, but for a split second I might have wondered, Is this it? After all our *angst* and worry about doing the right thing, trying to decide what was important, were we going to be cut down in that instant? Were we too late?

I opened my eyes fully expecting the lodge in front of us to be flattened, and ours not much better off. Miraculously, however, the lodge opposite was still standing. There was little damage, but it was almost buried by snow. The sign outside, 'Dream Lodge and Restaurant', peeked out at us. A powdery white layer covered the floor of our lodge; snow had blown in under the door at the point of impact. Nobody was hurt and everything seemed to be in place. We felt very lucky to have emerged from the experience in one piece.

The next morning dawned bright and clear. We came out of the darkness of our rooms, and the clear, crisp blue of the sky hit us. The sun shone. All seemed well. What would we do? Take the opportunity of this brief respite and retreat before any serious mishap? Or stay in the relative safety of Deurali? Dare we press ahead, and face the dangers? After all, we had come all this way. But the other question was, how long would this last? We knew the weather was apt to change quickly, dramatically, in the Himalayas. It was hard to know what to do. Our guide and porter were no help. We noticed now, more than ever, how young they were – two boys barely out of school, just trying to earn a bit of pocket money. If we had expected an archetypal Sherpa guide to lead us up cliff faces, we were mistaken.

In the end, a few of us decided to try to nip up to MBC, take a few photographs and quickly come down again. Eight from our lodge, including our guide and porter, went ahead, joined by a couple of trekkers from the other lodges.

And so we set off. The path started up a steep, narrow slope, and we had to climb in single file. Donal went ahead of me, as we walked beside a mountain stream. We had to pick our way slowly, choosing this boulder and that stone, taking care not to slip. The air was dense with moisture, and almost immediately a misty fog enveloped us.

'Donal!' I called out.

'I'm here,' came his voice, just in front of me. I could barely make him out.

We plodded on, talking, so that we could keep track of each other, if not by sight then by sound, as we moved in and out of patches of mist.

We were ill-prepared for these conditions. Two days previously, we had been trekking in shorts and T-shirts; now we needed snow gear. Some of the other travellers had heavy-duty Goretex jackets. I wore a light, cotton hooded top and Donal had to rely on his red and green rugby shirt. We wore layers of T-shirts under these garments and tried to keep warm as best we could. A photograph of that trek shows me wearing socks on my hands, as I had no gloves. My feet were frozen inside my hiking boots.

I had never skied, so all this snow was new to me. Some people took out what looked like ski poles to help them to climb. Our guide found us a couple of makeshift walking sticks. It was very hard going. Everything was covered by a deep layer of snow, which had buried any semblance of a path. We followed in the footsteps of the people ahead of us. We were all simply making a beeline in the general direction of MBC, hoping against hope not to be stepping into a crevasse.

Gradually Donal and I lapsed into silence. We were getting tired, at times sinking knee deep in the snow. Even though there was not as much climbing as before, progress was painfully slow.

I tried to take my mind off what we were doing. I wanted to think of other things. I thought about our move to Ireland. Words on the pages of my letter floated up to my consciousness. 'We don't know if it will work out, but at least we will have tried. We will have followed our hearts.' And then, in that instant, I felt more certain than ever that we were doing the right thing, whatever lay ahead.

Then we heard a crack in the distance. We stopped, afraid, expecting the worst. And then, nothing.

At last we came within sight of MBC. The clouds lifted momentarily and filled the scene with an amazing blinding light. A blanket of pure, smooth snow lay before us, crossed by a graceful line of dots – our fellow travellers, each moving slowly, inexorably, towards the first lodge at the camp. The line dipped into a valley, before it rose again, up a steep slope to the lodge.

I could hardly feel my toes. My fingers would not hold the sticks any longer. I cast them off desperately. With every step, my muscles screamed out in exhaustion and pain. And the lodge seemed so far away.

At last, we got to the bottom of the slope. Above us, the lodge held promise of warmth and comfort. Anything to get away from this private hell. I did not think I had any more in me to get up there. Every muscle cried for relief. And yet in a hazy, subconscious way, I knew I could not stop. The other enemy was the cold. There was no feeling in my toes now. As

I trudged towards the lodge, it was as if I were lifting heavy blocks of wood. Up, up, up.

Donal was behind me.

'I can't do it,' I said.

'Up,' he answered, literally pushing me up the slope.

I thought about the letter again. 'I know it will be difficult to remember why we left, once the hard times come. But they will come and all the more we will have to remember the reasons why, despite the comforts of Singapore, we felt we could never be truly happy, truly ourselves, and what it is that Ireland represents to us, the promise of the nameless things our hearts cried out for.'

And then it was over. We'd arrived, all ten of us. We collapsed onto the wooden bench outside the lodge. And as we turned to see what we had trekked through, the sun came out again, and we were blinded by the dazzle of white in all its pure majesty. The peaks of Machhapuchhare and Annapurna stood before us, clearly unmoved by our insignificant efforts. Another crack, and as we stood watching in amazement, one side of Machhapuchhare moved and slid off into a cloud of fine white dust.

Strangely, we got over our exhaustion quickly and soon we were all tobogganing in the snow with makeshift sleds. Donal and I used an IKEA plastic bag.

The next day, we left MBC and returned to Deurali. Only three had decided to press on to ABC. We wondered whether we should have followed suit, but we came across the three of them later in the descent and found that one was in a bad way. His eyes were bleeding from snow-blindness.

Despite losing a toenail from the cold and ill-fitting boots, I was so glad we decided to go up to MBC. We could have stayed on in the relative comfort of Deurali, just as we could have decided to stay in the comfort of Singapore, rather than move to Dublin. I thought of our little group huddling around the table in that lodge as a microcosm of life itself. I wondered at the coincidence of meeting Vittal, someone from a distant past in an alien setting. It occurred to me that we weren't the only ones on the verge of making a big change in our lives – one fellow traveller was a builder who was going to train as a paramedic; another was getting requalified as a lawyer and moving from the East Coast to the West Coast of America.

My grandparents had emigrated from China to Malaysia. Everything would have been different had they stayed where they were. I realised more than ever now how much we are the inheritors of changes made by our predecessors.

The end of our trip loomed in the horizon. We were to see Everest from a little plane, the greatest of mountains, almost imperceptibly higher than his brothers around him. We saw in our mind's eye a picture of our lives in Ireland. We hoped to meet the twinkles before too long and we wondered what they would make of our move to Ireland. We hoped they would value their inherited past.

When I think of our time in Nepal, I remember, not the beautiful mountains, although they were very beautiful, nor the hard life of the Nepalese, although their lives were very difficult. What comes back to me is the simplicity, the sincerity, the kindness and the good humour of the Nepalese people. They were centred, true to themselves. It seems we can learn so much from their lives. Stripped of material comforts, one seems to go back to the core of what one needs. All around me were examples of people whose deepest needs were clearly satisfied. Mountains stretched towards the sublime, just as we strive to return to that from which we came.

A woman who moved to Slovakia said of her life there that because people had very little, family was most important. I think that was also true in what I saw of Nepal. We met groups of Nepalese children on those endless steps, towels round their heads and over their shoulders for warmth. They had broad, shiny smiles and all were adept and at home with those steps, where elsewhere fear would have reigned. They were in harmony with life itself.

I pondered on the universality of our collective efforts to find meaning in our lives and our journey in looking for it. As we trudged along a path beside a little mountain stream under the lush rhododendron wood, it seemed God Himself walked with us. I sang with happiness and then I was quiet, awed and humbled.

I dedicate this story to Liadh and Ciara, the two twinkles, now four-and-a-half and two-and-a-half years old.

# SUZANNE POWER

## MEETING GILBERT O'SULLIVAN

We are in the middle of a desert at midday watching a listless, mackerel sky. It hurts even to move your eyeballs. It is south Peru and we are parked in a 1970s Pontiac V8, its receding dust clouds the only movement in forty degrees of dry heat. A man called Gorge is waving a 1,500-year-old human femur at us, and Gilbert O'Sullivan is whining on the tape deck. Gilbert is not whining because he is Gilbert – he is whining because the tape has been stretched from constant play and rewind. Gorge loves Gilbert. Do we know this? How could we not? We have listened to him for hours.

We drink two litres of water in twenty minutes and Gorge takes us on a tour of Chauchilla cemetery – just thirty kilometres south of the world-famous Nazca Lines. The lines have spawned a thousand theories, from the more fabulous notion that God was an astronaut, which suggests they were astral landing pads, to the modern-day celestine prophecy. They were amazing enough, for reasons I will go into later, but Chauchilla is a walk-on part into a Mad Max meets King Solomon's Mines movie.

The cemetery is a landscape littered with bones, ceramics, wool, human hair and fabric fragments. Gorge had picked up the femur outside the car door to show us what damage grave-robbers did when they vandalised the site a decade ago. We peer into open graves and see mummies resting in a very public peace, in the foetal position, clothed in shrouds, some skulls distorted by trepanning. Their hair is braided and as long as a horse's tail, coiled eerily around head and shoulders, jet black, unbleached by the desert sun. The reassembling of the bodies after the vandalism was somewhat haphazard. Heads of adults are placed on babies' shoulders. There are thousands of graves dating from AD600, evidence of a massive riverbank civilisation that predates the Incas by almost a millennium.

It's a feeling I never want to have again. To look at such remains and see how they are exhibited. To imagine that in one and a half thousand years' time a tourist may be peering over my graveside to stare at what is left of my hair, and my mummified skin. And there's the horror movie aspect of the little baby resting beside the mother, who may not even be his. The tomb-robbers had no respect for keeping families together. And the archaeologists have as little interest. They are as inundated with work in historical Peru as any stressed Irish city worker, and cobble together the grave sites to raise much-needed funds for further excavations, before the prospectors get there first. The heat, Gilbert, the desecration, the unbearable, luminous beauty of the desert; my head spins. Dali couldn't have painted it.

So I'm glad when Gorge advises us to retreat to the relative cool of the Pontiac. Its sticky leather seats are only tepid compared to the boiling stones. Gilbert is alone again, naturally and Gorge is almost in tears telling us about Gilbert's brother, who was also in this Pontiac, who also cried tears telling him what inspired Gilbert to write the song.

Someday Gorge plans to come to Ireland and to meet Gilbert O'Sullivan. I hope Gilbert is here. I hope Gilbert gets to meet Gorge in Peru. He will find a wealth of new, psychedelic material.

We have been here for six days and already have two novels and a feature film in experiences. I can't believe I didn't want to come, that I sat on the tarmac in the Caribbean and thought about disembarking with all the other Dutch and German revellers about to spend their Christmas break sipping pina coladas, listening to steel drums, limboing under poles held by bearers bored to tears at their ineptitude. At least, I thought on my four-hour stopover, they'll have fun. I'm off on another fecking adventure. Who needs adventure? I need a pool.

I asked. They wouldn't let me off. The option was clear. Fly to Lima or go to prison.

Arriving in any country after twenty hours of breathing recycled air and drinking duty free is enough to bewilder the most secure of senses. Arriving in Peru doubles the impact. The needle hits overload on the gauge. The most popular tourist destination in South America is so diverse that it feels like travelling to a different planet. If you are looking for a frontline experience in surrealism – Peru welcomes you. A place of deserts and jungle, mountains and ocean, slums and paradise, wealth and starvation, where temperatures range from sweltering by the coast to freezing at night in the unforgivably high Andes.

At the airport in Lima, our winter-tog sleeping bags have disappeared from our rucksacks. A man with more pockmarks than healthy skin, wearing a tie knotted so tight as to constrict his breathing, or maybe that is his eightieth Marlboro today, fills in a form photocopied so many times it is unreadable in any language. He has a faded name badge – Jesus. It is almost Christmas; soon it will be his birthday. Behind us are about twenty jet-lagged fellow travellers forming a disorderly and increasingly irate queue. Everyone has lost something.

Jesus looks at me with rheumy eyes, which appear to have clouded over with disinterest, practised diligently over the years spent behind the Lost Luggage counter. There are none of the usual shelves of suitcases, umbrellas, single gloves and vanity cases – the shelves are empty.

'Why are our sleeping bags gone?' I ask why rather than where.

'It is Christmas,' Jesus explains, with the beginnings of a hopeful smile. Perhaps I will be the first finger-snapping, instant-service-culture foreigner to understand. My evening-class Spanish does not stretch to emotionally incomprehensible explanations. Jesus retreats behind his disinterest again, defeated.

We travel into Lima by taxi and wonder what someone is going to do in forty degrees of heat when they wake up on Christmas morning to find that Santa has delivered subzero sleeping bags.

We do not understand the language. By the time we leave two months later, we are close to achieving an understanding that we don't need to understand. This is Peru. But for the moment we are still fantasising about what might have happened if they'd let us off in the Caribbean.

For most of my life, I've let my itchy feet run things. They went on one package holiday when I was twenty and they never wanted one again. It was the sunbathing that did it. The soles of those itchy feet got burned when I fell asleep. I hobbled from hotel to pool sunbed for four days, and bathed the blisters in the water. I looked miserably at my toes and they advised me: It's because the soles of your feet want to stay on the ground. You can point them at the sun when you can't walk any more. My enquiring mind agreed. Together they travelled for fifteen years at any given opportunity, foregoing new kitchens, a time when a sensible mortgage could have been obtained, nice cars and promotions. Instead,

I've lived for short spells in the hills of northern Pakistan; the back of a car in Australia; Phnom Penh; and Thailand. I've seen each continent for as long as I could afford to stay there, and my one prevailing thought? If you've seen one doss house, you've seen them all. A bedbug bite in Sydney is the same as one in New York.

Peru, I know, is my swansong as a backpacker. I'm thirty-bleeding-three and I want to have children. I want a nice kitchen and an okay house and a car that goes without me weeping at it and kicking its tyres. I want pesto and a bottle of wine and a bed that isn't a roll mat or a hammock. If I go away for long spells again, it will be to work, doing some vocational task. So I'm saying goodbye to all that went before in the country I've longed most to see. And I'm taking as much time as I can over this. I'm going to embrace the chaos once more and acknowledge that I'm unreasonably lucky to have an eight-dollar-a-day budget, when the poor of the places I've visited could survive a month on that sum.

I'm tired of watching extremes of poverty, altitudes, depths, beauty, isolation, over-population, history and future. If I see them again, it will be to help. For now, I need Peru's help to remind the weary traveller in me what excited me so much about seeing the world in the first place. I want a reason to hit the road again when the kids that haven't had time to be born to me yet have grown up a bit and either want to come with me or want to get rid of me to have a free house. So I'm on a Lima pavement and I feel like Paddington did when he was on a London platform. Lost. Exhilarated. Exhausted. Homesick. Too late – we are two months away from anything familiar. Why? is a question we will ask a lot.

Four days later, we will leave Lima – a city many do their level best to avoid. It is mad, crazy, filthy, outrageous, wonderful, and awful. On night one, fresh from the sleeping-bag incident, we find sleep hard to come by. A couple copulates under our hotel balcony, their moans and screeches resembling those of a couple of cats. The next morning, I wake up and trip over a tortoise outside my door. He doesn't even stir. I need a stitch to seal the wound. 'I want to go home,' I whimper to the nurse, who smiles and snaps the thread.

Nowadays some flights go straight to the epicentre of Peruvian tourism – Cuzco, the ancient seat of the mighty Incan civilisation. But I have wanted to see Lima ever since I heard about the treasures stored in the many museums, the dancing, the madness itself. And Paddington's Aunt Lucy lived there, so as a child, I made several requests to visit, after dinner. All were denied with a smile. And I grew up quite serious about seeing the place for myself.

By day three, I've acclimatised and remembered how much I love hot nights in strange places. Wearing summer clothes at midnight, listening to unfamiliar sounds, eating strange food, having no idea what lies three blocks away from where you've ended up sleeping. I have a whole month of memories in one day of visiting museums and galleries, markets and parks. All my senses are as open as my skin is bare to the prospect of all that's coming. It's December and I'm in cool linen. Yes, I do love that.

By night three, I've even grown accustomed to our overheated companions' loving under the balcony. It's much more interesting listening to them have sex than having it myself. Lima is a crowded place. Young people have nowhere to go. There is even a Parque D'Amor to allow the *limeños* the privacy they cannot get in their homes. When we take a stroll through it, there are couples necking, people of all ages, from early teens to early eighties. All overshadowed by a statue of two lovers in a very intimate embrace. His jeans are emblazoned with the motif 'VD' – she doesn't seem to mind.

It's enough to give me indigestion after the fabulous food we have eaten in and around the plush district of Miraflores, where we are staying. It is a million miles away from the shanty towns that have sprung up around the city in the wake of the terror induced by the Shining Path organisation during the 1980s. You may remember them by their Spanish name, Sendero Luminoso. Those who live there can only dream about the chicken breast beaten flat and coated in breadcrumbs, raw seafood marinated in lime juice and coriander, tamales (stuffed corn-flour rolls), stuffed jalapeño peppers, all washed down with a chicha morada (a soft drink made from maize) and really fine Cerveza beer. This does not seem to make them resentful. Lima is the people. The *limeños* are as eager to get to know you as the cockroaches which wanted to share our dinner. The owner, beside himself, beats them back out the door with a rolled newspaper. He brushes away our thanks – it is all part of the service.

Apart from the endless supply of crafts and hundreds of museums, the nightlife in Lima is tremendous; sometimes there is bullfighting, though we saw no evidence of it. One jaunt round the dance floor with a *limeño* in a nightclub and you feel you've gone ten rounds with a beast anyway. One unforgettable occasion sees me doing (something like) a rumba with an orthopaedic and traumatology (that's what it says on his card) specialist called Jesus (Jesus is alive and well and living in Peru). His height, a princely four feet eleven inches. By the slow set he is proposing marriage, but only if he can operate on my hips to give them some slight chance of rotational rhythm.

There are so many bars and clubs you could take a trip to a different one every night of the week and still not have been in them all in a year's time. Latin, Indian, African, even classical, music set to disco rhythms abounds.

There's a museum for everyone in Lima: for gore freaks, you have the Spanish Inquisition; for those who like wealth, the gold museum has just about every object under the sun clad in gold, apart from the sun itself. This is a private collection – the smallest fraction of what was here before the conquistadors came. We are just beginning to sense the amount of history that awaited us.

On the way to the bus station, we are warned by people in

bare feet to mind our possessions. The station has moved – twice – and both locations seem to be edging nearer the shanty towns, nearer to the people they serve. Street fortune-tellers shows us the ace of the spades, and crook inviting fingers. Traders are selling everything from corn on the cob to a single, used shoe.

We board the huge bus headed for Nazca and watch the goodbyes just as enormous. One car follows the bus for two miles, both sets of relatives hanging out every available window and screeching see-you-soons. The drivers of these monsters are a law unto themselves, taking off even as the baggage-handlers are still throwing luggage into the hold – a cooker, two beds, even a sofa. Someone is moving house.

There's a stifling heat, which means every window is thrown open and everything not pinned down flaps wildly. Beside me, a woman picks lice from her son's hair and flicks them out the window. I scratch at first surreptitiously and then with open violence. She regards me with the same disinterest the Lost Luggage Jesus wore on his seen-it-all skin.

The bus hurtles, stopping for tolls and police patrols and single passengers on the side of the Pan American highway, lined with rubbish dumps, sand dunes, slums and grottoes. People are washing in drainage pipes. Children are playing on raw sewage. This is Señor Jesus Cuavito's bus. He is very proud of it. For his passengers, he has even recorded violent videos featuring prerequisite amounts of sex, macho manoeuvres, black magic, nudity, and imaginative and very painful deaths. No advertisements to break the monotony.

Two mammas have a fight at the back of the bus, which rivals any in the video, and while they are screaming, a man gets up in suit and tie and begins to talk to the passengers with a fervency that convinces me he is a reactionary spreading dissent. He is, in fact, an entrepreneur using universal sales patter, a miracle-cure seller whose product is sold to us in body language alone. We are the only buyers.

His bottle of something will go down well as a gift to the receptionist in our hotel at Nazca.

Nazca is a dusty, dry little desert town with a definite lack of atmosphere and not a shred of its previous grandeur. But that desert turned out to be a sketch-pad for ancient Indians and one of the greatest scientific mysteries in the New World. The Nazca Lines are a series of drawings of animals, geometric figures and birds, ranging up to three hundred metres in size, etched into the arid crust of the pampa and preserved for about two thousand years, thanks to a complete lack of rain and special winds that cleaned, but did not erase, the desert. Their purpose is the subject of many a bar-stool conversation in Peruvian hotels and more than one Discovery Channel documentary. Books have been written, photographs taken, excavations carried out. But no one knows for sure.

In 1939, a North American scientist, Paul Kosok, flew over the pampa in a small plane and noticed the lines, which are hardly visible from the ground. He first thought they were part of a pre-Incan irrigation system, but he quickly concluded it had nothing to do with irrigation. He discovered that the lines of the sunset ran tandem to the direction of one of the bird drawings. He viewed the lines as the biggest astronomy book in the world.

A young German mathematician, Maria Reiche, was thirty-five when she met Kosok, not long after his discovery. For the next fifty years, she made the study of the lines her life. Many think they have something to do with alien navigation systems, made by creatures from other planets. Reiche firmly rejected these kinds of popular space theories. She died in June 1998, at the age of ninety-five, believing the lines made up a huge astronomical calendar, linked to the rising and setting points of celestial bodies on the east and west horizons. In all South American civilisations, and Peru had many of them, the heavens were consulted and studied on every issue. The whole complex, according to her theories, was designed to help organise planting and harvesting.

Apart from the lines, which are of far more interest to archaeologists, there are also shapes formed from a single line – a spiral-tailed monkey, a condor, a spider, tree, whale, humming bird, and so on. The best way to see them is as Kosok did in 1939 – in a light aircraft. If you are worried about not having booked a flight in advance, then don't be. Try leaving town without booking a flight – they'll follow you. For as little as fifty US dollars, you can spend thirty-five minutes hovering over this strange phenomenon that lies across five hundred square kilometres of bleak, stony pampa.

A giant canvas and revelation, the lines hold my fascination until I am somewhat distracted by the vomiting of a Hungarian woman sitting next to me on the plane. The sweat beads on her forehead. I smile at her sympathetically and give her some tissues. She doesn't look out the window, as she hands me the bags to mind for her. A little souvenir.

The most plausible theory, it seems for now, is that the Nazca Lines were a complex series of enticements to the gods for the one commodity all life needs to survive – rain. There is so little of it here, even the lizards are thirsty. Looking out the window, I am forcibly struck by the wonder of seeing what humanity will create in order to form ritual and meaning, in order to survive in a place for thousands of years where no one can survive today. Residents of the town of Nazca complain when the water is turned off for twelve hours, which regularly occurs in times of drought. Tourists at Nazca complain when the pool looks a little scummy. The engineers of the lines could wait years between rainfalls and still they developed a complex irrigation system that allowed their civilisation to flourish. But the years between rainfalls numbered too many. And all was lost. For a time.

Gorge is waiting for us with the Pontiac after the flight. The Hungarian woman comes with us. She never said thank you for the help. I ask her name. She shakes her head. I take this to mean that she doesn't have one. To Gorge she speaks in fluent Spanish and I hear 'O'Sullivan' mentioned more than once. He plays 'Matrimony' for her. He does not propose it.

We leave Nazca to head for the high country. The Hungarian woman looks a little lonely as she sits on the bus. As it gains altitude, the atmosphere changes. The hectic coastal influence is lost after a hundred kilometres: the tabloid papers with the pin-up's name printed across her bum; the cacophony of street sounds; the naked female billboards advertising everything from phone cards to private health insurance. All the tack is now replaced by a silence we had almost forgotten

Our destination is Arequipa, a city whose name is derived from the Quechua Indian, meaning: 'Let's stop here'. Even the conquistador Francisco Pizarro took time out from slaughtering and enslaving indigenous populations to build a villa here in the midst of an astonishingly beautiful natural landscape. A high plateau surrounded by volcanoes, it is the site of one of the most atmospheric colonial cities, 2,100 metres high in the Andes. We begin to see some of the ten million native Quechua who make up more than half of Peru's population but who have little influence.

If you are lucky enough to check into a hotel in one of the portals of the main square – the Plaze des Armas – you will have an unrivalled view of a colonial cathedral, which is floodlit at night. Inside there is a statue of the Virgin de Las Peñas in full white wedding dress, with gold embroidery, sequins, crown, and suitably startled expression. Beneath her, a Quechua woman breastfeeds her baby, and two women hold each other in a sleeping hug. For the Indians of Peru, who believe they are little more than animals after centuries of unabated persecution, the church is a source of sanctuary and comfort. They treat it as a home from home. Their statues of martyred saints and crucifixions are blood drenched. One priest who worked among these people for fifteen years believes that because they have suffered so much it reassures them to know their idols suffered in the same way. There is an easy alliance between the old beliefs of the Indians and the introduced Catholicism.

The cathedral has survived six earthquakes, one of which brought down the bell in 1960. Outside you see the people make use of their main square – fried corn, sweets, chewing gum for sale, benches to sit on, and life to discuss.

The Hotel Portal is a living monument, not to the days of the conquistador, but those of *Saturday Night Fever*. They haven't touched much since John Travolta slicked and adjusted his black hair and matching underpants. For the Spanish or mestizo Peruvian male, I would not be surprised if young John were a god. He is certainly worshipped in our hotel.

The main attraction in Arequipa is the Santa Catalina monastery, a convent, in fact, in which no man set a foot until the 1970s. It is a city within the city, and each quarter is named after a Spanish city. It was founded in 1540 by Maria de Guzman, the widow of a money-lender and renowned for her attachment to worldly possessions. 'Pray, work, quiet' was the convent's motto, and it became a retreat for the second daughters of wealthy families who were forced into cloister and Dominican sisterhood, regardless of whether they were suited to it or not. One hundred pieces of silver was a novice's dowry, 2,400 when she took her final vows – these were no ordinary nuns. Their surroundings might have been stunning, but it was a prison for many of them nevertheless. The only contact they had with their families and friends were the gifts which were left in a revolving wooden alcove. Each nun had her own house and was allowed to bring all her possessions, as well as a servant. Colonial furniture still remains in simple, white- or blue-washed rooms.

One of the mothers superior was canonised by the present pope. Her portrait hangs with that of thirteen other women who presided over this mini-empire.

The most atmospheric place in the monastery, despite all the wealth and finery of the cloister, is the open-air laundry, where the mestizo servants would meet under the fruit trees to thrash the habits of their mistresses against the steep hollowed sides of ceramic half-urns.

We leave Arequipa's cloister to climb higher into the Andes and the remote Colca Canyon, a place apart in many respects. This is where we first experience altitude sickness. Your head spins, you can't breathe and your gums hurt. Or so I am told. I haven't got it. Michael, the photographer, succumbs and is bedridden after a six-hour journey, which took us to five thousand metres, and which he only managed by munching his way through a bag of coca leaves. The leaves are the natural product from which cocaine is derived, but in this form they are harmless and help to relieve the symptoms. Even if you don't get ill, you still feel like you've aged fifty years, as the lack of oxygen slows you down. I've been drinking mate de coca, or coca tea, which tastes like dandelions in hot water with sugar, but it isn't helping. The Indians' lung capacity is almost twice ours, which explains why their upper bodies are so large compared to the rest of them.

The Colca Canyon is one of those places time has truly forgotten. It claims to be the deepest natural gorge in the world and is home to Quechua and Aymara Indians, all directly descended from the Incas of colonial times. Not that you'd know it now. They haven't a shilling. The people dress traditionally and it's obvious they don't like tourists, though they tolerate our intrusion. If you want to know what it was like to be a conquistador, then this is about as close as you get. Except now we come armed with cameras ...

There are terraces in this valley which date back to the pre-Inca period, huge herds of llamas, massive mountains, and condor eagles that rise on the early morning thermals and spend the day soaring the heavens before descending with the setting sun.

We have travelled by train to Cuzco, the seat of the Incan empire, situated in the Sacred Valley of the Incas. The Incas formed one of the two great empires in the Americas, at the time of the conquistadors, the other one being the more violent Aztec culture of Central America.

When Pizarro arrived in Peru in the 1500s, he discovered a splendour no European monarch could emulate. At the heart of Cuzco lay a temple – in itself, perhaps the greatest symbol of that wealth and power, and known to the Incas and their present-day descendants as the navel of the world. At the heart of the temple was a room made entirely of gold to venerate the sun. And beside it, one of silver to venerate the moon. Within months, it was stripped and shipped back on a Spanish galleon, to swell Spanish coffers and finance further expeditions.

How did such a civilisation flourish on thirsty soil so far removed from sea level? On stony mountainsides that reached higher than any known in Europe? The reason the Incas survived so successfully is that they were great organisers and agrarian engineers of genius.

After Pizarro's conquest, this wonderful civilisation was lost within decades. The Indians were enslaved, and to this day they live out their lives as second-class citizens. In the recent elections, one man of a poor family, who became a World Bank economist, ran for the presidency. He withdrew, but he is still in politics. The hope is that he will one day become what Peru has not had since Pizarro's time – a leader of Incan origin.

The trains in Peru at times ascend almost vertically, and after fourteen hours with a diesel engine doing all the work, I am tempted to call off the planned four-day hike on the Inca Trail to the famous Machu Picchu – South America's greatest offering. It is Christmas Eve and I am sure the Jesuses everywhere are celebrating. Arequipa has got to be the best city I have ever been in. Firecrackers are going off everywhere, scaring the living daylights out of me. Villagers who have travelled in for the special Christmas Eve artisan market are asleep in huts made from bales of straw. At midnight mass, a group of Quechua Indians mobs us, at the sign of peace, to shake hands.

The Plaza des Armas is a pageant of life all day. A collection of colourful Indian dancers spread out from the cathedral steps onto the streets, chanting, spinning rattles, holding their nativity dolls on trays covered with fresh flowers. Children bring their porcelain baby Jesus dolls to a doll doctor, who has set up a stall to fix them. There are food offerings, processions, cavalcades, and even a Santa Claus.

In the afternoon, I play table football – practically a national sport in Cuzco – and shop for alpaca wool sweaters and turquoise jewellery, all beautifully made. But beware – some sweaters are genuine synthetic. Light a match to check their relation to llama wool and lose your hair.

On the Inca Trail to Machu Picchu, the most intact remains of an Incan city, we travel on foot over sixty kilometres, across mountain valleys and passes.

On the first day, we camp among the ruins of an Incan fort, along with the local villagers' horses, pigs, donkeys, bulls, turkeys, geese, hens and cockerels. The hens and cockerels win the Most Noise in the Night Competition. The climb on the first two days is steep, but glorious vistas appear out of mists that rise and dissipate as quickly as Irish rain showers. The route is a testament to the Incas' civil-engineering acumen. They may not have formulated the arch as a concept, but they knew how to achieve the impossible. Unfortunately their road-building skills only made Pizarro's job the easier. But when you see a terraced field still producing a fertile crop at over five thousand metres, you have to admire the tenacity.

Two days' climbing leads us to a pleasant walk through high jungle with panoramic views of green peaks, butterflies and metallic blue birds. At Runki Rakay fort, the wind sweeps away the mist to reveal wafer-thin ridges of fields, jagged peaks, waterfalls, and flowers in abundance for the feasting humming birds, sparrows, swallows, swifts and blackbirds. 'How can Machu Picchu match this?' we ask. And the following day, we see that it can.

At dawn, we are at Inti Punku – the Sun Gate and point where Machu Picchu comes into view. We wait for the ubiquitous mist to clear. There is no way you can take views for granted here – they are with you one minute and gone the next. Three hours later, the first sight of this dramatic Inca citadel defies description – it is no wonder that this is the greatest tourist attraction in South America. It is perched between two mountain tops, surrounded by Andean peaks, swirling cloud and jungle. Two thousand five hundred metres below, the swollen Urubamba River snakes through the narrow valley. At this altitude, its roar sounds like distant thunder. It is New Year's Day.

A new year begun at such altitude, surrounded by such majesty, promises great things. We have two whole days to explore the ruins of one of the Inca empire's most important agricultural centres, in relative peace, before catching the train back to Cuzco. And we take full advantage. Walking the streets of Machu Piccho, a ghost city, it is as if the Incas left only yesterday. I find myself in awe of how they carved out such a place in this extreme environment. How they cut the stones and fitted them so closely together that a knife cannot pass between them; how they fed a population in such an isolated location for such a long time. On the first day, I examine the ruins, and when I catch the bus down to the town, I imagine that when I see it again the following day, I will be less impressed.

That night, I find myself aching to see it again, and when the morning comes, we are first in the queue to return, to climb up the hill from present-day dilapidation to the past glory waiting on the mountain top. I walk much as I did the day before, but this time I cannot escape the sadness, the futile fleeing, the driving of the Indians from dignity to the hardship they endure in modern Peru. I end up in tears and look for somewhere to hide them and myself.

I find it in a cave under the ruins. A cave with a view of unending mountains and mist. There is no Ireland beyond this place. It's a place where people have come to pray and light candles. I have one to light and I sit for an entire day, thinking of what happened here and what is happening to myself. Praying for the future of the Indians; and for my own future.

When I leave at the day's end, I don't look back. I know this is a place I'll never see again.

The train takes eight hours, a four-hour delay caused by a landslide which happened only an hour before we arrived at our destination. Like automatons, we get off, go to a hotel, sleep, get up, go to a train station, and spend another twelve hours travelling south to Puno, an adobe city on the side of the great Lake Titicaca.

Our visit to the lake is laced by lightning and a fear that it will find us. It seems almost a relief to disembark from our boat onto a man-made island of rushes. We photograph the people who live in rush houses. Their main source of income is small, tired fish, and posing for small, tired photographs; the children sell pictures they have drawn. Their smiles reveal teeth rotted by the sweets travellers give to them in part payment. I have read about this and hand out apples and a supply of toothbrushes. I can still hear the laughter, as we drive back into the city past the pink prison where the Sendero Luminoso are mostly held.

'Why is it pink?' I ask the driver.

'It is pink,' he says with a smile.

'Ah, yes. Of course.'

After almost two months, I am not just beginning to understand – it now makes perfect sense. If I don't leave soon, I think, I won't remember what Ireland looks like. I was born here. Wasn't I?

At Lima airport, we check in with as much reluctance as we felt when we arrived. We pay a visit to Jesus, the Lost Luggage official, just for the craic, to find out if our sleeping bags have made a dramatic reappearance. They haven't. But behind him, sitting in a cage with a luggage label attached, is a Yorkshire terrier with a red bow in its fringe.

'Why?' we ask.

'It's Christmas,' comes the laconic reply.

It is late January.

# NIAMH HOOPER

## HIKING IN THE FOOTSTEPS OF DRAGONS

A tatty little poster spotted through the window of a moving train was responsible.

There's no accounting for just why people choose to go to certain places on holidays. The weather, the sights, the culture, the shopping, the people, the drink or, in my case, simply the image of a red dragon set against a yellow background.

On an overcast October day, gliding through Booterstown train station on the DART, with crashing waves to my right, and on my left a wind-blown ad which caught my eye and tugged at my heart. 'Hike in the footsteps of dragons,' it said. My soul sprung to attention. Enticed by the majesty and magic of walking on the Great Wall of China, the serene appeal of the Eastern way, the saffron yellow of enlightenment and an opportunity to do some good for those less fortunate than myself and who have nowhere to lay their heads at night, I rang the Dublin Simon Community.

The personal physical challenge, and the requirement of having to raise at least €4,400 for a charity I admired greatly, appealed to me as much as it scared me. I delayed in returning my form. But never having taken on anything like it before, the sniff of adventure was enough. Eventually I signed up, paid my registration fee, and excitement fizzled through my body at the thought of the China Challenge on which I would embark: a seventy-kilometre hike in thirty degrees Celsius along the Great Wall.

The warm-up meeting two months or so before the departure date, however, turned that excitement to terror. Slides of a seventy-degree incline that could be approached only by scrambling on hands and knees put me in a state of paralysis, and my daily training walks came to an abrupt halt for several weeks. There was no escaping my delusions of adequacy. Regular walks on the flat pavement of Dún Laoghaire's sea front weren't going to be of much use to me when faced with steep, crumbling steps in the sweltering heat and carrying a big rucksack. Fitness was one thing; this looked like a hard-core assault course. But being a woman, I'm like a tea bag – you need to throw me into boiling water before you find out how strong I am. I wasn't going to be put off. And besides, by the time that meeting had rolled round, it was too late – I had already raised my money through the generosity of family and friends.

So months later, there I stood in Dublin airport. At that stage, I was definitely more apprehensive than excited. Beside me was a group of people, most of whom I'd never seen before. And the China of my dreams was very far away.

At the Aer Lingus check-in desk, a cornucopia of hikers had gathered, from the age of seventeen to sixty and in all sizes and shapes from throughout Ireland, North and South – boots tied to their rucksacks. No words were needed. The effervescent atmosphere said it all. Everywhere there were open smiles and a shared passion for jumping into life; within us all was a hunger for a challenge, for the unknown, for different cultures and different aspects to ourselves, on top of a love of nature. It was sure to be interesting, if nothing else.

We were the first of two groups to assemble and would meet up with the rest of the sixty-seven-strong group in Amsterdam for the long-haul flight to Beijing. Spotting the potential for truancy, the organisers hadn't left anything to chance, and in a letter notifying us about flight details came a warning that we were not allowed to leave Schiphol airport between flights.

As if.

Being one of the first group to leave Dublin, we had a couple of hours to play with, and it was inevitable that the opening words to tumble out in conversation with fellow strangers were along the lines of: 'Are you going to head into Amsterdam on the sly?'

With Dutch customs cleared, I boarded a swanky double-decker train with the first two people I'd met and clicked with in Dublin airport – Abina, an outgoing mother of two grown-up children, and her dry-humoured friend, Kenneth. Having laughed and chatted the whole way into Amsterdam city centre, we didn't discover until an inspector appeared as the train pulled in at our stop that we'd been travelling in first class because of a blissful ignorance of the local language.

The search was then on for angel cake, the confectionery made with cannabis, which I'd heard about and wanted to sample. What we did find in the hour we had to spare was the red-light district – you couldn't avoid it: trendy shopping streets and the dodgiest of drug café-cum-shops on the riverbank, full of stoners. But no cake.

As we tried to slink subtly back into the group in the airport without being noticed, a few giggly characters indicated we hadn't been alone playing truant, and the hash houses of Amsterdam had done well from their custom. Waiting to board, I changed the message on my mobile phone to say I couldn't take calls because I was in China. I had to record it twice; the first time I sounded too gleeful.

The adventure had begun.

After thirteen hours in the air, groggy and in need of uncrumpling, we touched down in Beijing, as plump grey clouds hovered overhead. A further three-hour bus journey north-west from the Chinese capital – home to twelve million – to the small village of Jinshanling had to be endured. Within ten minutes of us piling onto two smelly old buses, one of them broke down. The radiator had blown and water cascaded from its underbelly.

As we sat on the side of the dusty road, it was lovely to take a moment to drink in the scene around us. Elderly locals in torn slippers trundled by in bockety old rickshaws along the dirt tracks, and young lads hurtled past on bikes with buckets on the back, ready to carry any brave passengers. A super-duper six-lane highway sliced the countryside in half. On one side was a scene reminiscent of Millet's *Gleaners*, with men and women labouring in the fields. Everywhere was quiet and calm. This wasn't just a different continent, it was a different world.

A miracle by Western standards, the radiator leak was fixed by mechanics in fifteen minutes and we were back on the road. And stretching before us was the vastness of a Chinese horizon with verdant, dancing trees and feathery shrubs, a sprinkling of bicyclists, and figures squatting at bus stops (no one seemed to be standing) or toiling on the flat, arid land.

Eventually we arrived in Jinshanling. I don't know what I'd expected, but this wasn't it. It was remote, eerily quiet and secluded, and our cabin-style accommodation was in a drab, militaristic barracks, cheered up only by welcoming Chinese touches of balloons and a red and gold banner around the main entrance.

The first thing that I found hard to get my head around coming from the Western world was the poor level of sanitation. Toilet paper was not to be flushed away but placed in a bin instead. And to protect against disease, we were instructed to wash our hands in the big bowls of Dettol before eating. I think I wasn't the only one who went into shock.

We split into four groups, and were assigned a leader and two local guides per group. Tony, the expedition leader from Across the Divide, the British adventure company that organised the trek, then briefed us on the next day's hike – being forced to refer to a hand-drawn map because of the unavailability of printed maps in China. Advised to drink up to four litres of water a day, we were informed of the toilet etiquette for the week. It amounted to leaving your rucksack in the middle of the path whenever nature called and then a scramble off the wall to go. That way, the leaders or guides would know someone was missing. In the case of my group, that would be Emma, our leader, Gracie, our 22-year-old local guide from Beijing, or Dahou, the Mountain Man – a young, cheerful, light-of-foot character with an inexhaustible local knowledge.

We were free to do as we pleased after the briefing, and curiosity got the better of most of us travel-weary souls. Escorted by persistent-yet-friendly locals hoping to sell souvenirs, I walked up to a nearby section of the wall that was built in 1378. Suffice to say, I was awestruck.

And so, after twenty-four hours on the go and discovering to my amazement that mobile phones worked on the Wall – text messages could be sent and received loud and clear – the excited, sleepy group retired early.

At six thirty the next morning, when we arose for breakfast, the rain was pouring down. And it didn't stop. Prepared to walk a minimum of eight hours a day, we were taken by surprise by the weather. It wasn't in the plan and many didn't have waterproof gear. In the absence of the expected sunny thirty degrees, the first few thousand steps of the trek were amongst the most challenging of the week. But even before we took those steps, we were forced to use an alternative route to reach the setting-out point, because during the torrential rain the previous night, two huge boulders had become dislodged and were blocking the road.

In zero degrees, lashed by hailstones and unrelenting rain, we trekked through thick vegetation, walked on a restricted area of the Wall, and sang our way through farmland tilled by men and women pulling hand-drawn ploughs. 'Always look on the bright side of life' sticks out as that day's anthem. It's safe to say we were a miserable, bedraggled bunch.

And thus, at the end of day one, I stood fully clothed in the steady dribble of a shower that washed both the toilet and wash-hand basin at the same time as it washed me. It was easier to wash with my clothes on than peel off the saturated layers with wet wrinkled fingers numbed by the cold. Yet, bizarre as it may sound, the physical fatigue of the day dissolved into smiles in the process.

A visit with Kenneth to a few shacks selling souvenirs near home ended up with me trying on a selection of traditional hats. This caused the local families much amusement, perhaps because of the novelty of my strawberry blond hair and freckles beneath the Chinese headwear. After that, nothing and no one was safe. Kenneth was being pressured from various factions to buy a silk dress for his 'wife' – i.e. me. No doubt a sound marketing strategy.

After filling up my water bottles after a breakfast of water melon, bananas and eggs the next morning, I waited while fried rice was prepared for my lunch. The woman behind the counter gently took my hand to read my palm and smiled at what it said. I was glad she enjoyed what she saw there, but I was none the wiser about what it told her about me. Then came the chicken dish as part of the buffet – served Chinese-style, complete with head, eyes and beak. The horror on many faces persuaded the catering staff to remove them.

In keeping with Eastern spiritual philosophies and the importance placed on colours, red panels inviting in good spirits surrounded the doorways of all the homes and businesses. Whether such panels existed around the door of the local farmer who held us to ransom for walking through her land, we'll never know. Initially she appeared chatty and friendly, but soon enough – with hands deep in pockets, feet firm on the ground, gold tooth glinting – it was clear she wasn't for budging, and her fierce pack of dogs barked protectively in the yard beside her. Two hundred people had walked through her land, she said, and she wanted money per head – despite already having received payment from Across the Divide for access. A half-hour later, negotiations with four people ongoing, she agreed to release us.

Tales told and bellies full after dinner, we got the bad news and the good from Tony: more rain was forecast and, as a result, the next night's camping was called off – the ground was too wet to pitch tents. Things were looking up.

As wet fleeces, trousers, jackets, socks and day-bags dried on a cart (not all rooms had hot running water or a heater), Greg Maxwell, the chief executive of the Dublin Simon Community, gave the first of nightly talks about his organisation. He explained where and how the €200,000 we had raised would be spent helping the homeless. It was a touching and important part of each day and it grounded us as to why we were in China.

A campfire then lured us outdoors for a talk by Lao Tsung, a masonry foreman in the recent renovation of the part of the Wall we had walked that day, which stretched from Gubeiko to Jinshanling. Clearly it was one thing to walk it but quite another to build it.

An Irish singsong inevitably followed. Tall, blonde Sara from Galway started things off with a deep, husky version of 'Delaney's Gone Back on the Wine', and another dimension was added by the gentle, arty Maureen's ethereal Irish voice when she joined in. And with Darren's rendition of 'You'll Never Walk Alone' (he was a Liverpool supporter), we knew we were in for a good week.

The gods were obviously testing us, and the Irish

bonhomie won them over. Dawn broke through a clear blue sky. It was time for sunscreen and shades, shorts and T-shirts at last. In hindsight, the downpour, which had surprised even the locals, was the best thing that could have happened. From here on in, we enjoyed and appreciated the wonders around us, and as a group we had bonded early.

For me, day two was the most magical and the most challenging day of all. Plonked on the top of the back of sleeping dragons, lolloping along as far as the eye could see, the Simatai section of the Wall, with its 135 towers dotted at intervals, dates back originally to the Northern Qi dynasty (550–577) and was rebuilt during the Ming dynasty (1368–1644). Not for the faint-hearted, this section. The courage of those harbouring a fear of heights was impressive, especially at times when both hands were required to scramble, and cameras had been put away, so that there was nothing to distract you from the climb. And the pressure on knees descending the crumbling, narrow steps, while holding on to the side of the Wall for support, was incredibly demanding.

Built over two thousand years by different dynasties to protect the ancient Chinese empire from marauding tribes, the five-thousand-kilometre Wall snakes along from the Gobi Desert to the mountains of Korea. It was never fully effective as a defence system, but for a man-made wonder, it's out there on its own. Its construction involved tens of millions of people and legend has it that the bodies of deceased workers are buried in the 180 million cubic metres of rammed earth within the Wall. The structure is a massive feat of engineering. The age of modern machinery hasn't yet reached some parts of rural China, but even if a JCB were available, the variety of terrain would undoubtedly prove too much for it. There were times on that day's sixteen-kilometre hike when we trod a narrow ridge of crumbling stone not much wider than our hips and with sheer drops on either side. One three-minute stretch, for example, took more concentration than a full week at work just to reach the other side.

It was at stages like this that the easy-going conversation had a tendency to dry up, and helping hands and shoulders were offered and willingly taken. Lose your footing and not only would you fall but also everyone on the sections below you – anything up to sixteen fellow walkers. And there was nothing more likely to cause you to stumble than the stunning views all around, as mountain range upon mountain range, in varying hues of green, blue and brown, stacked endlessly behind each other into the distance. At times, all I could do was swivel slowly and carefully around and around, trying to take it all in.

At various stages that day, I couldn't help but look at what was ahead of me – an interminable number of steps, getting steeper and steeper – and doubt my ability to meet the physical challenge. But equally there were moments of pure bliss, when I felt I could have walked forever, with the Wall's magnificence and majesty at my feet.

Part of the hike was to cross a wooden, chain suspension bridge, swinging in the wind, before attacking the day's final challenge. But word filtered back that it was being called off – because of high winds, the cable car was deemed too dangerous to use. On our alternative route home, we passed a high-wire trapeze act above the valley. A notice beside the cable-car lift-off quaintly warned that such daredevilry wasn't for those who were 'horrifying of heights or liquor heads'. In any case, our insurance didn't cover the adventurers among us who were keen for a go, and we had to give it a pass.

After our warming-down exercises, we piled into buses to the Reservoir Lodge. My cheerful room-mate for the night, Conor, and I took a dip in the reservoir, much to the amusement of the incredulous hotel staff, and later that evening karaoke got the better of us. Ken and Darren, the jokers of the trip from County Kildare, kicked things off by crooning 'California Dreaming'. They didn't win the competition but Darren's talent as a masseur won him friends before the night was out, as he massaged many a pair of tired aching feet with someone else's prize of foot balm.

On day three, we climbed about eight hundred metres to the highest tower in the province and one of the highest on the entire Wall. The Wang Jing Watchtower, 120 kilometres from Beijing, is so high that the lights of the capital can be seen shimmering in the distance, or so we were told. Doing our warm-up stretches in the car park before the morning's long and steep hike, our leaders pointed to where we were going to have lunch. It didn't look possible.

In the sweltering heat, I decided to go native and invest in a traditional hat, tied on with a piece of wool. During the climb of the steep, rugged rock face came the scariest moment of the trip. Someone tossed aside an unsteady rock rather than have someone else fall on it, but their thoughtfulness almost backfired, and the rock bounced down the mountainside, gathering speed as it went, and eventually landed perilously close to people in the last group. That episode behind us, we scrambled the final ascent on our hands and knees, expecting to be greeted by a plateau on which we could relax and enjoy the view. But when pulled over the top, we found ourselves perched on a narrow ridge, where all four groups had lunch. If you hadn't experienced vertigo by this point, you did then.

The afternoon trek was downhill through thick vegetation to the rural village of Ganfang where we camped overnight in the school playground. For many, this special evening was the highlight of the trip.

Initially reticent, the kids soon discovered that we enjoyed playing games. Although their living conditions appeared bleak, the brightly dressed children were the picture of happiness as we played together for hours. Many were orphans and stayed in the school overnight. As a gift from her young son's classmates, Maureen had brought a tape of them singing Irish classics such as 'The Fields of Athenry' and 'The Irish Rover'. It was lovely to experience the mixing of the two cultures, and the children played tug-of-war, marbles, German jumps, arm wrestling, and gave themselves up willingly to being spun around till we were all dizzy. Their jackets and caps, both local and donated, were emblazoned with Western labels such as Coca-Cola and Nike. Their small faces were lit from within, and they simply wallowed in the affection showered upon them.

A beautiful little girl in yellow came over to me, took my journal and pink pen, and using my knee as her table, started to write in Chinese characters. She was trying to communicate, but because the extent of my Chinese was *Ni Hao* (hello), she was getting no more than smiles from me. Undeterred, she continued, with her schoolmates gathering round to read what she had written. Gracie translated it – the child's name was Lili Pui and she wanted to know mine. She'd written, 'If you can't tell me what it is, you can write it down here.' Then she sang to me – music was her favourite subject, I was told.

That determined little girl lived several kilometres away, but to ensure that she wasn't going to miss out on our visit, she had 'developed' a back problem that meant she was allowed to stay overnight in the school with the other children who had to walk up to ten kilometres daily for classes.

When it was time for bed, we made our way to the fifty-five odd, two-man tents crowded into the playground. They were so closely pegged together that it was like sharing one tent with seventy others, and with temperatures below zero, sleep was not an option. Acting on the clever advice of my tent-mate, Abina, I wore my thermals, trousers, socks, three tops and a fleece, as well as using my water bottle as a hot-water bottle, but it was still too cold. And instead of rising with our normal six thirty wake-up call, we were all wide awake at five.

Everything about the trip was perfectly planned, but being given a taste of real Chinese life not usually enjoyed by tourists, just when we were getting used to the beauty of our physical surroundings, was the icing on the cake. Not only did we get to experience some of the world's most breathtaking scenery, but we got to camp in rural China – witnessing Chinese life at the foothills of the Great Wall in its most natural state, among some of the friendliest people I've ever encountered.

And by welcoming groups such as ours, the school at which we stayed received three new computers and was about to go online. Observing a culture so beautifully pure, I was uneasy about the introduction of the Internet, which would make them aware of things they didn't have. But then, who are we to stop their advancement?

We watched the flag-raising ceremony, performed each day by the children, who stood in line saluting, and listened to the recitation of a very touching letter from the pupils, thanking us for our gifts. And after lots of hugs, it was sadly time to leave.

As the leading group on day four, we were joined by the respected Lao Tsung, who, in Hansel-and-Gretel style, tied red ribbons on shrubs, laying the trail for all to follow. The local guide in the final group collected them when everyone had passed through.

Enjoying being up front, Maureen led the singing as we approached one of the highest towers in the province at four hundred metres and then climbed under the Wall at Bailingguan. Lunch was held on a spectacular rock, and an official photo was taken of the entire group. There was an air of finality to it all and, as we set off, we thought we were just a jaunt away from home. But what Tony had described as 'undulating hillocks' turned out to be eight kilometres of mountain ridge after mountain ridge. I had a dodgy tummy and, for me, that afternoon was the lowest of the trek. But it was nothing that couldn't be sorted out by Kathryn and her homoeopathy kit when we got to camp.

Curious hotel staff joined us in our warm-down session, and with cups of jasmine tea and biscuits in hand, the group was happy again. Before bed, I went for a stroll by the breathlessly still reservoir, surrounded by pyramidal peaks and ridges lit by a full moon. Day five, the final day of the walk, beckoned.

The next morning, we began our trek at the earlier hour of six, and walked through a nature reserve not normally open to the public. As the hike was coming to an end, our break that day included time-out for twenty minutes, and each of us found our own space on the mountainside to reflect.

Ten minutes from the end of the trek, all four groups joined up, and together we walked across the finishing line as gunfire crackled to celebrate our achievement, followed by glasses of bubbly, the awarding of medals, and hugs and kisses from our fellow hikers.

Beijing and the party that lasted till the wee small hours; the Forbidden City and Tiananmen Square; the peals of laughter in the Pearl Market as the two Kens and I modelled a selection of wigs; delicacies such as dog with 'Chile' sauce and crispy bun with ants – all awaited us. Not to mention me being a freak because of my fair hair and freckles, which were enough to prompt children to squeal and touch me just to see if I was real.

But as the buses pulled out, leaving the sleeping dragons behind, I was engulfed by sadness. The experience was nearly over and, like the photographs that couldn't capture the stunning vistas we had had the privilege to enjoy, words can't begin to describe the emotions I felt towards the many people – leaders and local guides included – who had made up my family for the trip. Since that first night, it had been impossible to get 'You'll Never Walk Alone' out of my head. It became the anthem of the China Challenge and I will never hear it without having the fondest memories of everyone who shared the wonder of China with me.

Little did I know that windy October day how a tatty poster in a train station would open up my life in so many wonderful ways.

# GRACE WYNNE-JONES

## THE QUEST

The information leaflets from the Heyokah Retreat Center made it clear that this was no ordinary holiday. I was going on a Native American Vision Quest in a 'majestic' canyon in New Mexico. And not only would I be sitting alone, surrounded by nature, but I would also be entering the 'Cave of the Bear'.

'Do I have to enter a *real* bear cave?' The question had to be asked before I booked my plane tickets.

'No. Not unless you want to.' Although we were on the phone, I could hear the smile in the voice of the centre's founder and medicine woman, Julie Rivers. Native American teachings are rich in metaphor and have great reverence for nature. 'Entering the Cave of the Bear means "going within",' she continued calmly. 'We sometimes need to enter the void in ourselves to find the deeper answers we seek. It is a time of introspection and healing.'

One September evening, some weeks later, I arrived at the centre's home, an adobe building called Buffalo House, located in the high desert outside Santa Fe. I was glad that I was going to stay there for a while before entering the Cave of the Bear. After all, I was only just getting used to the large buffalo head that presided over the hallway.

Buffalo House was attractive and welcoming and its rooms were liberally adorned with Native American fetishes and 'medicine objects', including large dream catchers, huge drums, a turtle shell, and many paintings of 'medicine animals', such as wolves.

'Wow!' The exclamation gives a sense of the almost electric jolt of excitement I felt when I stepped outside Buffalo House in daylight and surveyed the magical high desert country for the first time. The mountains and land were a glorious red and the high clear sky, a vibrant, singing blue. D.H. Lawrence once declared that New Mexico was the greatest experience from the outside world that he had ever had. It seemed like the perfect place to go on a Vision Quest, or West Direction Retreat, which was the main focus of my holiday.

Apparently many people are drawn to these quests during times of transition. I certainly felt I had reached a point in my life when I needed to step out of my comfort zone for a while and ask who I truly was and what I truly valued. I think all of us need to ask those questions every so often. Catch up with ourselves.

The feeling that I wanted to know more about Native American culture had occurred some years before when I'd been on a Celtic spirituality retreat in Glendalough, County Wicklow. I'd been spending a lot of time in the company of nature and books, and then I came across the Sacred Path Cards created by a foremost Native American teacher, Jamie Sams, with illustrations by Linda Childers. A book accompanied the cards and I found them nestling intriguingly on a shelf in my bedroom. 'The Discovery of Self Through Native Teachings', proclaimed the cover. Each card presents a 'teaching' and one often picks a card that uncannily contains the advice and wisdom one needs to read. I put the cards on the floor and chose one.

Though I can no longer remember the card I picked, it spoke to me at that time and that moment, and I somehow got a sense of comradeship. A sense that what sometimes seemed a lonely personal journey was not so lonely after all. As I read the book and looked at the cards, I saw that they understood my fears and questions and yearnings. I felt I was in touch with something very old and very wise.

I wanted to learn more about these ancestral ways, and decided to write to Jamie Sams. She passed on my letter to the women who run the Heyokah Center. They contacted me some months later. It was a lovely surprise. When I said I wanted to visit them, they suggested I go on a Vision Quest, which is one of the oldest tools tribal people use to seek direction in life. I knew from my reading that Jamie and many others actually experienced visions on their quests but that lots of people were happy simply to come away with a deeper sense of their own truth and place on the 'Good Red Road' of life.

A Vision Quest. It seemed quite an adventure but, yes, I wanted to do it. I felt that in some way I was being guided. I already believed that guardian angels, and many other enlightened beings, can help us humans. Now I also believed in what Native Americans call 'Great Spirit'. And I wanted to be out there in red rock country. In recent years I had come to love red rock with a passion. When I saw photographs of it or it appeared on television, I felt a great longing in my heart. I was sure it had healing and grounding properties, as well as looking so splendid. I later learned that Native Americans tend to revere that beautiful rock too.

Our Vision Quest was to take place in the remote and picturesque Cochiti Canyon, south of Santa Fe. On the evening before we all set off together in cars and rather ancient jeeps, we took part in an equinox new moon sweat lodge, followed by a feast. At the time, I was a bit too nervous about what the sweat lodge might involve to observe closely how it was constructed. It looked like a low circular tent and appeared to be covered with heavy canvas. I learned later that the frame is composed of bent saplings, and that the sweat lodge is probably the oldest form of purification used by humans. We wore very light clothing and sat in a circle. The lodge became extremely hot as water was poured on the heated rocks that were placed in the middle of the circle. They had to be volcanic rocks in order to withstand such high temperatures.

In some ways, the experience was not unlike an exotic and demanding sauna. We sat in darkness and sang or talked, shook rattles or pounded drums. There were several rituals associated with the ceremony, and I would have noted them more carefully if I hadn't spent much of the time hoping I wouldn't have to make a bolt for the door. It was claustrophobic, but something else was going on as well. Something that was spiritually uplifting and energising and even reassuring. When I became frightened, I stuck my hand under the canvas into the cool night air, and Jo, one of the women who run the centre, noticed and gently squeezed my fingers comfortingly. It made all the difference.

Early the following morning, we set off for the canyon. My companions were all female and, like me, they were both excited and nervous about our six-day adventure. We knew that each day we would spend at least four hours sitting alone in the wilds in our Sacred Spaces. Nature was to be our teacher, though the three women from the centre would be on hand to offer support and advice. Julie, Dona and Jo have devoted their lives to sharing Native American teachings with women from around the world. (Men in search of their female side can also join in.) They believe that women, in particular, often tend to put others first and that the retreats help them to recognise and honour their own needs and find ways to nurture their true selves. They run four retreats a year in different locations, and visitors can also undertake personal retreats at Buffalo House.

The canyon was beautiful and not at all what I'd expected. Quite verdant, in fact, with an abundance of tall leafy trees and a stream near the camp. It has its own micro-climate, caused by the spectacular jutting red rock on each side. During the day, it was hot, but not the sweltering heat of the desert. The two tepees were already erected, along with a large tent to store our belongings. There was a makeshift shower heated by a solar panel, but toilet arrangements involved a spade and a long walk.

Sleeping in the tepee that first night, I looked up at Father Sky through the hole at the top and wondered how I would feel when I was out in my Sacred Space with my whistle, water, and a large supply of Ritz crackers. I knew that the quest experience had been simplified for us novices, but it seemed high time to call on the power of the Bear to help me face my fears. After all, it seemed the Bear had already helped me feel less nervous on my long-haul flight and in the sweat lodge.

Julie Rivers helped me to find my Sacred Space. It wasn't far from the camp and seemed welcoming. A stream flowed nearby and there were large rocks and big trees and a sunlit clearing in the centre. We had learned how to make our spaces sacred by performing a ritual. Stones were placed at the four cardinal points, and then we asked for protection, healing and guidance from each one. Native Americans believe that each 'direction' has special attributes and represents a different time of year. They also believe that they are all part of the Medicine Wheel, or circle of life, which helps us to respect and balance the many aspects of our nature. During the Sacred Space ritual, Great Spirit was also asked to help and guide us, and the burning of sage cleared the space of its energy. Then we made tobacco offerings of gratitude.

Native American teachings 'can come from such diverse things as cards, animals, stones or even clouds – they are all metaphors for spiritual principles or ideas,' Marie Herbert explains in her book, *Healing Quest*, which includes a section based on her experiences at the Heyokah Center. 'The medicine people I knew were not encouraging people to "become Indian" but rather to develop their highest potential.'

A strange routine commenced. Every morning, I felt very reluctant to go to my Sacred Space. When I reached it, I felt alone and jumpy and started to devour my snacks. What on earth would I do if a bear turned up? Stuffing Ritz crackers into my mouth provided a welcome distraction. What was making the leaves and twigs crackle continuously? More often than not, it was some unseen creature. Occasionally my skin prickled with fear but after a while I felt less alone and there were times when I felt extraordinarily calm. I learned how to tell the time by the position of the sun and how to recognise bear droppings. They always seemed liberally festooned with small seeds, and the old droppings were dry and scattered easily when they were kicked. This was a welcome sign because a fresh dropping meant ... well, the implications are obvious. I urinated in my Sacred Space every so often to 'mark my territory', and I had time to examine the small creatures that shared my circle and the butterflies that air-danced in and out of it. It was good to have the time to just be. (And to get a tan on the back of my legs.)

Sometimes I cried and sometimes I was happy. The mixed emotions did not seem strange. We were supposed to be developing faith and trust, among other things. And there was no choice but to try to trust. The feeling that Great Spirit was watching over me faltered from time to time, but there were intervals when my faith and trust were extraordinarily powerful. Certainly something seemed to be protecting and guiding us all. I didn't experience visions, but sitting in my Sacred Space helped to clarify what didn't really matter and what needed to be cherished. And every day, I felt sad when it was time to return to the camp.

At night, we gathered to share stories or create rituals. My companions were sturdy and gentle and a few of them spent whole days and nights far away in their Sacred Spaces. A camaraderie developed. There was much laughter but there were also tears. That was what the quest was about. It was a safe place to be open about our feelings and to acknowledge what needed to be healed.

Soon it was time to leave the high desert and I knew that I would want to return one day. Before I left, I asked Julie why she thought so many people are drawn to quests like this.

'Because when you get away from the mechanical world, you start to just be,' she replied. 'Nature doesn't have a job apart from just being what it is. It can help bring us back to our own truth.'

And what can we learn from the ancestral ways?

'That we are all one,' she said.

It's hard to convey how the Vision Quest affected me. Much of it happened at a level beyond my ordinary understanding and it would lose some of its meaning if I were to attempt to analyse it intellectually. It is simply something that I experienced and now it is part of me. It provided glimpses into the duality of our human nature – both mind and body; and gave me a definite sense of my inner spirituality. And an insight that we are all united in the Great Family of creation.

I brought some red rock home with me and I cherish it. I hold it in my hands and feel its special energy. And now I know that Jamie Sams was right when she wrote, 'the Language of Love ... can be understood only through an open heart, for it is a way of living life rather than a system to be mastered.'

# ANNA CAREY

## THE YOGA-MEISTERS

The summer we lived in the yoga-meisters' apartment was the hottest one in nearly twenty years. Back home in Dublin, as we were told in every letter from gloating friends and relations, it was like the French Riviera. And we were in the heart of Berlin, where it was like an oven. There were three of us – Jane, Lucy and I, friends since our Drumcondra school days, and all totally unable to live in such heat, something we had suspected beforehand. We were all also completely incompetent at housekeeping, although we didn't discover that until we were there.

It was our first summer away as (supposedly) independent young women. We had all just finished our second year at Trinity, where both Jane and I were studying German, and had decided that if we had to go to Germany for the summer, we were going to go somewhere cool (as in 'chic', that is). And where could possibly be cooler than Berlin, a city of legendary craziness which had been divided by a wall up until almost six years before? And so a Berlin-resident friend of

Jane's uncle arranged a sublet with a pair of yoga teachers who were away conducting a yoga camp on a Greek island, and for the entire summer we called them the yoga-meisters.

And yoga-meisters, we soon discovered, had different needs from the rest of us. Jane and Lucy went over the day before me, as they were flying via London and I was flying via Düsseldorf. That night, they rang me to arrange where to meet the next day. I asked what the flat was like.

'It's beautiful,' said Jane. 'You'll love it. But it's very uncomfortable.'

'What do you mean?' I asked.

'Well,' said Lucy. 'There's nothing squashy in it. You'll see when you get here.'

But the only thing that stuck in my mind was the fact that the flat was beautiful and that I would love it. The reality of a place where nothing was squashy didn't really hit me until the next night. That was after I had arrived and gazed in awe at what would be my home for the next two months, a series of blissfully cool, high-ceilinged, white-walled rooms with old wood floors and big windows. The main bedroom was astonishing; there was a four-poster made of a silvery, matte metal, hung with a canopy of pink gauze. In a corner of the room was a lovely old green-tiled oil stove. The sitting room was almost empty, apart from a simple couch, covered in a piece of black silk. There was a tree in a pot in one corner, hung with paper stars and moons. The kitchen was equally enchanting, with its old black-and-white tiled floor, cheerful yellow walls, and Otto Dix poster. There was a tiny, book-lined study, and a room with cute little bunk beds, which presumably belonged to the yoga-meisters' children.

Then I sat down on the couch, and yelped with pained surprise. Under its silk covering, it was simply made out of two flat boards, one being the seat and the other, the back. The two could be flattened down to make a bed. But there was absolutely no give in it at all; it was like sitting, and lying, on hard ground. Further investigation showed that the beautiful four-poster was no better; instead of a mattress, it had a thin layer of compressed foam on top of more flat boards. There wasn't a single cushion in the house.

I can safely say that that night was the most uncomfortable one I have ever had. It was terribly hot, even with the large bedroom window wide open, but I could have borne that if only I had had something soft to sleep on. I thrashed and turned and got all tangled up in the one sheet I had to cover me. I was ridiculously skinny in those days, only about seven stone, so didn't have any fat to cushion my poor bones, which seemed to dig into my flesh. I was horribly, painfully tired, and craved sleep like a drug. I remember eyeing the yoga-meisters' wardrobe and debating whether to take all their clothes out, pile them on the bed, and sleep on top of them. But I didn't. (Although I was tempted again on several occasions, until I finally got used to sleeping on the boards.)

We were all slightly nervous about living in someone else's house, but we were determined to be the perfect tenants. The yoga-meisters, we vowed, would come back to find their house exactly as they had left it. They wouldn't be able to say that we had exploited their hospitality; we would leave their cupboards untouched. We would ignore their tempting herbs and spices, and their oils and vinegars. We wouldn't even use their salt and pepper. Unhappily, we also decided not to touch anything in the fridge. For the whole two months.

Looking back, I can't explain our behaviour. Somehow – don't ask me how, all I can suggest is that maybe we were suffering from heat stroke – we assumed that if the yoga-meisters had left anything in the flat, they expected it to be there for them when they came back. Although how we thought they would be rejoicing at the sight of the two-month old vegetables, which had, by the end of our stay, given the fridge a rather distinctive odour, is beyond me now. But leave them we did. We also left their long-life milk, whose life was not as long as we hoped. After the first week, it looked like a hideous sort of cheese. And still we didn't throw it out.

We didn't stop at the food, either. Our determination to make the entire flat some sort of June 1995 time capsule extended to the washing machine. When we arrived, it was full of just-washed clothes. We had no idea what to do with them, and assumed the yoga-meisters wanted us to leave them there. So we did. We didn't need to take them out to wash our own clothes because – shameful to relate – at the age of nearly twenty, none of us really knew how to work a washing machine. We were terrified of doing the wrong thing and accidentally shrinking all our clothes or dying them blue. Although we had been hoovering and washing up and dusting our respective homes for years, somehow clothes washing was something that was always done by our long-suffering parents. So we handwashed everything, which meant that we found ourselves endlessly rewashing the same few easily washed garments for the whole summer.

After we had been in the flat for a few weeks, we noticed an appalling smell coming from somewhere in the kitchen. Ignorant of the effects on wet clothes of three weeks in a closed washing machine, we became convinced, even fearful, that there was a gas leak. We rang the gas company, which sent out an engineer, who agreed that there was a horrible smell, but it wasn't gas and we were in no danger of imminent death. And so we decided that the smell was something we would just have to live with. We only got to the bottom of it all when the yoga-meisters made several furious phone calls to Jane's uncle's friend, having discovered the rotting clothes on their return from their Greek idyll.

Really, though, they weren't perfect themselves. The male yoga-meister had agreed to leave the phone line connected, because he, like the good yogi he was, believed in universal trust. He thought that if we were left with both an open phone line and the knowledge that we weren't to use it, we would live up to the trust placed in us and refrain from making ten-hour phone calls to friends in America. Apparently, however, we couldn't be trusted with a stereo. Or a telly. Or a video. Or indeed anything with a plug. For the yoga-meisters had hidden all of these things.

Who knows what they thought we would do if exposed to such temptations? Perhaps they thought that such a cornucopia of electronic items would go to our poor Irish peasant heads, and that we would be over-stimulated by it all and have nervous breakdowns. Perhaps they thought that given the opportunity, we would run amok, blaring loud music on the stereo and keeping the television on twenty-four hours a day. Maybe they thought they were saving us from ourselves. Whatever their motivation, we discovered their nefarious scheme on our first night when we looked around in vain for a cassette player. The many photos strewn around the flat showed that the yoga-meisters did indeed own one, as well as all the other aforementioned electronic goods, but they were nowhere to be seen.

So we did what anyone else would do. We rooted them out. The stereo was found first, hidden under a coat, but we were outraged when we discovered that the yoga-meisters, obviously expecting such a discovery, had taken the plug off it. We couldn't find the plug or anything resembling a screwdriver to put one on with. At this stage, fuelled by our new resentment against our churlish landlords, we were desperate for music and determined to find something on which to play our tapes. Finally, while standing on top of the desk, I discovered a small dictaphone-type tape recorder lurking forgotten on the very top of a bookshelf, and I bore it in triumph to the others. We put on a Beastie Boys tape to celebrate.

A few minutes later, there was a knock on the door of our flat. It was the woman who lived in the flat across the landing, holding what remains to this day the most hideous baby I have ever seen. The child was round and red and evil-looking, with hair that stuck up in tufts like a devil's horns.

*'Die Kleine schlaft,'* said the woman apologetically. Clearly the Little One was no longer sleeping; it was glaring at us

with a perfectly foul expression on its horrible red face. How it could have been woken up by a dictaphone is beyond me, as we, who were in the same room, could barely hear it ourselves. But apparently it had, and was angry. So we apologised and turned the music down to an inaudible murmur, feeling sorry for the woman, who seemed as vaguely appalled by her horrid child as we were.

Soon after that, we found the television (in a laundry basket – there were no depths to which we would not sink). Despite not watching lots of telly at home, we were determined to watch it now, in a spirit of defiance, whether there was anything good on or not. MTV played 'Alright' by Supergrass a lot that summer, and the jaunty song seemed to suit our mood. We were young and in Berlin, away from our parents and college work and (in my case) a particularly tormenting boy. The world was our oyster. Or rather, it would have been if we had had any money. Jane's uncle's friend had promised jobs in the Irish pub managed by a man she knew, but it turned out that there were only two jobs going, and they had been offered to, and accepted by, Jane and Lucy on their first night in Berlin. This left me unemployed in a city suffering from an employment crisis thanks to the relatively recent collapse of the East German economy, which had sent thousands of economic Ossi migrants looking for work in the supposedly wealthy capital. Needless to say, I didn't get a job for the entire summer.

The others weren't earning much money from the jobs in any case, and so we were each living on about five Deutschmark a day (around two pounds fifty, I recall). We constantly ate a particularly horrible meal made from a vile packaged bolognese sauce with carrots and pasta, or, for some reason, rice. Lucy had suggested the carrots, saying that someone she knew in college always made bolognese sauce with carrots and that they would provide essential vitamins. We must have got addicted to it after a while, because I seem to remember us eating it far more than was really necessary.

I bet we could have made a much nicer meal for the same price, but no, every day, we'd chow down on the hideous carrot/pasta or carrot/rice combo. Unsurprisingly, we literally dreamed of good food; I remember the three of us standing next to a food stall and just breathing in the delicious smell, the nearest thing to actually eating the food itself.

In my memory, it is always early evening in Berlin, and the tall, lovely houses are suffused in that perfect golden light. On our first evening there, we walked around the streets near the apartment, where we were genuinely shocked by the sheer number of astonishingly sleazy sex shops. Considering the apartment was on a beautiful shady street next to a primary school, we hadn't expected to turn the corner to be greeted by the Erotik Kaufhaus. Of course, at that stage we hadn't seen the bizarrely attired prostitutes who plied their trade on Juni Strasse, near the Siegesaule, the famous angel statue. Later we regularly walked past their spot on our way home from a night out, us in our battered second-hand cords and little 1970s T-shirts, they in their thigh-high, scarlet PVC boots and matching corsets. And, incredibly, we were harassed by kerb-crawlers. Perhaps they were jaded by too many hours in the erotic supermarket and found the sight of scrawny little Irish indie girls with no make-up suddenly appealing.

Still, the sleaziness never stopped us from exploring, and we spent hours just wandering around. We met up with Carol, a friend from home, who had decided to join us and who got a room in a flat just round the corner from ours, and together we roamed the city. We especially loved East Berlin, which had not been so meticulously restored after the war as the West. In Mitte, you could see wartime bullet holes in nearly every building; in West Berlin, they had all been painstakingly filled in and were no longer noticeable. Once while walking around Mitte, I stuck my finger into a hole and felt the bullet, still there after fifty years. The most amazing buildings, all in a beautiful state of crumbling decay, were in

Prenzlauer Berg, a district beloved by artists and hipsters. It was utterly magical.

We couldn't afford to go clubbing much, but sometimes we would go to Tacheles, a bar-cum-art-space in Mitte. Tacheles was situated in what had been a department store before it was bombed during the war; at some stage, people had taken over what was left of the bombed-out building and made a wonderful party space in the ruins, selling cheap, but good, alcohol and hot food. There was a large yard next to the main building, which had become a sculpture park, filled with a variety of amazing creations. Best of them all was a swing, suspended from long metal bars. Attached to the bars, at shoulder level, were two huge, beautiful angel wings. When you went on the swing, you looked as if you were flying.

After just two hazy months, it was all over. The yoga-meisters were coming home to their, by now, odoriferous flat, and I couldn't afford to pay for another month's rent elsewhere. So I left the other two behind in Berlin and went back to Dublin and job-seeking and the stupid boy.

I hated leaving. I loved Berlin. I loved its oddness, its beauty, its golden light, its friendly people, its cheapness which made it possible for even poor students like us to survive in the heart of the city. I even felt kindly towards the yoga-meisters. After all, despite the lack of cushions and their frankly childish behaviour with the electrical goods, our accommodation could have been a lot worse. Carol's German flatmate, for example, had a calendar on his wall, illustrated with photos of himself doing naff things, like jogging and mountain-climbing. At least the yoga-meisters weren't that bad. Or so we thought.

Of course, on the last night we found all their self-taken, naked yoga photos, images so awful that I'm surprised we weren't struck blind on the spot. Ah, Berlin.

# CAROLINE MORAHAN

## VIVA LAS VEGAS

It's something every girl should do – at least once. We compared calendars, bribed bosses for extra time and eventually settled on September. A leg wax and two facials later, I was all set for my first ever girlie holiday.

I was never part of the J1 generation. The concept of eleven students sharing a two-bed apartment in Ocean City didn't seem like an ideal way to spend my summers out of Dublin City University. There was also the fact that, despite surviving on high spirits and minimum wage, everyone seemed to return to college a stone and a half heavier. Not a good option for me who had remained on the wrong side of ten stone since age twelve. But I wasn't going to blanket ban a trip to the land of opportunity just because of the threat of super-sizing for fifty cents. I was a gym-goer now, ready to head straight to the birthplace of the all-you-can-eat buffet, without fear.

The girls had formulated a plan: a no-boyfriends, no-holds-barred, three-week trip to remember. 'Girls on Tour

2001', we christened it. Eight bottles of nail polish each was a standard travel requirement, I was told, and although space in the rental would be tight, twelve pairs of shoes were not excessive. This was going to be momentous!

Finally the red crosses on my calendar outnumbered the blanks. It was time to go.

As is customary in the Morahan clan, I left everything to the last minute and was forced to pull an all-nighter. After a few 3 a.m. calls to suss out who was packing the hair straighteners, I was ready.

Arriving at Dublin airport at some ungodly hour, I observed I wasn't the only one with more bags under my eyes than on my trolley. But it would take more than sleep deprivation to dampen our spirits. Handing over our boarding passes, we were united in a spontaneous squeal of excitement.

The four of us: Caoilfhionn, Dara, Suzy and I. With two-litre bottles of water and eight-hour cream in our bags, we were all set for the impending half-day in the sky. Destination – sun-drenched San Diego. But our first surprise was waiting for us a lot closer to home.

Suzy, a frequent flyer who's always over and back to her family home in the Bahamas, had the inspired idea of checking our baggage for the entire journey. No hauling the Samsonites round a tour of Heathrow. We checked in at Dublin for our connecting flight and spent our time in London elbow deep in bronzer at the Lancôme counter, instead of queuing for boarding passes.

At the gate, the blonde with the pursed lips wasn't expecting us. 'I'm afraid there's a problem.' She delivered the line with all the emotion of the speaking clock. Apparently, the seats we had reserved in Dublin had not been communicated to the desk. The flight was full.

Listening to the gloom in her voice, I was certain we'd be grounded for hours or find ourselves doing the next leg of the trip in cargo. When all seemed lost, she uttered the most exquisite collection of words, though her monotone droning meant it took a couple of seconds for the meaning to catch up. But as I looked at the grins spreading across my friends' faces, I knew I'd heard right: 'We'll have to upgrade your tickets to business class. Please board immediately.'

I'd seen the ads on telly: 'The first airline to introduce flat beds in business class.' They meant nothing to me. The furthest I'd flown was Tenerife. The 4 a.m. flight time meant I didn't need a bed to facilitate sleep – the clip-up table and a rolled-up cardi worked a treat. But this was a far cry from budget travel. While the sardines behind the navy curtain were handed the in-flight mag, our attractive flight attendant, male and not apparently homosexual, presented us with beauty kits. Hand cream, lip balm, moisturiser, face spray, eye covers, ear plugs, nail kit. I'm sure I'm forgetting something.

While we busied ourselves with manicures, watching Nicole high kick her way through *Moulin Rouge* on our personal television sets, Karl brought our drinks menu. His sexual persuasion was no longer up for debate. The glances he shot in Caoilfhionn's direction during the safety demonstration put any doubts to rest.

Kir Royales before take-off. Goat's cheese parcels to start. Seafood risotto loaded with shellfish as we cruised at 62,000 feet. And Belgian chocolate ice cream just as we settled in to *Heartbreakers* with Jennifer Love Hewitt and Sigourney Weaver. This I could get used to.

Refreshed after perfect sleep, with glowing skin, we glided into San Diego. For me, the sunshine city was just somewhere to get over our jet lag before the real holiday began. I can do surf and sand in Donegal, but 24-hour gambling in a hotel fitted with a roller coaster? There's only one place on earth for that. The girls made the mistake of introducing me to a few websites and now all I could do was fantasise about winning big in Vegas.

Our journey over had given us a taste of how the other half lives, but in San Diego we were about to witness it first hand. Suzy's sister worked as a travel agent in the city and managed to swing us a great deal at a beach-front hotel in La Jolla. Dubbed the Beverly Hills of San Diego, it was Lamborghinis left, right and centre. Any plans of going on the cheap were soon out the window. Drinks, even in small bars, doubled the going rate at Lillie's.

'No problem,' said Caoilfhionn, who had just decided to do a post-grad and was feeling the pinch a little more than the rest of us. 'We'll just have to get blokes to buy us drinks!'

We did one better and went straight for the bar. It didn't take long for me to shed my feminist ideals and switch my eyelids to flutter. Was it the power of four? Was it the Irish accents? Whatever the magic ingredient, we became best friends with whoever was manning the taps.

After a couple of lazy days enjoying the sunshine, it was time to once again make a three-month supply of clothes fit into one small suitcase. A couple of nail breakages later, we waved goodbye to the sea.

Flying over charred desert, you're sure nothing could exist out here. Valleys meander within valleys where water once flowed. It's as if the entire landscape has been cremated and left to blow away. Then suddenly, sprawling in the distance, there's life – but not as we know it.

I'm distracted with excitement. Looking out the window, I imagine this is how Neil and the boys must have felt before that first lunar landing. The strangeness of the environment they'd soon inhabit, the awesome sights waiting for them. Granted, a forty-foot neon cowboy doesn't quite evoke the same emotion as witnessing the earth from space, but I was riveted nonetheless.

As the nose of the plane dips slowly downwards, we are treated to our first close-up glimpse of a familiar scene. How many times have I seen Nicholas Cage tearing through these streets or Elvis waving to the crowds outside the MGM? It's all laid out before you as you land. Like an impressive Lego city, crafted by some *Come Dancing* contender on speed.

Everything is glittering, shimmering, larger than life. It's only twelve thirty in the afternoon. Imagine this place at night! We grab our bags as the doors open. Hot air slaps us, clinging to our necks like a molten scarf. I take a deep breath, relishing the extreme heat. Caoils has already peeled off her white cotton cardigan and is looping it round the tortoise-shell handle of her bag.

Inside the airport is its own tourist attraction. Moving billboards on every available flat surface entice you to the Bellagio for a one-off performance from Siegfried and Roy or to the MGM Grand for Janet Jackson in Concert. A giant screen shouts not to miss 'the Big Fight, Saturday night'. But I'm most intrigued by multicoloured scenes of gondoliers and opera singers moving through the canals of Venice.

'I've heard about this,' squeals Dara. 'The Venetian Hotel has a life-size canal running through it – identical to the real thing!'

Caoils adds that she heard the eccentric proprietor of the hotel, having spent tens of millions on its construction, had the entire thing pulled down. 'He said the water wasn't the same shade as that in Venice.'

We pause, looking at each other in disbelief before bursting into fits of laughter.

Suzy returns from her expedition to find water, carrying two half-litre bottles and sporting a huge smile. 'There was a queue, so I put a few dollars into a slot machine. Whirlwind or something. Next minute, all I know is quarters start shooting out and I've won twenty bucks!'

I love this town.

A quick cab ride takes us to our home for the next five days. We have seen the Sphinx from the plane – a monstrous carving too tall to fit into a wide-screen snapshot. The towering pyramid he guards would alone take a day to discover.

My door swings open as I fidget for change. 'Welcome to the Luxor, ma'am.' The super-friendly door staff see to it that our luggage is ferried swiftly to our rooms. With so much teeth on show, I half expect to find our bags unpacked and clothes neatly put away. But the courtesy doesn't extend beyond the gums.

Strolling into the foyer of the hotel, I think I've landed on a film set. Statues of pharaohs stand thirty feet high, gold-embossed escalators rise up from perfect marble floors, water fountains dance in every corner. But the most arresting sensation is undoubtedly the noise.

I close my eyes to take it in. All around me, I hear gasps, the basic unconscious response the crap or roulette table always elicits. It's as though the body thinks a sharp intake of air will slow the ball onto black twenty-two or suck that second dice back in time so it won't land on five.

Then come the sounds I haven't heard since Funderland. Casino music. Electronic, loud, constant but inviting. The xylophone of the slot machines, bing, bing, bing as a lightening bolt foils the trio of dollar signs you were waiting for.

Most desirable is the sound of winning. Screams of pleasure, chants of 'yes, yes!' Despite their surroundings, some lucky folk choose to thank their Maker for their good fortune. An odd practice, given I can't think of a more godless place. The celebrations are different; the fruits the same. A three-second pause, followed by the inevitable crash of coins, as another machine parts with its precious load.

'Never work a slot that's just paid out,' Suzy advises as my eyes light up, drinking in the scene as an overweight couple from Florida jump up and down by their singing machine.

In an instant, all my prejudices about mind-warped Americans are confirmed. Everyone around looks like typical fodder for a Jerry Springer special. We've got the you're-too-fat-to-dress-like-that mob, pioneered by a band of disturbingly huge black women in mini-dresses and stone-washed hot pants. They're whooping and high-fiving at the crap table, performing all sorts of pre-toss rituals on the dice. There's the I-was-a-geek-in-school-but-look-at-me-now brigade – silicone enhanced Barbies who've forgotten what their natural hair colour is and have probably picked up a new name along the way.

My favourite by far are the sixty-plus grannies who appear to have Cindy Lauper as a stylist. Often tangerine from a life spent split between sun and scotch, they're always colourful. Leopard skin seems to have been elected chief wardrobe staple. But you'll find plenty of sequins, even at ten in the morning. Bony legs advertised in purple lycra with matching bum bags, they nurse giant paper cups full of quarters. Quickly you realise these are the ones to tailgate. They'll plug their life savings into a machine until it pays out. If you see one moving off without the shrill bells ringing and silver lining the tray, then get parking. I can't fathom how they can operate the one-armed bandits with so much gold around their wrists, but manage they do.

I'm already picking up the lingo. One-armed bandits are the slot machines that work by popping in your change before pulling down the handle at the side. Most dangerous of the slots, the simple action itself becomes hypnotic. Suddenly the forty dollars you bagged at poker has morphed into a paperclip, lighter and crumpled receipt in your pocket. The magic of Vegas.

After a day, I'm still not acclimatised. It's nearly forty degrees outside and utterly freezing indoors. I give it three days before I get a cold sore. I'm told the excessive air conditioning in the casinos is to keep gamblers awake.

Bubbly blonde twenty-somethings dressed in metallic tank tops and micro-minis tour the casinos with their drinks trays. They're all waiting to make it big as a dancer or model but, until then, are happy to wear too much make-up and a can of hairspray apiece. Frozen margaritas, JD and coke. Whatever you want, they've got it. Of course, you must be twenty-one to play here but you'll find the question's asked only when the money starts coming your way.

The system is genius. You're plied with so much free alcohol you forget how much you started with on spin-the-wheel, while the cold air ensures you stay upright just long enough to take another shot. Another handy design feature is the absence of clocks. You won't find a watch on any of the Tammys with the trays.

Natural light is another no-no, so even if you are sober, your body has absolutely no idea what time of day or night it is. Four hours in front of Fireball can pass faster than an episode of Corrie. The twenty-four-hour all-you-can-eats are yet another ingenious time-defying invention. Burgers and nachos at 9 a.m? 'No problem, ma'am!'

As soon as you step out of the technicolored trance that is the casino, you're swiftly reminded that, yes, you are still on planet earth. In fact, you're in the middle of the desert, and water would be a great idea right about now.

Each hotel has a fabulous pool area, with all the excessive design features reminiscent of what's happening inside. The high rollers have their own cabanas fully stocked with champagne and nibbles, cold towels and TVs. A sort of hi-tech sprinkler dispenses a subtle, cool mist whenever they feel a sweat coming on. The rest of us are frying on a grill; only a rare breeze provides respite from the searing heat. After my seventh trip to the pool in under an hour, I resign myself to finding a closer spot tomorrow. If I'm planning to travel from my sun lounger to the pool every eight and a half minutes, surely I should be working on cutting down the transfer time.

Our hotel room is gigantic! Egyptian columns are on either side of the telly, one of those super huge screens you see only on the likes of MTV Cribs. Despite acres of space, within half an hour the place is strewn with glittery tops, white trousers and pencil skirts.

A vote decides Suzy looks better in the turquoise chiffon top and white mini than in the gold bustier with the trousers.

But what skirt will I wear if she's borrowing my mini? Caoilfhionn to the rescue with a long, beaded, pink skirt and baby-pink silk vest. In spite of all the phone calls reminding her to pack them, Dara's managed to forget the straightening irons. We call for the real thing. She contorts her slim frame in such a way that a yogi would be impressed. Just the right angle to get her forehead to the tip of the ironing board, avoiding the dreaded crease line in her hair.

Suzy doesn't need ironing. Her poker straight Timotei blonde locks fall perfectly, *sans* serum. As for Caoils and me – we're going for curls. Hers are God-given; I'm struggling with Velcro rollers that appear to have lost their sticking power.

Two hours and a half-dozen Captain Morgans later, we're ready to leave. Tonight, I was lucky and found an outfit early on but the girls have gone through more costume changes than Gisele Bundchen on a busy day in Paris. As the pile of halter necks, faded jeans and little black numbers grew on the bed, I set about more advanced cosmetic preparation. In a giant beauty supply warehouse in San Diego I had found myriad sparkly wonders to stick to my toe-nails, body, finger-nails, wherever. At those prices, I was forced to buy ten of everything. These weren't your common-or-garden bits of dull imitation diamond à la Claire's Accessories. These babies would fit in quite happily on a P. Diddy ensemble, or Puff Daddy, as he was then known.

Having jewel encrusted my two big toes and their nearest partner, I set about decorating elsewhere. To my delight, I rediscovered a gold dollar sign I'd added to the booty back in San Diego. With Nelly's contagious brand of singalong hip-hop blaring from MTV, I was suddenly inspired.

The triple X marking on either side of the skull didn't dissuade me. Nor the underlining of the word 'TOXIC' on the front of the box. At a quarter past twelve that night in Vegas, squeezing noxious, highly flammable nail adhesive inside my mouth seemed a perfectly excellent idea. With the precision of a respected orthodontist, I swabbed the chosen incisor with a cotton bud before dabbing on nail polish remover. Why stop at one lethal solvent? I thought. Once the area was clean and free of foreign bodies, I fixed my golden dollar sign onto a toothpick, this time with Blu-Tack as the bond.

Then came the tricky part.

Deploying bathroom magnifying mirror, I coaxed a single droplet of glue onto the back of the dollar. Too much, and I'd be left with dollar, Blu-Tack and cocktail stick jutting from my mouth. Two little, and my good-luck charm would be lost to a bowl of chicken wings before the night was out.

My steady hand didn't fail, and a single perfect dome of glue spread to all edges of the dollar sign. Until now, my face had been frozen in its best Elvis impression to ensure my lip didn't touch and moisten the targeted tooth. Now holding the pose, I gently fitted the tiny jewel onto my favourite fang. Disposing of toothpick and Blu-Tack, I used my finger, covered in tissue, to ensure my artwork would stick.

Stick it did, so well that I was left with a fan of tissue clinging to my tooth like a ballerina hanging from a top-floor balcony. Ten minutes of tooth brushing was all it took to loosen the visitor's grip. Underneath sparkled my new lucky charm.

The girls applaud my efforts: 'A toast to the girl with the golden gum!' Whoops, we'd run out of rum.

On to the majestic Bellagio, where my lucky charm finally earns the title. After blowing a few twenty-dollar bills in a variety of locations along the strip, I am overdue a win. But the routine of entering a hotel and hotfooting it to the casino is broken on this occasion. My win is to come after another treat.

Stepping into the foyer, I am rooted to the spot by the sight of what has to be the largest vase of flowers in the Western world. A football team would just about circle it. Wait – there are dozens of them. Gigantic stems of every variety clamour for space. Orchids, lilies, roses, freesia – more than I can name. It's too much to take in but once my eyes accept the scene, my nose takes over. Lavender fields in the south of France, sun-ripened peaches, old roses from my nan's front garden, the white lilies my boyfriend first gave me.

The fusion of fragrances is intoxicating. But it isn't restricted to the foyer. It spills down the lengthy corridors of the hotel and through the vents and air-conditioning system, serving as a delicious reminder of the beauty downstairs. Following my nose, I discover that the spectacular entrance hall was merely a *petite entrée* preparing us for the feast that awaits inside.

Just when you think you've seen it all, Las Vegas goes one bigger. Not content with an entrance hall reminiscent of the Chelsea Flower Show, the Bellagio has devoted an entire ballroom to every conceivable bloom. But these flowers aren't static displays lying in rows or pretty flowerpots. They're living 3-D art, grown in spectacular designs. Gazebos are constructed entirely from flowers of every shade of yellow. A wishing well and water bucket sing in purples, pinks and blues. A canopy of dazzling colour lures the eye towards the ceiling.

The owner of the Bellagio spends a reported million dollars a month on flowers for the hotel. We learn this from Donna and Steve from Kentucky. Steve's digital Canon is getting such a workout I imagine there mustn't be either flora or fauna in the fried chicken capital of the world.

The next day, we witness once again the unfathomable excesses of Las Vegas. Yesterday's spectacular scene, that olfactory delight is utterly demolished. Uprooted and torn down. Summer wishing wells and pretty tulip swings have lost their appeal. The manager wished to move on to the next mind-blowing floral extravaganza. Yellows have made way for orange and greens have become gold. Though still thirty-plus degrees outside, the ballroom of the Bellagio insists that autumn has now arrived in Nevada. September 10th was the last day of summer this year.

Three laps of the ballroom work up quite a thirst. Tammy to the rescue with vodka and Sprite. This time Tammy's name is Lou-Anne. She has yet to commit fully to the course of blonde highlights. Still, the skirt doesn't deviate from the eight-inch customary ra-ra.

Three of us drop anchor at the nearest roulette wheel. Meanwhile, Suzy is ready to rumble with the big boys.

We catch up with her at a poker table, one of the many that line the entrance to the casino. She is a lone female, the advantage of which becomes immediately apparent. Her fellow players are easily distracted. Any piece of eye candy teetering by sees the lads lose a hand. As they admire the view, the soulless dealer plays their round without blinking. Suzy is up ninety dollars.

A troop of hens from New York sees two gents go bust – literally. Nancy from New York, as advertised across her chest, and her team of twelve merry man-eaters, are enjoying the attention that tight, matching T-shirts can bring.

And the boys are a willing audience. One of Nancy's many attachés helps fluff out the spectacular cerise-pink veil she's wearing. Her over-sized tiara is in perfect keeping with the surroundings. All the girls have fabulous legs and are wearing skirts that could pass for belts.

Ogling the passing cloud of oestrogen, Jed, the bank clerk from Wisconsin, and Christian, the marketing exec from Paris (Suzy does her research), soon find themselves out of the game.

Bored with poker, I head off in search of a windfall. Licking my dental dollar for luck, I settle upon a three-roller slot with boots, cherry buns and dollar signs flying past. The object of the game is simple: match three and you're a happy camper. A four-roll slot is more than I can cope with. Just when you think you're on to a winner, window number four settles off centre – and it's some symbol you've never seen till now, a ring or an anchor.

My rules are simple: I never go above a quarter machine; I

stay until I either win something, or run out. But it's never above a quarter. Plugging dollar after dollar down the bottomless pit would be just too depressing. Imagine how fast you could lose a week's rent or, God forbid, your holiday money. I am half tempted, though, at the Mandalay Bay when I sit two slots down from a sixty-year-old with hair darker than mine. Five minutes after my arrival her machine goes mental. The seemingly endless jangling into the tray signals a win of nearly five grand!

Back to the Bellagio. Despite witnessing the dream, I still can't stomach anything more than a quarter a pop. Every five or so shots is rewarded with a two-coin drop. I have no idea what the signals in red lights mean. All I know is, the shrill ringing noise means cash is on the way.

Dara doesn't even wait for the coins to drop – she's straight back pulling on the handle. Repetitive strain injury is definitely on the way. But she looks happy.

My giant paper cup has been refilled twice. Sadly, both times at the cashiers. You hand over your notes (mostly twenties in my case) and they transform them into change. How they can handle such vast wads of cash and cope with their tiny wage packet is beyond me. They don't seem bothered; although, come to think of it, they are the least friendly bunch in the place.

I'm back at another machine: the Lucky Diamond. I have no idea how long I've been here but I've got a good feeling about this one. Suzy reckons the slots nearest the doors pay out more often. The sight of people winning is an obvious attraction to those walking past. So here I am. Parked metres from the foyer, feeling lucky.

Twenty-two dollars, seventy-five cents degenerates to nineteen dollars fifty. Then, without blinking, another ten bucks goes down the Swanee, followed by a swift loss of eight dollars in a row. (I gamble four lots of doubles, hoping to recoup my losses, as at this point I am absolutely sure a win is on the way.)

My plan is foiled – once again I can see the bottom of my paper cup with just six lonely quarters staring back at me.

I take things a little slower now, savouring the action and concentrating my mind on the inverted triangle-shaped diamond I'm hoping will turn up with two of his friends.

Fifty cents, twenty-five, twenty-five. Oh go on then, one last double! I close my eyes, certain that St Anthony, whom I have just consulted, won't fail me now.

Opening an eye, I notice one diamond. Slowly I move to roll number two and, yes, it's another poxy cherry. St Anthony, it would appear, was busy and I'm left with a diamond, a cherry and a two-hundred-dollar sign. Fantastic.

Caoilfhionn pops her head around and offers a slurp of her strawberry daiquiri. 'All out, huh?' She sympathises with a knowing nod. 'This is all I can offer you.' She squeezes round to my side of the slot and pours the remains of her paper cup into my hands. Three quarters slide out and land confidently in my palm. 'Use them wisely,' she jokes.

I take another slurp of her day-glo concoction and fix a stare at my machine, the machine that's already swallowed nearly twenty-three dollars of mine.

Double or a single? I ask myself. Deciding to try and make my pocket money last thirty seconds instead of ten, I choose for the single option. In goes my first quarter. Never to be seen again, says the voice in my head.

Something's different. The lights haven't faded out waiting for the next feed. I look up at the rolls. Holy shit! Is that, is this ...?

Caoilfhionn swings round and in one deafening shriek confirms: 'Oh my God, you've won! You've won!'

My mouth's gone dry, but I'm still able to get the words out. 'How much?' The coins keep coming, flooding the little steel tray as we fill our cups.

Frantically searching the machine, we see that in the top right corner numbers are flying up in red. 'Oh my God,' Caoilfhionn laughs. 'I think you're getting two hundred and fifty!'

'Good for you missy,' wave an eighty-year-old and his wife, both wearing Stetsons.

Recognising the screams, Dara and Suzy scramble to the scene. Suzy gets the camera going and we're all smiles and full paper cups.

Silence descends on my beloved machine: my silver waterfall runs dry. 'But that only says one eight four!' exclaims Caoilfhionn. 'You're due two fifty.'

A little man in a navy uniform appears, asks for ID, examines our passports and then disappears. One minute later, he's back carrying a white canvas bag and a key. We're asked to step away from the machine while he fiddles with the back of it. Finishing the operation, he returns to the front of the slot with an empty bag, enters a code on the machine and asks me would I like to press the green button.

'Here comes the money!'

It was 5 a.m. on 11 September when we finally hailed a cab to take us back from the Hard Rock, still high from the win and with a belly full of onion rings and vodka. Had we stayed up any later, we'd have seen everything, live, as it happened.

The manager's timing to end summer at the Bellagio proved to be frighteningly accurate.

Barely in bed, we awoke groggily a couple of hours later, blinking to come to terms with the unfolding events.

I can't say what woke me – a scream, someone shaking me. Bleary-eyed, I leaned over to see what the others were looking at. None of it made sense.

Together we watched as the first plane smashed through the side of Tower One.

Convinced we were watching a local channel, I asked was this a freak accident at New York New York, a hotel just metres from our room at the Luxor.

Nothing could have prepared me for the answer. This was no accident. And then came the unthinkable: another plane.

Dara started crying. No noise, just tears.

The rest of us sat frozen, our eyes searching each other for guidance on how to react. Then panic took over.

Still in my pyjamas, I scrambled to buy a phone card to check if all my cousins were safe in New York. It's odd how irrational the mind becomes when fear invades. I needed to have a family roll call. I knew none of them worked at the World Trade Center. But what if they happened to be in the area? What if Steven had moved offices, or Kelly was meeting someone for breakfast?

I fled downstairs to find an unoccupied phone in the lobby. My sister Olivia, distracted, told me none of the family was anywhere near. I was to learn later how many friends my cousins had lost.

Long after Olivia had hung up, I stood clutching the phone.

Three single tears found their path down my face as I turned away from the booth to face the casino.

To my utter disbelief, the scene was unchanged. It was business as usual in Las Vegas. Slot machines kept on chiming, while the catastrophe played out on the big screen.

Hollow from shock, I surveyed the room.

Waitresses in blue and gold ra-ra skirts still ferried to and from the bar servicing thirsty spenders. Hundreds of lone gamblers stood grasping their paper cups in one hand and feeding the machines with the other. Their eyes fixed straight ahead.

My gaze settled on a dangerously overweight woman who was busy concentrating on a pay-off.

She wore a grey Mickey Mouse T-shirt and denim shorts and was tucking into a hot-dog at the Snowball slot. While she munched through the greasy onions, asking her husband for more change and ordering a vodka and ginger from the passing waitress, the fire-fighters began bringing out bodies.

My thoughts turned to Nancy, all smiles last night in her pretty pink veil.

I prayed she hadn't lost a husband.

# ANNE-MARIE O'CONNOR

## PILLS AND SPILLS

I hate flying. Ask anyone who's ever had the misfortune of sitting next to me on a plane; I'm an absolute nightmare. It's not like I've never been on a plane and have a fear of the complete unknown; I've flown a thousand times; I know all the statistics – I know there's more chance of winning the Lotto or being run over by a bus. But quite frankly, if I get squashed by a bus, then chances are it was my own fault. I was obviously dawdling across the road and probably deserved it anyway.

Flying is different. Call me a control freak, but I can't fly a plane. I don't know what gets it off the ground; I don't know what keeps it in the air (although I have a sneaking suspicion it has something to do with me scrunching my eyes shut and grasping the armrests with my sweaty palms, while counting to ten repeatedly). I don't know what you have to do to land it, and as a result, I am constantly suspicious that if *I* don't know, then nobody knows, really. They're just pretending, all these airlines and flight attendants and pilots. I know their game. I'm on to them.

So it was after a number of long-haul flights and no light at the end of my flight-fear tunnel that I decided to seek professional help. Well, semi-professional. Always one to try and do things on the cheap, cut corners and generally make things more difficult for myself in the long run, I enlisted the help of a friend of mine, Andrew, who is a hypnotherapist. Despite the fact that he warned me repeatedly that because we were friends it might be more effective if I went to someone I didn't know, I soldiered on regardless.

I went to his practice, laid myself down and was almost childish in my scepticism of all things 'alternative'. Go on then, I thought, quite pleased with myself, do your best, mister, you won't hypnotise me! That was the last undirected thought I had until Andrew was telling me that I could now open my eyes and that I had been there for nearly an hour. I sat up, mesmerised, as he told me that he had directed me through a typical flight, covering all the things that made me anxious: taking off, levelling off, landing, the whole shebang. He had then suggested while I was still under hypnosis that I would now be calm in these situations. I made a mental note to ask mutual friends if he was actually a witch.

The following day, I skipped into Terminal One of Manchester airport with the zeal of the converted. Helen, my friend who was accompanying me on an eight-week jaunt around Thailand, was waiting for me. We had some romantic notion that we wanted to be somewhere fantastic for the millennium, and so we had scrimped and saved for the previous millennium to finance this trip.

Helen was understandably sceptical about my new-found confidence. We had gone on holiday a few years before and as the wheels came down and the plane began its final approach, I had shrieked 'What was that?' To which she had nonchalantly replied, 'The wing falling off.' My irony detector was switched off that day. By the time the plane landed, I was almost on the floor with a straitjacket on and a flight attendant's knee in my back. So as I winged my way through check-in, then customs, then through Duty Free and the Sock Shop, Helen eyed me suspiciously. I hadn't mentioned flying once.

We got on the plane and I chatted away breezily. I took out a book, and rather than pawing it, making it dog-eared and smudging the writing with palm sweat, I began to read it.

The flight attendants showed us what to do in case of emergency and I glanced up once or twice. Usually I would watch their every move intently and envisage myself like Kate Winslet at the end of *Titanic*, bobbing up and down in the sea with my life jacket on, half-heartedly blowing a whistle and clutching my toggle that I had so diligently pulled down on as instructed.

The plane taxied down the runway and I didn't feel even slightly anxious; the nose of the aircraft lifted and there weren't even mild palpitations.

By now Helen's eyebrow was so arched that she looked like Roger Moore. 'Are you all right?' she asked in disbelief.

'Fine!' I blithely replied.

Helen turned to her magazine, mumbling something about frontal lobotomies as I smiled, as happy as a dog that had just poked its head out of the window of a moving car.

The fasten-seat-belt sign was switched off and the flight attendants began to busy themselves, sweeping up and down the cabin. Normally I would be consumed with envy as I watched them, silently laughing in my petrified face as they ignored all the noises and bumps. They were like the young, generally mulleted, men who worked the Waltzers at the fair. There you were puking your guts up and clinging on for dear life, and there they were, moon-walking around the place, like it was the most normal thing in the world. But this time I just smiled politely as I was handed my in-flight meal. This was usually my favourite bit anyway, because it gave me something else to think about. But now it was as if someone had given Helen and me a free meal at the very posh Morrison Hotel, and I tucked into my All-Day Rubber Breakfast as if all my birthdays had come at once.

I finished my meal, had a coffee, watched a film and even nodded off for a bit. But then it happened. Four hours into an eleven-hour flight, and thirty-five thousand feet over Turkmenistan or somewhere else equally preposterously named, we hit turbulence. To say I lost the head is an understatement. The only thing that stopped me running up and down, flapping my arms like a chicken and trying to open the door shouting, 'Get me out of here', was my low embarrassment threshold. So I reserved my fit of lunacy for Helen, who, having been rudely awakened from her slumber, by her right arm being nearly yanked off at the shoulder, was saying to me in low, stern tones, 'Breathe in, count to ten, breathe out.'

I followed these instructions for a good ten minutes. She later informed me, once we were on terra firma, that she didn't know what breathing in and out did, it just sounded right and it had allowed her a little time to think of something more practical to do.

In the end, she grabbed a flight attendant and explained that I was a hazard to myself and everyone else on the plane. The nice woman came over to explain that there was nothing they could do; that they were not allowed to administer medication of any type to passengers, whatever the circumstances. But after seeing the rabid-dog lunacy in my eyes, she hurried off and brought back two tablets from her own stash of horse tranquillisers, and within twenty minutes I was in a coma. I was still drowsy as we came into land, but by the time we were in the open air, I felt fine.

As a result of this glowing feeling of well-being, I vowed that the flight home was going to be a different experience altogether. I was going to go to a chemist and buy the strongest sleeping tablets I could find. I put my bad reaction down to the fact that I was beyond help, and even though hypnotherapy could assist people in overcoming the most deep-rooted psychological problems, it had yet to do battle with my irrational brain, and, as such, was not to blame.

We dragged our backpacks out onto the street in front of the airport and waited for a bus to take us to the city. Bangkok assaults the senses; as soon as you step off the plane, the noise, the smells and the heat hit you. It's like walking through a wall of just-toasted marshmallows. The roads are constantly busy, horn-beeping is compulsory, and tuk-tuks, the little motorised rickshaws, are ready and waiting to take your face off whenever you attempt to cross the road as they speed past. It's one of those places that you either love or hate, and I loved it. Street traders on every corner, people shouting over the noise of other people shouting, who themselves are only shouting because they can't hear themselves think.

To begin with, we stayed in a little guesthouse that was slightly off the beaten track. It had a small garden with a waterfall by the entrance, and the sound of running water drowned out the chaos from the street outside. It was like a little oasis, and we threw ourselves on the bed with delight. The place was very basic, but as we had an accommodation budget of about five euro a night, basic was at the top end of our price range.

It was soon time to move on; we had to get to the south of Bangkok for what was going to be a sun-drenched, non-stop party for the millennium (in our heads anyway). Heaving our over-laden backpacks on to our backs and buckling under the weight, we headed for the train station to catch the train to the southern islands.

We arrived at our destination twenty-eight hours later, frazzled shadows of our former selves. This was only partly due to the fact that we had travelled, overnight, on a train that looked like something straight out of *A Passage to India* – the smells from the streets creeping in through the windows being half-heartedly pushed around by the fan that hadn't read its job description; the shouts from each station as we went past and my insistence on pointing out every village we went through in the style of an embarrassing Westerner – 'Ooh look, Helen, people picking rice!' – all did a fairly good job of keeping us from slumber.

The overwhelming reason for our bleary-eyed arrival at our destination, however, was that we were joined – no, more than joined, we were assaulted – by someone who definitely had themselves down under the title 'traveller'.

'Hi!' She had bounced over to us at the train station as we sat on our backpacks, a cacophonous vision in her multi coloured, tie-dyed top and purple, fish-print sarong. 'My name's Jazz, and I've been sent over by my mates back in London to get the party started!' she announced, pulling out a set of three juggling balls and proceeding to throw them, rather amateurishly, to the four winds.

I looked at Helen, who was busy gnawing her way through her own leg, out of embarrassment at having been lumbered with this self-confessed, social-butterfly-cum-circus-reject.

That was only the start. By the time the train had finally turned up (I think we'd been waiting for it to be built), we had been loudly subjected to Jazz's life story. She had given up her 'fab' job in London working in PR, 'because, like, it's the facking millennium, yeah?' She spent her entire time on her mobile phone back to England, announcing to her friends in an even louder voice than she was employing for our benefit that Thailand was going to be a 'facking blast'. We were drawing stares – people looking at us with pity and gratitude, thankful that we'd been lumbered with the human foghorn and they hadn't.

More than a day later, sleep deprived, after two trains, one coach, and a boat that was less seaworthy than the coach, we arrived at our destination, Koh Samui. It was here that we managed to shake off our new-found friend, safe in the knowledge that we knew everything about her, from her favourite film – 'It's gotta be *Scarface*, yeah?' – to her inside leg measurement. 'OK girls, going to the north of the island to get me a nice spot on a secluded beach, you take care.' She had waved animatedly, as if she were guiding in a plane. 'Oh yeah, and what are your names again?' After this, we vowed to talk only to people who appeared to have the propensity to listen.

As we wandered along the road in search of accommodation, Helen looked up at the sky and then turned to me and asked, 'Is it raining?' The answer was yes, it definitely was and it wasn't about to stop, any month soon, so it transpired.

Like the pair of worldly wise travellers that we weren't, we hadn't bothered to check the weather. I'd seen the front cover of the *Lonely Planet* for Thailand; it had a nice wooden boat bobbing on still azure seas and there wasn't a cloud in the sky. That was what the weather was going to be like, I had ignorantly assumed. However, it was to lash rain for the best part of three weeks and on more than one occasion we were to lose the will to live, as the electricity went out for the fifth time that week and we were forced to play Connect Four by candlelight.

We were staying at a place called Coconut Bungalows. The name conjures up images of tropical huts on a balmy beach; of sitting on a balcony and gazing at the emerald sea, sipping a cocktail from a hollowed-out pineapple. It doesn't suggest a mosquito-ridden flea pit, with barely running water and a gaggle of men from Leeds, staying in the adjoining bungalows, hiring prostitutes (they liked their women loud – that's all I'm saying on the subject). We stuck it out for a good few days, spending a cold Christmas Day on the beach. When the weather turned from monsoon to deluge and the creaky roofing all but gave way, treating Helen and me to a spot of sleeping alfresco, we decided it was probably time to move on.

During this time, I sent umpteen postcards home. Postcards, Connect Four and reading and rereading *Tales of the City* were what kept us going. One of these cards happened to be to Andrew, saying, 'We're having a good time ... weather's great (lie) ... lost the head when we hit turbulence, but thanks for the help anyway.'

We had decided to head to Malaysia, in the hope that a different country might mean a different weather system, and, for a time, it did. As we stood outside the bus station, waiting for a coach to take us across the border, I noticed a chemist across the road. I pulled Helen over to it and asked in my best Thai (which means that I ordered a beer and he spoke perfect English back to me and asked me what I really wanted) for some sleeping tablets. I purchased them, probably illegally, over the counter and went on my merry way.

Now, not being a great fan of prescription drugs, I wasn't particularly *au fait* with the intricacies of taking sleeping tablets. So I decided I'd give one a bash, to see if it was enough to knock me out for the flight home. We were about to embark on a twelve-hour bus journey, so I thought that it would be a good time to perform my experiment.

I took one at six o'clock in the evening and awoke as fresh as a daisy at six o'clock the next morning, an hour before we were due to pull into our destination. My jumper was a bit soggy, which was a mystery to me, but other than that, I was perfectly happy. I could see that my fear of flying might be temporarily and, in hindsight, rather insanely dealt with by this pharmaceutical method.

Helen opened her eyes and pushed herself up in the chair. 'Awake, are we?' she asked.

'What?' I replied, the muscles in my bum clenching as, from the way she was looking at me, I had an instinctive feeling that I had probably done something wrong on a rather grand scale.

Then she started laughing.

It transpired that I had got off the bus at a service station to buy some crisps (of which I remembered nothing) and had instead gone careering headlong into a stack of shelves. Helen had had to come to my rescue and direct me to the bus as I weebled around. She had guided me back, like an infirm granny, and sat me in my seat thinking that that would be an end to it. It wasn't. I had started demanding to know who told her that she could go and work as a teacher for ten pence an hour in Thailand (and other inane questions) and halfway through my rant, my eyes had glazed over, I had thrown coffee all over myself and fellen asleep.

But instead of doing the sensible thing and binning the tablets, I kept them just in case – I told myself, just in case – I was petrified on the plane on the way back. I could just take half.

Malaysia was to prove to be sunny (hallelujah!) and beautiful. We stayed on the island of Langkawi, hunting out the only backpacker accommodation available. It was run by an eccentric ex-model who vogued around the place calling everyone his babies, and persuading us all to dress in togas for the New Year celebration. We did as we were told. As the midnight hour drew near, the owner of the hostel brought out a large pole with the number 2000 made from wood and cloth attached to the top of it, and proceeded to douse it in petrol. As the countdown began, he set fire to it, which in turn set fire to the fence next to it, and within minutes there was chaos, as people desperately tried to unravel their togas so as not to go up in flames; the Sydney Harbour Bridge firework display, it was not. Once this was dampened down by a lot of frantic running around with hoses and buckets, we went to the beach and sat by a bonfire, drinking some cheap champagne and watching everyone dancing round in the heat as the waves lapped the shore. We finally felt very pleased with ourselves that we were somewhere so beautiful.

A week later, we ventured back to Thailand with our goldfish memories and were rained on for the rest of our time there.

Heading home towards the end of January, Helen and I summarised our travels. We'd been eaten alive by mosquitoes and worn nylon knickers. (I didn't realise until I got them back to the guesthouse. The knickers I had bought, due to my inability to pack, were like fifteen denier tights with the legs cut off. If you have a vivid imagination, then you will realise that this is not a good look and, as such, the knickers were binned forthwith.) We had been harassed by prostitutes and Leeds boys hiring prostitutes. We had nearly frozen to death in an opium den and been up and down the length and breadth of Thailand three or four times. But we'd had a great time, and we had laughed our way through the eight weeks, only going insane once or twice.

And strangely, once again on the plane, I was as calm as I had initially been on the way out. The plane took off; I was calm. Drinks from the bar; calm. Pilot announces that we are cruising at an altitude of thirty-five thousand feet; completely calm. And then it happened. Again. We hit turbulence and I was almost up the wall and trying to climb into the overhead locker. It was useless, I decided. I couldn't go through the next six hours frightened out of my wits. And this time, Helen couldn't even placate me with her breathing techniques because I knew that she had made them up. So I rifled around in my bag and found the sleeping tablets.

'Oh God!' Helen groaned, but then I could see her do a quick calculation in her head. Six hours of me hopping around like a lunatic or two minutes of me ranting insanely about teaching rates in Thailand before falling asleep? 'Just take half if you're going to take any at all,' she advised, resignation creeping into her voice.

So I did. After a bit, I felt slightly calmer. The turbulence didn't last for long and soon the flight attendant offered me an in-flight meal, and my eyes lit up joyously again at the prospect of some rubbery chicken and a bit of stale cake.

'Are you sure you should be having that? I'm not wiping coffee off your face again,' Helen said.

'I'm fine,' I protested.

And that was the last thing I remember. When I woke up,

the seat to my right, which had been occupied by an American woman, was vacant and I noticed that she was now occupying the seat in the aisle opposite. My jacket was on the floor, the sogginess and the brownness of it leading me to believe that I might have had another 'accident' with a cup of coffee. I went into mortified panic. I shook Helen wildly, desperate to know what had happened.

She woke up and shook her head. 'Give me those tablets – I'm putting them in the bin,' she demanded, and then proceeded to tell me what I had done.

I had opened my bottle of sparkling water, followed by the peanut-replacement dog-biscuit-textured snacks that I'd been given and had poured them both into my plastic glass.

'Fair play to the American woman,' Helen said. 'She stuck that little incident out.' Apparently just giving me a dirty look, and Helen a dirtier look – as if she should be looking after me properly. She even stayed seated while I tried to balance my coffee cup on top of the plastic cup and ultimately threw the coffee all over myself before promptly falling asleep while Helen and the flight attendant disposed of my meal and mess.

'What did the flight attendant say?' I asked in shame.

'Nothing,' Helen said. 'She just gave me a look of complete sympathy.'

'Fair enough,' I said. 'And the American woman – when did she move?'

'When you started dribbling.'

Lovely, I thought. I am so attractive. Get me an upgrade at once; I want to dribble with the stars!

So that was the end of my glittering sleeping-tablet career. I decided to try to deal with my fear of flying as best I could without the help of pharmaceuticals. I'd rather be utterly petrified than utterly mortified.

When I got home, pale and weary, someone had posted a note through the door. I threw my bags down, picked it up and slumped on the settee. It was from Andrew. 'Did you pick up any e-mails when you were away? I was trying to get hold of you. In the script, I forgot to mention turbulence!'

So the hypnotherapy had worked after all; if he'd mentioned turbulence, I'd have been fine. But I mulled it over in my head; with an irrational fear like mine, it could never cover every eventuality – turbulence is one thing but what if one of the flight attendants were wearing a pair of dangly earrings that I didn't like the look of? That might set me off. It could be anything. I just have to accept that I'm never going to get on a plane and get off at the other end without breaking out in a cold, clammy sweat.

So, next time you're on a plane and there's someone clinging, limpet-like, to the headrest in front of them, sobbing silently and saying the rosary, feel free to ignore them; it's probably me.

# MARITA CONLON-McKENNA

## SAINT-TROPEZ

Paris for a week, then down south to Saint-Tropez for the rest of the summer. It sounded like the dream job, the opportunity of a lifetime, too good to refuse for most seventeen-year-old colleens. All that was needed was a bit of French and being able and willing to mind a dotey one-year-old. My French was fine as I had once stayed with a French family in Rheims on an exchange, and being mad on babies and kids, I regularly baby-sat for neighbours and cousins – so how hard could it be? It certainly beat hanging around Dublin for the summer, like most of my pals.

It only got better as information about my prospective employers filtered through. Both worked in the chic French film industry, and they had a massive luxury apartment in the centre of Paris, and an enormous old house in its own grounds in Saint-Tropez, with a swimming pool and Brigitte Bardot for a neighbour. My friends were green with envy, and my head was filled with notions of a jet-set summer revolving round *la crème* of the film world. No other Irish nanny would have it so good!

Before I flew off, my mother gave me the talk about French men. Up until then the worry had been French boys, but now she was definitely talking men. Me secretly hoping she was right. I had been on the usual family holidays around Spain and Italy and Portugal, but this was trip of a different colour, *sans* relations, totally solo.

Paris basked in the June sunshine, and the apartment was even bigger and better than I had imagined. Monsieur *et* Madame welcomed me, dressed in expensive black, oozing jaded Gallic charm. Polite and pleasant, and *très* intense for an Irish greenhorn.

The baby was beautiful, as all French babies are – no dirty noses or ruddy teething cheeks. French babies seem to avoid all the unglamorous traits of their Irish counterparts and smell and look divine. Thea had perfect blond wispy hair and big blue eyes, and, thank God, took to me immediately. We all sighed with relief, as nanny and baby quickly bonded.

Along with my other baby-minding duties, I was personally to prepare and cook Thea's food. Madame took me into the kitchen after dinner to show me the ropes. She insisted that everything the child ate must be macrobiotic. I did my best not to look nonplussed. What did 'macrobiotic' mean? Nothing packaged, coloured, processed or refined, I was told. Thea would eat only the purest food ingredients, grown without trace of chemicals and fertilisers. A whole press was given over to the baby-food production area, and meal preparation and cooking must be followed *exactement!* No sweets, no biscuits, no chocolate. Pure, pure, pure. I thought of the Smartie-coloured monsters I'd minded back in Dublin, multicoloured with chemicals, chocolate digestives squashed in one hand, screaming for tomato ketchup on every meal that was served up to them. There was a lot to take in but I was determined to make a gallant effort and change my ignorant Irish ways.

Thea went to bed easily, and returning to the sitting room, I hunted for the baby-sitter's staple – a television to flop in front of. There didn't seem to be one, so I sat down with my hosts and was expected to join in their chat about the state of French cinema, praying my French would be up to such intellectual conversation.

Madame *et* Monsieur had to work for the rest of the week, so Thea would be in my care.

With my designer-clad baby in buggy, I explored the city – the parks, the shady streets, the hippy markets – and window-shopped outside elegant boutiques. I became an automatic Parisienne, people stopping to admire my beautiful little girl.

One night, Madame, Thea and I visited Montmartre, the warm narrow streets crowded with artists and musicians.

On Friday, Monsieur packed up the silver Mercedes with all the luggage and baby equipment, and I mean *equipment*, because for some bizarre reason they did not want Thea to have any toys. She was likely the only child in the universe with no teddy or cuddly toy, nothing squeaky or shiny or plastic or coloured. Perhaps there were two or three carved wooden shapes but the baby had no interest in them whatsoever. For similar reasons, they did not want her exposed to anything but classical music, and I was forbidden to use the radio or the record player. They detested *le pop* and I was banned from listening to any form of pop music within the hearing range of my charge. I was forced to sing under my breath for fear of upsetting the delicate artistic balance of my employers.

We drove through France during the night, the huge service stations and autoroute lit up like broad daylight, the baby and I sleeping in the back.

I awoke to the azure skies of Provence, the warm air rich with the scent of lavender and grass as we headed down towards the coast. Black cats cleaned their paws on the doorsteps and window ledges of steep hillside villages. Monsieur followed the busy twisting coast road and turned off just before *la ville de* Saint-Tropez, then drove up a private roadway that led to what they called the *château*. I held my breath as I took in the sun terraces, the veranda, the huge castellated house. The baby woke up and yelled, anxious to get out of the car. I walked her around the gardens and lawn, as the gardener appeared to help carry in the luggage.

My room had a high ceiling and French doors leading to the terrace and gardens. I had my own private bathroom and a study area with a library of books and a chair and a desk. The baby was to sleep in the room beside mine, in a large cot draped with mosquito netting. Monsieur *et* Madame were upstairs in another wing of the house, where they could not possibly hear the baby. The sun scorched outside, the ground was dry, and the sound of cicadas filled the air, but inside, the shutters stayed closed and the tiled floor and marble stairs remained cool.

In the kitchen, the baby-food preparation area was again kept separate, and Madame explained that most of the vegetables would now come from their own vegetable garden. If I was in need of something, I was just to go and get it or ask the gardener.

With no work or demands, Madame insisted that she and Monsieur needed to rest, relax, and remain tranquil, and they were relying on me to deal with Thea, who was beginning to show a sudden determination in her attempts to walk. An American housekeeper in her late twenties came in every day, and an Algerian maid did the heavy cleaning once a week.

The days slipped into an easy routine, and the baby and I spent all our time together. While Thea dozed and napped, I swam in the large, old-fashioned pool, serenaded by the frogs. In my room, I left my doors open to the sun. The bookshelves were crowded with crime books and Agatha Christie novels *en français,* and I devoured each one in turn. Bored eventually, I took out my pad and began to sketch and write.

I was warned that when I walked up and down the long driveway I could wave to France's most famous film star at a distance, but under no circumstances was I to engage in conversation with her or try to be familiar with her. The millionaire Germans who had built a disgusting modern villa nearby were to be ignored.

At night, for the most part, we ate dinner on the terrace, shaded by climbing vines and bougainvillaea, the only disturbance, the lizards that plumped on the table every now and then and stared at us with curiosity.

Madame asked me only two or three times to accompany her to the local market, where she bought huge melons, and cheese and fish. We bought rope sandals and she surprised me by buying a delicate, embroidered black caftan for herself and making me a present of a green one.

In the first few evenings in Saint-Tropez we ventured down to the port, admiring the yachts and the chi-chi boutiques with their enormous prices and tiny bikinis and denim mini-skirts and dresses. Handsome French boys on scooters prowled the streets, as girls with golden tans paraded up and down past the trendy cafés and bars, dogs and big cats on bejewelled leads panting in the heat.

Only a short distance away were Port Grimaud and Cogolins aspiring to be like Saint-Tropez, with yachts jostling for position in the busy marinas and speedboats plying up and down the coast with skiers in tow.

One day, we left the sea behind us, and the Mercedes climbed inland towards Grasse, the village home of French *parfum*. The air was scented by miles of lavender fields. The steep, cobbled streets were quiet, and shutters were closed on the narrow, sun-drenched houses. Madame disappeared inside one to buy some favourite perfume essences before Monsieur treated us to lunch in one of the most expensive restaurants in France, where breathtaking views spread out below us.

Two weeks, then three weeks had passed and still I had not been on the beach. Usually Madame *et* Monsieur disappeared there for the morning. One day, they relented, agreeing that the baby and I should accompany them. I wondered where we were going when the car swept by the popular *plage* close to the house, Monsieur making a sneering comment about *les touristes*. Our beach was definitely more off the beaten track and we walked through a wooded area of pine before putting foot on the almost white, bleached sand.

I had the buggy and baby bag, plus my own beach bag. I sat down, undressing the baby and putting on her sun hat, as Monsieur *et* Madame stretched out two sunbeds. I suddenly realised that both were naked and they were instructing me to leave the baby *au naturel* as well. I didn't know where to look, and tried frantically to pretend that as a young Irish woman of the world I was not fazed by such things. I stretched out on my towel feeling totally overdressed in my bikini.

The beach began to fill up with generations of French nudists, grandfathers and grandmothers, fathers and mothers, sons and daughters. I had never seen anything like it, as they hugged and kissed and wished each other *bon jour*. I tried to ignore my surroundings and lie on my stomach and tan my back, but Thea wanted to play and I had to sit up and mind her.

Beautiful young women lounged in the sunlight and splashed in the water, shrieking at the top of their voices, while their mothers and grandmothers sat naked and gossiped on the chairs and sunbeds. The French men, on the other hand, didn't like to sit and preferred to stand or promenade along the waterfront, proudly displaying their manhood. Having no brothers, my only glimpse of such things had been my ageing father in his stripy pyjamas. Confronted now with every shape and size, *grand* and *petit*, young and old, handsome and ugly, grizzled grey, weary, *erect*, I was mortified. I thought of my mother and aunt back home in Dublin and knew that I was certainly experiencing more of French men than my mother had ever imagined.

'Strip off,' Madame suggested to me.

I looked at Monsieur lying only a few feet away and decided definitely no. I could not face him.

To my relief, we returned home at lunch-time and the next day there was no invitation to join them on the beach. The baby and I stayed at home.

The temperature soared in the afternoons and Monsieur *et* Madame retreated to the privacy of a shaded room overlooking the terrace on the far side of the house. The baby and I were ignored. A small red ball was the only diversion for little Thea, unless we chased lizards or watched the frogs. She was beginning to take her first faltering steps, and on the day she walked alone, I ran to call her *mama* and *papa* to see, disturbing them as they drank coffee and smoked funny-smelling cigarettes.

'Come and see Thea!'

I brought them down to the lawn, placing my prodigy on the dry grass as they watched her, and I called to her. Thea took one step, two steps, three ... then oops-a-daisy! down she went on her bottom.

Incensed, Madame flew towards her and looked at her hands and knees, the baby laughing and slightly marked with dry clay. 'Wash her! Clean her immediately!' she ordered, demanding that I take Thea inside for a bath, insisting that from then on I was to keep baby wipes or a damp towel with me at all times, so that she was at no risk from germs or dirt or disease from the garden.

Madame's behaviour was becoming more bizarre by the day and I couldn't fathom why Thea was being treated so strangely. Trying to teach a baby to walk without it falling or sitting down or touching its hand to the ground was an impossible task.

Pale and wretched and dressed in her *de rigueur* expensive black, Madame fought with the American housekeeper, who quit, and screamed at the maid, who hissed at her employer behind her back. She gave out to me because I had spoken to the German family one day, as I returned from a walk with the baby. They were lolling around their shiny new pool, and on hearing my Irish accent, they had asked me about Ireland

and told me I was welcome to use their pool any time or to join them for a cool drink or a barbecue. In a frenzy, Madame had cursed the Germans and forbidden me to fraternise with such uncouth people.

The atmosphere in the house became heavy and tense, Madame *et* Monsieur leaving a trail of black clothes on the floor and the stairs for me to pick up and tidy away or put in the wash, as the other help would no longer work for them. I had worked for almost two months, and my requests for a day off or a night off had been ignored.

I bumped into the housekeeper, who had come to collect money owed to her, and she asked how I was getting on.

I was dying for a night out, I told her. I longed to hear loud music, to laugh and sing, have some fun. Do what seventeen-year-olds do!

'Come and have dinner with me tomorrow,' she said. 'Take a few hours off.'

The next day, I summoned up courage and told Madame I would not be having dinner with them as I was eating out. I took no notice of her sulks and bad humour and fed the baby, cleaned up after, washed her and put her to bed, before setting off on foot for the American's house. She lived with her French boyfriend close by.

A simple meal was served – chicken and salad and bread. I had forgotten what it was like to feel relaxed at the table.

'Come out with Jean-Luc and me later on,' she offered. 'We will go to a disco.'

'I can't,' I wailed. 'Madame would not give me a key, so I can't be late.'

The talk turned to my employers.

'They both like drugs,' the American said with a shrug. 'She was an addict. She gave up when she was pregnant, but now ...'

I was appalled. Poor baby Thea.

It was getting dark and, checking my watch, I decided to make my way home. Approaching the driveway, I was surprised to see the house in darkness. The back door was locked. The terrace door was locked. I knocked and knocked for Madame or Monsieur to let me in. Scared, I began to call them. Why had they locked me out? I had been away for only three hours, after all.

Eventually Madame appeared in her black silk kimono, her face pale. Her dark hair tumbled to her shoulders as she screamed and roared at me. How dare I go out! How dare I leave the baby!

Thea was still asleep.

Madame cursed and swore at me, and switching on the kitchen lights, she ordered me to wash up everything left from their meal, the pots and pans, and clean the huge kitchen floor before I went to bed.

'No,' I protested. 'I'm not your maid.'

She flung the dirty plates from the table onto the floor, oil and grease and lettuce smearing the tiles, then, out of control, she proceeded to fling plates from the dresser at me and on the ground. Monsieur appeared in his matching black silk kimono to see what the noise was about.

I longed for the sanity of my own crazy parents and home as I watched her smash their expensive plates and bowls. Monsieur eventually led her to their private wing of the house, and I stayed up to sweep and clean, listening to the cicadas outside and wondering how paradise had become such a hell.

Alarmed by it all, I phoned the American and told her what had happened.

'Get out,' she advised me. 'It will get worse.'

I phoned my mother, told her I was coming home, and managed to book an expensive one-way seat on a flight from Nice to Paris.

Madame was quiet and drawn when I told them the next morning that I was packing up and returning home to Ireland the following day. Monsieur insisted everything was fine, furious that I would dare to leave them. I asked him to drive me to the airport. I was worried sick about the baby and would have bundled her up in my baggage and stolen her away if I could. Perhaps with me gone, they might actually look after their little daughter and talk to her. It was all I could hope.

He was silent in the car, smoking his usual Gauloises, and dropped me off on the roadside outside the airport, flinging my bag on the tarmac.

I sat on the plane as we flew out over the Mediterranean, watching the Riviera disappear from view, and longed for wet, wonderful, dirty Dublin and to be home.

# ANN MARIE HOURIHANE

## WORST HOLIDAYS

I have only two pieces of advice to offer on the subject of holidays. The first is self-explanatory: do not try to learn to ski whilst suffering from premenstrual tension. In fact, I can shorten that: do not try to learn to ski. The second piece of advice is even simpler: do not go on holiday to any country where the people are poorer than you. I realise that this leaves us with just Western Europe, North America, Australia and the Antarctic to play in, but they are large land masses. It is all right to holiday where the penguins are poorer than you.

The problem is that the word 'tourism', like the word 'charity', has come to justify anything. We Irish know this from our own experience. Remember when we were poor? Brash Americans roared around us, spraying cash. Remember how we hated them? Well, in some parts of the world even adorable Irish people are regarded as brash Americans now. Take Morocco, for example. A beautiful country with a rich tradition of hospitality, full of lovely people who are eager to share their varied cultural history with you. Sound familiar at all? Well, this is how they're selling Morocco now.

We landed on the Prophet's birthday, a public holiday. On the way in from the airport, we passed through miles of wasteland, travelling on a pristine new road. The towns were so desolate that they looked as if they had been hastily reconstructed after an earthquake – which was, in fact, the case. Agadir, once an interesting port, was destroyed by an earthquake in 1960. Fifteen thousand people were killed. Fifty thousand were left homeless. The travel brochures just didn't have room to include that fascinating piece of information.

As we drove, we saw families eating their picnics in olive groves. Their cars or their camels standing patiently beside them. In the rush to get on a plane, in the search for the most inexpensive package deal, we had forgotten that there might be a reason why Morocco offered the cheapest five-star service and wonderful massages: the people are dirt poor.

Agadir was reconstructed as a tourist resort for Western visitors. It is now a run-down, ramshackle, concrete town, and we were staying in one of its cheaper hotels. A lot of Germans were staying in the hotel and most were on their second holiday of the year. In this, they differed from most of the Irish people, who were on their first. There were quite a lot of Irish people, we discovered, who were there for just a week, prior to going on their real holiday later in the year. There were several 'girls' holidays', as my grandmother used to say, groups composed entirely of women. Believe me when I say – and I am a regular attender at an annual girls' holiday – that Agadir is not the place for it. Before the week was out, one of these women had been dragged down a flight of concrete steps by the strap of her handbag, mugged by a young man. He succeeded in stealing her bag and breaking a bone in her arm.

The woman, who was middle-aged and shy, was, naturally, terribly shocked by this attack. In the reception area, we Irish murmured about poor tourists in Ireland who had suffered similar fates, and worse. However, we were unprepared for what came next. A couple of days later, a group of young men was led in to the lobby of our hotel in chains. The woman, with her arm heavily bandaged, was asked to identify her assailant. To her eternal credit, she said she was unable to do so, as it had all happened so fast. Hotel staff unofficially informed us that this wouldn't make any difference to the authorities, because one of the boys would be sent to prison anyway, so that a crime against a tourist would not be seen to go unpunished.

I hadn't witnessed the attack. At the time it took place, we were wandering the blindingly concrete streets, being chased by men who ran up to my companion shouting, '*Conas tá tú?* Howaya? *Conas tá tú?*' This led us to suspect that Irish tourists were not the charming underdogs of Agadir, as we all know ourselves to be elsewhere, but, on the contrary, rather routine. My companion was the one who suffered the complicated verbal assaults for money because, as a woman, I was ignored during these exchanges. He is an unaggressive person. So, while I would have bopped these Gaelic-speakers in the eye, he remained perfectly friendly. There is a downside to being perfectly friendly. The downside involved walking across three miles of Agadir in blistering heat. We were being led by my companion's new friend, who said that my companion simply had to meet his cousin. I followed.

Back on the Prophet's birthday, we had been warned not to buy spices of any kind in Morocco, except from a trader recommended by a tour guide or the driver of a tourist bus. As it happened, my companion's family had been left at the commercial mercy of the drivers of tourist buses in Ireland, back in the bad old days when you had to bribe them in order to get them to stop at your craft centre, or your roadside café, or whatever. As a result, his kind heart rebelled against the awful power that could be wielded by tour guides and coach drivers. But he wasn't planning to buy any spices, oh no.

Eventually we came to a massive indoor market. I was the only female under its huge corrugated roof. The cousin insisted that we have a glass of mint tea, which my companion then would not let me drink in case it was laced with narcotics. Then my companion spent forty pounds on spices. And not just spices either.

'Oh, oh,' said the stall-holder. 'Fantastic aphrodisiac. Oh, oh, all night long. Ha, ha.'

We were mortified. Did we really look like the sort of people who needed an aphrodisiac? I suppose people who buy aphrodisiacs must always feel like this. No wonder they are so expensive.

The aphrodisiac was thrown on a mounting (you know what I mean) pile of ecologically unsound white plastic bags, which contained, amongst other things, paprika, mint tea, an unnamed combination of spices – 'Very good with lemon or fish' – and saffron. We had been very sternly warned about buying anything purporting to be saffron. So naturally my companion, bamboozled to the point of passivity, bought it at once.

We left, gasping as we emerged into the blazing sunlight. We had our first row of the holiday before we turned the next corner.

In my considered opinion, holidays are bad for relationships. They are like Christmas: you are obliged to have a good time. If you don't enjoy holidays, then there is something wrong with you as a family, as a couple, as a person. You wake up every day to the terrible burden of enjoying yourself.

We had very nice rooms on the shady side of our hotel, which meant they looked over the main road. We had a little living room where we could watch the Moroccan equivalent of *Fáilte Isteach*, a television programme which taught us more about Moroccan folk music than we had ever thought existed. We had two bathrooms, which, believe me, by the end of our holiday, was not one bathroom too many. On arrival, we were presented with a basket of fruit, which (I knew by the way our maid looked at it) amounted to untold luxury. But she wouldn't take any fruit, and I think it must have rotted away. We couldn't eat it all and I couldn't pack the rest of it into our little fridge.

There is a beautiful beach at Agadir and my companion thought he might like to hire a little dinghy to mess about in. Agadir is on the Atlantic coast, the water is icy and the waves are rough, so I was quite relieved to discover, once we had walked the not inconsiderable length of the beach, that only the more expensive hotels hired sailing boats. The only way you could go sailing was to hire a local person to take you out for a terrifying spin on a catamaran.

Then there was drinking, which in Morocco, as in most countries, is a minefield. Either you could drink by the swimming pool, served by endlessly courteous barmen. Or you could drink in the bar at night, where tourists eventually forgot that the barmen spoke perfect English and cheerfully swapped stories about the ludicrousness of Moroccan social codes.

There was table tennis by the swimming pool. Our daily matches were the high point of the day. 'I said a prayer that you would win,' said a young Irish woman to me. I had won that day, so I was pleased. This goes to show how low our horizons had fallen.

And there was always the nagging thought that really we shouldn't be in the hotel at all. We should be on Morocco's very efficient public bus system, exploring the Atlas Mountains. But the companion, who had been working like a dog up to our day of departure – it was I who had forced him to take a holiday – declared himself too exhausted. Instead, we explored the Atlas Mountains on a tourist excursion, with a guide who was more educated and sophisticated than the President of Ireland, and who seemed on the edge of a very genteel despair. Wherever we stopped in the mountains, children ran up to beg money from us, or even ballpoint pens. We bought a silver ring for me in a town so poor that I would have thought it incapable of supporting human life. We were shepherded from carpet showroom (not that sort of carpet showroom) to metal workshop to bric-à-brac outlet with a firmness that was humiliating.

Then I had the brilliant idea that we might go home after one week, instead of two. 'Do your best,' said the companion. 'Do your best.' Throwing dignity to the winds – or a little further to the winds – I told the airline that we simply had to be back in Dublin for a number of spurious reasons that are too embarrassing to repeat here.

When that plane left Agadir airport, containing the poor mugged woman amongst many others, we were virtually clinging to its undercarriage.

'Another week,' groaned my companion.

I was beyond words. I don't think we've ever been so low. I had nothing but a large biography of Winston Churchill and my convent training to sustain me. He had nothing but his guitar and the World Cup.

The high point of our holiday came when the transmission of the big match – I think between England and Argentina – was interrupted for the broadcast of Friday prayers. Everyone, men and women, tourists and Moroccans, jumped into taxis in a dash for a bigger hotel which had satellite television.

My companion and I settled into a routine. He got up at five to watch the team he was supporting; I remember many anxious days worrying about Senegal. Every day, I got up at eight and went to a patisserie round the corner for breakfast. Moroccan patisserie is wonderful and I'd bring some back for his breakfast. Every day I inspected the tomato plants that bravely grew against the concrete walls of the high-rise buildings, carefully avoiding the stray cats, which I feared were rabid. I spent a couple of minutes each morning looking in the window of the saucepan shop, which had excellent pots on display, but never opened once in the fortnight we were there.

Then we went to the pool. There was a major sensation one day when some bare-breasted German women decided to sunbathe.

Every night the companion went to the local shop to buy cigarettes, and there we saw the lowest of Agadir's low – the drinkers in a Muslim country, buying alcohol.

To us, Morocco did not feel like being on holiday. It felt as though we were participating in someone else's social experiment. The best memory I have of it is the sight of a man pushing a satellite dish through the kasbah of Marrakesh – a wonderful place, like the New York of Africa – in a wheelbarrow. But Agadir felt like some other people's idea of a good time. Which of course it was. Whoever they are, I hope they enjoyed it.

# CATHERINE DONNELLY

## TRAVELLING HOPELESSLY

During my life, I've had holidays I loved and holidays I loathed. On the whole, the bad ones were the best value because at least you have something to talk about when you return. No one wants to hear about the perfect restaurant, the idyllic beach, the wonderful hotel. But come home armed with horror stories of cockroaches and food poisoning, robbery at knife-point and attacks by jellyfish, and people perk up. A good holiday is pleasant at the time – a rotten one is a fund of anecdotes that can get you through a whole year of boring dinner parties.

The first holidays I remember were taken in the company of my nurse, Eileen, in various Irish seaside towns. When I say 'nurse', she was actually a nanny. Perhaps it was because she differed so radically from the other nannies around our part of the country that the word 'nanny' seemed inappropriate. At children's parties, the nannies would sit having tea and gossiping. They wore blue or grey uniforms, with starched, white cuffs elasticated at the wrist and elbow to protect their sleeves. They wore thick, grey stockings and stout, laced shoes with no-nonsense heels.

Eileen wore a skirt and blouse and shoes that suggested she was prepared to put up with the occasional misdemeanour.

The nannies drank their tea daintily and when they talked of their charges, they did so with unashamed bias. 'He's very small for his age,' they would murmur casually of another child and then feign annoyance at the number of times they were obliged to let down the hems of *their* little boy's trousers.

Eileen didn't need to boast about me. We both knew I was the best. She'd give me this look. It made us complicit in that awful world of tulle and lace and nasty small boys clad in velvet. Small boys who pulled your hair and spat a powder of sugar in your face during tea. When the ordeal was over and we were home again, we never mentioned the party. They were something we both had to endure. A bit like holidays.

What I remember most vividly about those childhood holidays was the cold. The soft sand of the dunes with its skin of wet from repeated showers giving onto the concrete-hard beach that skirted the grey sea. A wind whipped along the beach, creating mini-tornadoes; the sea clasped ankles like ice. I remember the constant background music of my teeth chattering like castanets. I grew used to the sound just as, I suppose, someone with tinnitus becomes accustomed to the sound of bells.

People weren't so well equipped then. For example, you owned one bathing suit – not a whole wardrobe of them. You might have a second suit but that would be last year's and a little too small for you, the straps cutting into your shoulders like wire. So generally I stayed in the same bathing suit, cold clammy – its jolly little skirt clinging limply to my legs. I erected rather poor sandcastles, surrounded by muddy moats. Eileen made better castles – volcanoes that really worked. You built a tall mountain-shape out of damp sand, hollowed out the centre and drove a hole through the top. You filled the centre with newspaper, lit it, and if the wind was in the right direction, you had Mount Vesuvius! But mostly I waited for the arrival of lunch-time: salad sandwiches and Club Milk biscuits.

I was always voraciously hungry – a phenomenon Eileen put down to the sea air and the fact that I was growing. I think it was mainly because the introduction of food into my mouth stopped for a moment the cold clamour of my teeth. The day would pass with immersions in the sea, vigorous drying of hair and then a damp half-hour or so covered in the sand, which adhered to damp limbs. We would have a walk mid-afternoon, down past the dunes in which clutches of families roosted with their picnics – elaborate wickerwork affairs with china plates, or cardboard boxes containing newspaper-wrapped sandwiches, depending on their circumstances.

In the evening, we had high tea in a dining room that smelt of polish and cabbage. There must have been some choice on the hotel menus of the time but all I can remember is 'mixed grill', which I thought was a pretty spectacular dish. After this, there would be cakes. I think they were called 'fancies', and my favourite – butterfly cakes, which had little wings of sponge and a filling that resembled a mixture of marshmallow and soap.

These holidays blur in memory into long, cold days and long, boring nights. After high tea, Eileen and I would go for another walk, this being 'good for us'. We walked up through the small town, past shops selling buckets and spades and seaside rock, and then back down again, purchasing an ice-cream on the way.

In one town, a river ran to the sea under a bridge of faded wooden boards that gave access to the dunes beyond. Some evenings, we might linger at this bridge, from where the men of the town shot with pellet guns at the myriad rats that inhabited the river – but my nurse didn't much care for this simple spectator sport.

The next morning, it would start all over again. Only very heavy rain kept us from the beach. On those days, we played snap or she read to me from books by Patricia Lynch about tinkers and horses and, the best in my view, *The Grey Goose of Kilnevin*, which, as you might gather, was about a goose.

My parents holidayed abroad but often they took an Irish holiday as well and I would go too. These were more elaborate vacations, with hotels that served dinner rather than high tea, but very similar to other holidays, in that the climate remained the same. Eileen came along as well, so that my parents' time wouldn't be marred by my constant presence and even more constant reminders to them that I was bored. Sometimes I was allowed to have dinner with them rather than children's tea and I would relieve the tedium by commenting on the food. I would claim, for example, that there was spit on my corn on the cob (it was melted butter), thus mortifying my mother and amusing my father, who would by now be two or three whiskeys to the good.

Occasionally a tiny drama would highlight a particular holiday. Once, we stayed at a hotel frequented by golfers and, because of the fine courts, people interested in tennis. At a table near us, there were two young men on a week's break. In their twenties, they filled their days with swimming, beach football and, of course, tennis. They were kind to me in the way big brothers are kind to small girls. They allowed me be ball-boy for their tennis matches. Around the tennis courts was a thick, tightly packed hedge ten or more feet wide.

One evening, because they were so jocular and full of fun themselves, I got overexcited – started throwing the ball away from rather than to them. At first, they were amused. Then, when I threw the ball into the hedge, they got a little cross. I didn't know how something that had seemed such fun, so full of giggling from me and laughter from them, could have changed to this coldness, this impatience. I crawled into the hedge to retrieve the ball and when I couldn't find it, I started to cry. I stayed in the hedge for some time, while, from the tennis court, they called to me. Their voices became placatory. I could hear them chuckling encouragingly but I couldn't face them. Not without the ball. Eventually, I crawled out to the other side and went back to the hotel; their voices, still calling, receded.

For the remainder of the holiday, every time I saw them, I ran away. People were suspicious – it was strange that one day I had followed these two young men about constantly and the next I seemed terrified of them. Then there was the matter of the cuts – my tussle with the hedge meant I was covered in scratches and cuts. Were it today, the assumption would be that something terrible had happened but those were more innocent times and eventually my cuts healed and the two young men left, puzzled at the way things had turned out.

My first holiday abroad took place when I was thirteen. My father had business connections in Europe – he was a wine merchant. I was sent to a family in Salou in Spain, which supplied my father with wine. It's a huge tourist resort now. Back then, it didn't even have one hotel – just streets of sleepy villas which families from Zarragozza rented for the summer. There were four children in the host family, all older than me. We had a staff of four to look after us – one each, if you like. El Señor and la Señora came down at weekends.

None of the family spoke any English and I didn't speak Spanish – not one word. We started the day with breakfast – milky coffee into which (I discovered this from watching the others) you dipped your bread spread with butter and honey. I rather liked that but couldn't bring myself to drink the coffee with its slick of butter and crumbs when the dipping ritual was over. The maids decided that I didn't like milk, so thereafter I got a tiny cup of espresso instead. I used to drink it like medicine, terrified of what they might produce if they decided I didn't like this either. Then we went to the beach, where I immediately started to burn. No one seemed to have heard of sun protection. I turned red all over, it peeled off and then I went brown. I can't remember it hurting too much. Midway through the morning, hawkers came around selling sugary sticks of dough or chips in cornets of white paper.

At around 1 p.m., we returned to the house for lunch. The four staff were obviously taking a bit of a holiday too because the food was like something you might expect if you were 'doing time' (which, in a way, I was). Invariably there was soup to start – a pale yellow, tasteless broth in which there floated the odd pasta shape or bean. Not too many – three beans maybe, as though there were a shortage of some kind. Afterwards we might have boiled rice with tomato sauce, or pasta with more tomato sauce. The sauce tasted of nothing except tomato purée – no flavourings, no herbs. At the weekend, when the adults arrived, the food became more elaborate and there would be things like *paella* and stuffed squid. I longed for the weekends.

The plan was that I was to stay there for three weeks and then my parents would pick me up and bring me with them to spend two weeks in another part of Spain, but the three weeks drifted into six and then ten. The modest sum my father had given me to cover the original time frame soon evaporated and I didn't know how to ask Señor to lend me some. Actually the only thing I needed money for was to buy books. There was a little shop near the beach that sold English books. I dealt with this problem by reading really fast and then returning the book, explaining to the proprietor regretfully that when I'd got it home I realised I'd already read it. I did this quite a lot. I occasionally think of that kind old man who chose to believe me and always provided another book. *'Hasta luega, guapa,'* he would say to me – 'See you later, pretty one.' I wasn't particularly pretty and appreciated the compliment almost as much as the replacement book.

The book purchases took place during the hours of siesta, which I found intensely boring, and when everyone was asleep, I would slip out into the heat of the afternoon and the long, dusty streets empty of people. I always made sure that I got back in time for the wake-up snack of a roll filled with sausage or, even better, big chunks of chocolate. I'd never tasted chocolate in bread before. I thought it a very fine idea. For dinner we had more soup.

At around midnight, we went to the cinema – a huge outdoor arrangement that looked like a handball alley. Maybe it was. This was the highlight of my day, as all the films were American. True, they'd been dubbed into Spanish but it was almost as good just to see familiar faces like Debbie Reynolds and Rock Hudson and to try to lip-read the original English.

Eventually, after twelve weeks rather than the original three, my parents did arrive, and the Spanish family drove me to Sitges to meet them. My parents were unapologetic for the delay. Time goes more quickly for grown-ups, I suppose.

The following year, I went to France. I was very agitated before going – again the plan was to stay three weeks. I was somewhat reassured by the fact that on this occasion I had a return ticket, which I kept in my purse and checked daily to make sure of the date. The family was a big name in the wine business and there were two large châteaux on the estate – one occupied by the grandmother. I stayed with her. I got the impression that she wasn't too pleased to have a guest. Neither was her maid.

The grandmother complained to Monsieur that I was a vulgar, common girl because I left my shoes outside the wardrobe. I also refused to eat the breakfast, which the maid delivered ill-humouredly each morning. The reason for this was that the tray and everything on the tray was covered with ants – live ones on the bread; dead ones in the jam. I decided to go hungry until elevenses in Monsieur's house – a snack that appealed to me, consisting as it did of mulled wine and biscuits. I was always pleasantly squiffy by eleven thirty.

I spent the rest of the day, until bedtime, in Monsieur's house, together with his two daughters, both of whom were funny and full of ideas for elaborate games and trips into the nearby town. Best of all, they spoke English – possibly rather better than I did. I remember being very impressed by the older girl's sentence constructions, but maybe that was the effect of the wine.

But everything paled into insignificance beside the food. Nowadays, when every food you can imagine is available from Bangkok to Ballsbridge, from Milan to Monaghan, its very ubiquity has jaded our appetites. You would no more have found a green Thai curry in France than you would have found cannelloni in Carlow. I'd never tasted an avocado before, never tried ratatouille, never eaten fish flavoured with saffron or sampled fresh goat's cheese. And we thought we were a rather sophisticated family. Back then, countries stuck to their own cuisine, eschewed imports, followed the seasons. So, while I was well used to asparagus, lobster and fresh prawns, all these other things were as new to me as the idea of having mulled wine for elevenses.

The food was amazing. I'd never known anything like it. I ate for Ireland. For the last week of the holiday, we went to a hotel in Juan-les-Pins on the Côte d'Azur. My appetite had infected the younger daughter of the house – a girl my age. Lunch was taken at the hotel pool. There was a vast cold-room containing literally hundreds of hors-d'oeuvres, which the other guests picked at languidly, their long lithe bodies giving testament to their self-discipline. We piled our plates high; we tried everything and went back for more. The holiday was an epiphany – I came to French cuisine like someone who has lived her life in the darkness and on a diet of dry bread. Everything was a revelation.

The hotel was enormous and expensive. I shared a room the size of a football pitch with the younger girl, and by day two we'd discovered room service. We would manage a large dinner, *en famille,* in the open-air restaurant that looked out on the sea. Then when the family had gone off to attend the rather dull French parties they favoured, we would retire to our huge room and ring for some little snack. This would be delivered by a minimum of three waiters – all of whom did their best to ignore the fact that they'd just served us four courses down in the restaurant.

One day, we went to a party in a large villa in the hills. 'It's very casual,' they explained, dressing as though for a cocktail party. At lunch-time, we went to a restaurant. It looked like a stable yard with long trestle tables laid out in rows. I'll never forget what we ate: we had plates and plates of shellfish, including creatures I didn't even recognise but I ate them anyway. Then there were tarts filled with frazzled onions. Afterwards there was more fish – huge, white fish filled with branches of some kind that gave off a fragrance I now know to be fennel. There were *frites* like shoelaces, and a salad that looked like dandelion leaves but I didn't care, I ate them as well, and waited for them to bring on the daisies and the buttercups. Then there were little sweating cheeses, whiter than the whitest linen, and finally a lemon tart. The company who had ignored me pretty much up to then were awed by my appetite – my delight. The two young men who sat on either side of me began to chat to me in a most amiable way. I discovered in France (at least, the France of that time) that sometimes a healthy interest in food is as attractive as a pretty dress.

In just three weeks, I put on a stone and a half. When my mother saw me in the airport, she burst into tears. I had left looking rather waif-like, wearing a little suit made of plaid that fell in folds. I returned filling every pleat and seam and square of it. My face was moon-shaped. Fortunately weight so quickly gained is easily lost, especially when you're welcomed home with lamb chops and stewed apple.

I once had a particularly unpleasant holiday in Cork. My older sister was taking this holiday. In order to get permission, she had chosen as a companion an intensely serious girl, which calmed my parents somewhat. But they were still dithering. Then my sister played her trump card. Me. She would take me.

My parents were relieved – delighted even. They had failed me in not providing a holiday that year and now, out of the clear blue sky, a holiday had been provided.

We stayed in a hotel overlooking the sea. My sister drank beer in the bar and had unsuitable relationships – one with an undertaker who would pick her up in a hearse, which she found hilarious.

It rained. God, how it rained. I went to the beach in the rain, my bathing suit wrapped in a towel, tight as a drum. Every day, I went through that hideous ritual of an Irish person getting undressed in public. The meek removal of knickers under the cloak of towel, the shrouding of tiny breasts.

Were they living in a different decade, my sister would probably have advised her friend to lighten up. As it was, they rowed most of the time.

Meanwhile, I appeared every morning for breakfast in my clean gingham pedal pushers (of which I had any amount) and ate a full Irish breakfast. The waitresses treated me like a pet – something I played on. My eyes were always full of unshed tears. I would leave a tip. Sixpence.

The hotel shuttled us between rooms. We were always moving. From one room to another – then to the annexe. There was a monkey puzzle tree in the annexe. No wonder I hate them.

Dank, miserable, wretched. The awful monotony of an Irish summer.

And then it was over. We came home. My sister brought a present for our mother. I don't think there was a malicious intent. I think she thought they were so sweet that my mother would overcome her phobia about mice. That she'd unwrap the box and be ... well, won over.

She wasn't.

My father drowned the two mice and their offspring (they hadn't been idle in Cork) in the dogs' water bowl. And then he cried, because circumstances had made him be cruel and he was not a cruel man.

Looking back over the years to those small towns in Ireland, I think perhaps the sun did shine occasionally. In fact, now that I think about it, I can see myself running over the slatted bridge where the rats cavorted happily and the sun glinted off a sea as blue as the sea in Crete or on the Côte d'Azur. And thinking back to the three months in Spain, I remember that there came a moment when, almost without realising it, I was talking enough Spanish to understand the jokes the other children told. I remember that when I finally got to Sitges to meet my parents, several people in the town assumed I must be Spanish because of my dusky skin and my ease at ordering in restaurants.

When I stayed in that hotel in Juan-les-Pins, I would sit on the balcony at night and look at the beautiful people far below. How I envied them their perfect clothes, their insouciance, their confidence. I vowed that one day I would return and I wouldn't be a plump fourteen-year-old – I'd be just like one of them. And do you know – one day, I did – and I was!

# MARY HENRY

## IRAN AFTER THE FIRST GULF WAR

In 1991, after the first Gulf War, many refugees fled Iraq for Iran. The International Red Cross appealed for aid for these people and the Irish nation responded with its usual generosity. The aid was to be distributed by the Iranian Red Crescent, a long-established organisation with branches all over Iran.

I was the chairperson of the Overseas Committee of the Red Cross, and as the money poured in, we bought food, drugs, tents and blankets, and chartered planes to send them out to Tehran. Donations of dried milk, baby-food and other useful commodities came too, and eventually we had seven planeloads – internationally acclaimed as 'a very good effort'.

But when one sends aid to a country, it is always advisable to ensure that it gets to its proper destination. And that's where I came in.

Iran was not very enthusiastic about visitors at that time, as the Iran–Iraq war was not long over. It must be remembered that most Western countries had supported Iraq during that war, and many Westerners were *personae non gratae* there. Ireland had not been involved on either side, so the committee of the International Red Cross decided that no one would be more suitable to fly to Iran to check on the situation than an Irish person. And a middle-aged Irish woman would be even better. 'Who, me?' I asked, and, full of excitement, off I went.

The dress code for women in Iran is very strict (even more so then), and there being a shortage of chadors or burkas in downtown Dublin, I assembled my own outfit – a long wool Micheline Stackpoole skirt, a Bernadette Madden batik headscarf and a long plastic mac I bought years ago at a Swiss airport when I was caught out in heavy rain. Fashionably, if curiously, dressed, I was seen off from Shannon airport by the Minister for Defence, Brendan Daly. The cargo plane belonged to Air Egypt, and being the only passenger was a novel experience. I felt like I should be serving tea, coffee and sandwiches to the two pilots, but they took turns in doing the catering honours. To be honest, the plane was so large I'd have been happier if they had both concentrated on flying it and allowed me to deal with the housekeeping.

We travelled south across France, Italy and the Mediterranean and towards the Middle East, flying into Tehran in pitch darkness. When the city's lights loomed, the pilots let me sit between them and, as we swished down onto the runway, I was still there, probably against all official airline rules. We taxied to a halt and pulled into our allocated space. It was then that the diplomacy started. The plane's door opened automatically and the pilots explained that it would be preferable if I stood in the doorway rather than one of them, this being the first Air Egypt plane into Tehran since the end of the war. Egypt had supported Iraq, after all.

I stood in the darkness for what seemed like hours. The pilots told me that the Irish ambassador in Iran, Frank Cogan, was doing his best to make the airport staff send out a stairway. Now and then, I waved to the authorities like the late British Queen Mother and, at last, the ambassador managed to persuade someone that, despite my odd outfit, I was not a threat to anyone, and the steps arrived. My gratitude to Frank Cogan and his wife Pauline, not to mention my admiration for their professionalism and ingenuity, was to grow during my time in Iran.

The Iranian officials insisted on driving me to the Irish embassy, where I was to stay while in Tehran. On the way there, as dawn was breaking, they took me to see a fast-food joint called The Bobby Sands Take-Away. This bizarre memorial to the first of the IRA hunger-strikers to die in 1981, erected so far away from Ireland, made me very sad, but my hosts clearly felt I would be pleased to see the way they had honoured him. Some time later, I discovered that the road on which the British embassy was situated had been renamed Bobby Sands Boulevard.

The Irish embassy was lovely and the Cogans were very hospitable. Sean Finn of the United Nations was there too, and after a few hours sleep, I went to visit the relevant ministries to obtain the documentation I needed to leave the city and travel to the mountains in the west, where I would check that the Red Cross supplies had arrived safely.

All the women in Iran, in offices and on streets, wore chadors or long coats and headscarves. The weather was delightful – just the day for a light summer dress – and there I was, trussed up like a turkey ready for the oven. An unexpected problem arose – I found it difficult to think in a headscarf, especially indoors, and thinking was essential with these officials, whose favourite word was 'no'.

Eventually I managed to sort out my travel papers, was detailed a pleasant driver who would also act as interpreter, and off I went to the airport to see how the unloading of the plane had progressed. All had been safely put onto lorries, which had left for the refugee camps. And it was then that I first met the man from the Dutch Red Cross who was looking for a field hospital. Our paths were to cross many times over the forthcoming week.

That night, I met some of the diplomats who had remained in Tehran. The Irish embassy was taking care of people from many different countries, as their own diplomats had already left. We had a meal together, which was both exotic and elegant, right down to the nets of spun sugar that balanced precariously, like delicate spiders' webs, on top of each individual pudding.

At five the next morning, I set off with my driver and all my papers. Iran is beautiful – a country of pale greens and yellows, and in the soft dawn light it looked magical. On the way out of the city, I asked the driver why so many large buildings stood unfinished and he told me that they had been like that for many years, ever since the Shah's time.

Once we left the city, there was very little traffic on the roads – bicycles and donkeys were the favoured modes of transport. I remembered reading Dervla Murphy's book about cycling across Iran and was glad I was cruising along in a Peugeot 504. It was a fascinating trip, if a little bumpy, and my eyes were glued to the windows as we passed through the stunning Iranian countryside. Frequent roadblocks and paper checks punctuated the journey, and, many hours later, we reached the province of Kermanshah. And here the real trouble began.

I spent hours with the officials, beseeching them to stamp my papers and allow me to travel onwards. I knew that Frank Cogan couldn't help me. He had had to go back to Ireland with an Iranian minister. But his wife was still in the country. I mentioned her name and there was an immediate, spirited jump to attention, which took me completely by surprise. She was obviously a woman of influence, and the officials stamped my papers without further delay.

I thought my problems were over, but then my driver decided that his feet were sore because his shoes hurt him and he couldn't possibly drive on without new ones. I gritted my teeth and said nothing. Grim-faced, I took him to the local bazaar and bought him a new pair.

I think he was anxious about our safety, as we were now heading towards an area not totally under government control. We were about four hours behind schedule and darkness was falling – not the best time to be driving on the winding mountain roads. In a way, maybe I was better off not seeing where we were going – several days later, in bright daylight, I suffered an attack of vertigo just looking at the precariously steep roads we had been on.

We were met with more roadblocks and paper inspections but eventually we reached a small town, where we spent the night. And once again I met the Dutchman, still in search of his field hospital. I told him I'd seen an operating table in an office in Kermanshah, and he wasn't amused.

The following morning, we set off again before dawn, driving up into the mountains. As we climbed higher and higher, the sun began to break and I saw the refugee camps in the distance. Here, a new and different-looking group of men stood at a roadblock – the men who controlled this area. They said we could not proceed, despite the fact that I had produced all my papers – from the UN, from the Red Cross and Crescent, from the Irish government, from the governor of the last province. Had I no other form of identification, they asked? Personal identification. I was a woman travelling alone, after all.

I was livid. I was so near the refugee camp and yet so far. What could I do? Then I had a brainwave. I wondered if my credit card would cut any ice. All my travel documents were in the name of Mary Henry, but my Visa card was in my married name. I produced it with some ceremony and showed it to the men. I explained that in my professional life, I travelled under my maiden name but that the card, in my married name, had been given to me by my husband, who expected all men to honour me in his name and all the banks to give me money in his name – no more than the truth. Without this, I told them, I could go nowhere.

Well, talk about an improved atmosphere! They could see at once that I was a right-thinking sort of woman, with proper respect for my husband. 'Go on, madam,' they said immediately. I bowed my head humbly and we drove on.

We travelled up the mountain road until we met a group of Red Crescent workers, sitting at the verge, fingering their worry beads. It transpired that the workers were afraid to go up to the camp because the refugees were stoning them with the bread they had been given.

'Surely the bread can't hurt you,' I said.

'The bread's in tins,' they explained.

This was an unexpected complication. There was a date on the tins containing the bread, which the refugees thought was a sell-by date, and they were angry that they were being given food past its best. I found that the tins had originated in Italy and that the word *fabrique* preceded the date. My Italian ran to knowing this meant 'made', which put a better complexion on the situation. We opened a tin and headed up to the camp to explain, with me enthusiastically eating the bread.

About eighty per cent of the refugees were women and children, as is always the case. The men leave to fight; the women and children flee to safety. These refugees were Kurds, mainly from Arbil in northern Iraq. The women were wearing the lightest of clothes, rather like evening dress, certainly not appropriate for mountaineering.

We studied the supplies that had arrived in the camp and there, to my delight, were all the boxes and bags from the Irish Red Cross. Some enthusiastic young medical students were in charge of the drugs and they were pleased with what we had sent, apart from the nit preparations. Apparently head lice aren't a problem in that part of the world.

During my time at the camp, several well-dressed men approached me and offered me money to get them or some of the women and children out of the camp. Obviously I couldn't help them. The local workers told me that the people had expected President George Bush, mark one, to come to their aid – after all, he had asked them to rise up against Saddam Hussein. But, instead, Saddam's army arrived and they had to flee. Some of the locals tried to supplement the refugees' diets by selling them their produce – tomatoes, for example, seemed to be especially plentiful. Others had made stews with chickpeas, and the samples I tasted were delicious. There was an air of the travelling market about the place. In view of the problems with ethnic minorities that the Iranians were having at that time, I feel they have never been given enough credit for their help to the refugees, some of whom are still there twelve years later.

I remember little of the journey back to Tehran. I was suffering from exhaustion – less than five hours' sleep a night had taken its toll. But at least I had been well fed and many of those who provided the food were reluctant to take payment. Yoghurt, tomatoes, nan-style bread, tea and more tea were generously provided.

I returned to Ireland on a regular commercial flight, via Istanbul and Frankfurt. I embarked in Tehran, along with many women in chadors, and slept for most of the trip. When I changed planes in Frankfurt, not one woman was still wearing her chador – they were now all in elegant clothes, high heels, red, painted nails and full make-up. And I was still in my modest outfit. Indeed, I had become so used to my headscarf that it was still in place.

How sad that, as I write, more refugees have had to flee across the mountains, following the invasion and occupation of Iraq by the troops of President George Bush, mark two.

# CLARE DOWLING

## MIAMI VICE

He wore a jacket like Don Johnson's. He laid one elbow on our table, flicked back a whole load of hair and leaned over in a cloud of Brut.

'How are youse doing, girls?'

We stifled giggles. 'Very well, thank you. Very well.'

He looked from Viv to me, then back to Viv again. 'Haven't seen you in here before.'

'That's probably because we haven't been here before,' Viv answered cheekily.

She added, 'We're on holiday.'

'You're on holiday?'

'That's right.' Viv tossed back her head airily. 'We just said to ourselves last week, we'd really fancy a couple of days up in Dublin – didn't we, Clare?'

I just nodded.

Don Johnson looked at us suspiciously. 'In January? Are you taking the piss out of me?'

'Not at all. We wanted to catch the sales.' We both choked back laughter again.

It was touch and go for a minute, then Don Johnson decided to play along. 'Seeing as you're on holiday then, can I buy youse a drink?'

We looked down at our glasses. Nothing left but some watery froth from the bottle of Stag we'd split between us, and only the price of the bus fare back in our purses. But still, to accept a drink?

'Yes, please,' Viv said boldly.

He looked at me now, recognising a novice when he saw one.

'And what about you?'

'I ...'

'You're very quiet.'

Both he and Viv were looking at me now. I bluffed something about it being the quiet ones you had to watch. He laughed. Viv smiled graciously. I felt like I had passed some kind of test.

'Two bottles of Stag, then,' he said.

'Make mine with ice,' Viv told him.

Don Johnson skewered her with a look. 'Need cooling down, yeah?'

Cooling down! I nearly exploded again.

But Viv said, 'Maybe.'

Don Johnson lifted himself off the table. 'Don't go away, girls.' He swaggered off to the bar.

Viv turned on me. 'What were you sniggering like that for?'

'What?' I was stung. 'I didn't realise you *fancied* him.'

She readjusted her cleavage. 'I don't fancy him. He's ancient for starters. I just don't want him thinking we're a couple of silly schoolgirls, that's all.'

We were schoolgirls. We were sixteen. But then Viv looked about twenty in her mini-skirt and heavy make-up. I was wearing a leopard-print top that was low cut and scratchy. It had made a big dent in my post-office savings book, but Viv had said it looked terrific on me in the shop. Viv knew about fashion. She knew lots of things, like how to light a match on the backside of her jeans, and how to sneak in and out of the emergency exit at the hostel without alerting every nun in the place.

She fired up a fresh cigarette now and waved it about with great style. 'Want one?' she asked.

'Actually, I ... yes, please.'

'If you're going to keep scabbing fags off me, then you'd want to start buying your own.'

We sat there swinging our legs and puffing away, trying to ignore the looks we were getting from Don Johnson at the bar. He was surrounded by a group of his mates, all of whom were dressed like extras from *Miami Vice*. There was a buzz of excitement about them now. We were the cause of it.

'Don't gawk, for God's sake,' Viv said, with a little sigh.

Viv knew about men too. She'd had about seven boyfriends to date if you were to believe her. But Cork apparently was teeming with gorgeous fellas, all of them with cars and big wads of money to spend on girls like Viv. There were no such fellas in rural Kilkenny, or at least none that I'd met. My first kiss had been with a guy with no front teeth, called Fish. Viv had laughed so hard at this misplaced confession that I'd had to hurriedly invent a couple of ex-boyfriends with jobs and cars.

It was obvious from her tone of voice now that she hadn't believed me. 'And for God's sake, don't go on about theorems or anything when he comes back with the drinks, okay?' she said bossily. 'Or Henry the Eighth and his six fecking wives.'

'I wasn't going to!'

'As far as he's concerned, we're on holiday, all right?'

Her superior tone was starting to bug me a bit. 'But we're not on holiday,' I said.

She stubbed out her cigarette and reached for a fresh one. '*I* am.'

Viv's attitude to the Pre-Leaving Certificate Intensive Course in Leeson Street had never been in any doubt. 'It's a load of shite,' she'd declared that very first day, as we'd set out for the college from our hostel, school books under our arms. Scandalised but trying not to show it, I'd said, 'But the exams ... are you not worried?'

Everyone knew that if you didn't do well at the Leaving Cert, then you didn't get the right course in college, and so your qualification was more or less worthless and you would end up selling chips from a van on the side of the road and become an alcoholic who would die at an early age from some terrible disease that could easily have been avoided had you got that B in geography.

I felt the weight of pressure on me that cold first week in January 1985. At considerable expense to my parents, and with great expectation and hope on their part, I had been sent all the way up to Dublin to do a crash course in history and mathematics, my weakest subjects. The nuns would take me in, feed me shepherd's pie and ensure that I studied my books and didn't die of homesickness. I would return home six days later with a head bursting full of knowledge, do a very successful Leaving Certificate exam, and go on to live happily ever after.

That had been the plan anyway, until I had met Viv.

'Let's go into town,' she'd said the second morning.

'*Town?*'

'Yeah. Go shopping or something. We'll ask one of the others to save us the notes. It's all photocopied stuff anyway; that's what you're paying for.' She saw my reluctance. 'Unless you *want* to join the swots?'

Suddenly it became a bigger choice: to be cool and grown-up in the big city, or to bend childishly over my books. I felt the first stirrings of rebellion deep in my pious, swotty soul.

Viv must have seen this. 'It's the Christmas holidays, for God's sake,' she'd added.

And all around us, there was a great air of gaiety. The city was still coming down with decorations and lights and Christmas trees. People walked along with a spring in their step. The pubs in town were heaving at all times of the day and night.

Viv was right: we *should* be part of it. We were sixteen and had never spent a week away from our parents. It didn't matter that it was only Dublin in January; suddenly we had the same heady sense of freedom, of daring and adventure, as if we were on a beach in Majorca.

We went into town that day. And the following day too. Guilt made me attend the odd lecture now and then, but the exams seemed less and less important as we window-shopped and walked up and down Grafton Street and sat for hours in Bewley's over coffee and girls' magazines. Viv pointed out to me the proper way to put on make-up; apparently my main fault was not applying enough. She took me shopping too, and I bought a mini-skirt, and a black lace top à la Madonna, even though it was hard to know when I'd wear them at home.

'Let's go out to a pub or something, will we?' Viv said one mid-week night. 'I'm dying for a drink,' she added dramatically.

For all my new-found sophistication, I was a coward at heart. 'The nuns would murder us if they found out.'

'How will they? It's not as if we're going to *tell* them.'

In the end, we decided we'd only go for an hour, just in case the nuns suddenly took a notion to do a head count at bedtime or something.

They didn't. And the next night we ventured further: into the city centre, where we had two bottles of Stag each, and we had to sprint for our last bus back, giggling and tipsy.

Tonight was our last night in Dublin. Perhaps that was why Viv had pushed the boat out with her choice of pub: it was very glitzy and smoky, and the people seemed very loud. I wasn't sure I liked it. But I didn't say anything; there was no point in underlining yet again what a country hick I was.

'Now, girls.' Don Johnson was back with the two bottles of Stag. He jerked a thumb over his shoulder. 'By the way, this is Mick.'

Mick wore a pastel jacket too, rolled up to the elbows. He had dark hair, and chewed a piece of gum.

'Hi,' he said, looking very bored.

'Do you fancy him?' Viv whispered after a bit.

I didn't really. But it was obvious that Viv and Don Johnson were getting quite pally, so I agreed that Mick was gorgeous.

We spent the rest of the evening with Don Johnson and Mick. They turned out to be a good laugh. And quite okay-looking too, Viv and I agreed in the loo, if you saw past the jackets and the big hair. There was still the matter of them being quite a bit older than us, but Viv said there was nothing worse than an immature man. Oh, nothing, I concurred.

'Don Johnson wants us to go to a party with him,' Viv announced, leaning into the mirror over the sink. He'd told us his real name but neither of us could remember it.

I asked where the party was.

'Some house somewhere. He says it's going to be great fun. Free drink and everything.'

'You go.' I was feeling the effects of three bottles of Stag. And I wanted to be up in time to catch the last lecture in the morning – I couldn't face my parents off the train otherwise.

Viv ringed her mouth with bright red lipstick and put the top back on a bit crossly. 'I can't go without you.'

'Can you not?'

'Of course I can't!' She added, casually, 'Mick's really into you.'

'Is he?' He had started to look more attractive as the night had worn on.

'He told Don.' She handed me the lipstick. 'Here, better put on some of this.'

Mick was delighted I was going to the party. He didn't look bored any more. He held my coat out for me, and bought four more bottles of Stag at the bar to take away, and a six-pack for himself, and we all tumbled out into the cold January night.

'It's snowing!' Viv squealed, pointing at the ground.

'Don't be stupid. That's pigeon shit,' Don said, and the pair of them fell around laughing.

Mick shook his head at me, as though such childish jokes were beneath the two of us, and I felt quite grown-up. He hailed a taxi. He really was very purposeful – not like Don Johnson, who was draped drunkenly over Viv and tripping over himself. Mick gave the driver directions to an address in west Dublin, and squeezed in beside me in the back seat.

The house where the taxi dropped us was in darkness.

'Where's the party?' I asked.

'We're the party,' Don said. He must have thought I looked disappointed, because he said, 'Lighten up, for God's sake. We'll stick on a bit of music and have a dance – will that do you?'

He opened the front door with his own key. Viv gave me a look as though I were spoiling all the fun. I followed her into the house.

And Don did put on music, and we opened more beers, and in no time at all, Viv and I were dancing around our handbags to Duran Duran, best friends again. Then Mick and Don produced two guitars and began to compete with the stereo – or record player, as it was in those days.

'Mick's in a band,' Don told us.

A band! We were very impressed, even though neither Viv nor I had heard of the band when he told us the name of it. They still had to make it big, Mick assured us. Then he began to play some mushy ballad on the guitar. Viv and Don took this as their cue, and started to snog very noisily on the sofa beside me. Then Mick threw away his guitar, jumped on me, and we began to snog too.

During a minor interval in all the snogging, Viv threw a look over her shoulder at me, as though to say, Isn't this great? I nodded back enthusiastically, even though I didn't think it was all *that* great. I had hardly any experience in the sexual department, but I knew instinctively that Mick wasn't a great kisser. It was all a bit wet and sloppy and at the next available opportunity I excused myself and found the loo.

All my red lipstick had worn off. I didn't much care. I was very tired now, and drunk, and I wanted my hard little single bed in the hostel dormitory. I wondered whether Viv might be ready to leave. I hadn't a clue how we were going to get home, but we'd manage.

When I got back, Mick was arranging the sofa cushions neatly on the floor.

'Where's Viv?' I asked.

'Gone to bed.'

I thought he was joking. Then I looked around.

'Where's Don?'

'Gone to bed.'

Even I couldn't miss the implications of that. I stood there feeling stupidly surprised and utterly abandoned by Viv. Somehow, deep down, I believed that she was a bluffer just like me. I hadn't realised that she would actually go *through* with things. But, then again, hadn't I given her the impression that I would?

'We'll sleep down here,' Mick said.

He was covering the cushions with a blanket.

I stood there, nodding and smiling, my prudish, shocked little brain wondering what he meant: did 'we' mean the two of us together, but not actually 'together'? Did 'sleep' mean sleep, or did it really mean wild, unprotected sex that would lead to pregnancy and possible VD and those feelings of worthlessness that the girls' magazines of the day warned could happen if you weren't ready for it and didn't do it with the right man? *More* questions: was I 'ready for it'? Was Mick the 'right man'?

The answer was a swift no in both cases.

Maybe I should have said something then; that I wanted to go home or something. But there I was, in a strange house, in a strange city, wearing very few clothes. My new best friend had disappeared. It was pitch black outside and I had forty-five pence in my purse. Worst of all, I had given the come-on to a man I didn't know from Adam, and who I instinctively knew wouldn't take that kindly to a bald rebuttal and a request for a taxi fare.

'I'll just go to the jacks,' he said.

I was left looking at the makeshift bed. I took off my shoes, but on second thoughts put them back on again. I lay down on the cushions and pulled the blanket up to my chin. I shut my eyes tight.

The toilet flushed down the hall. Then I heard him coming back in. The light snapped off. There was a rustle of clothing, followed by the sound of him unzipping his boots. More clothes were discarded. Then I felt the blanket lift up and he got in beside me.

I lay very still, trying to breathe in and out very evenly and deeply, hoping that he would think I had conked out due to a surplus of Stag. Whether he did or not, he wasn't going to let it stop him. I felt hands on me; he was groping me and trying to turn me over.

'Mick, I'm feeling a bit tired,' I said. I made some little joke about having had too much to drink.

'Come on,' he said. He wasn't going for it.

'I'm tired,' I said again, more insistently.

'Oh, for God's sake,' he said, and kind of flung me away.

There was a very long, dangerous moment. I could feel him looking down at me in the dark; I could smell the alcohol and cigarettes off him, and the sense of being cheated. I didn't know what was going to happen. I didn't know what I would do if it *did* happen. Maybe Viv would come and rescue me if I called for her loudly enough. But maybe she wouldn't. We didn't owe each other anything, by the looks of things.

Then the blanket was thrown back and he got up. I heard him grabbing his clothes. He muttered something under his breath – prick-tease, or a variation on it. Then the living-room door slammed shut behind him. I don't know where he went after that – home, maybe, or upstairs. I never saw him again, even though I stayed awake most of the night afraid that I would.

I woke the next morning with a vicious hangover. So did Viv, judging by her pale face and sullen silence as she came in looking for her shoes and bag. We kind of lingered for a bit, but Don Johnson never appeared to say goodbye to her. I thought that maybe she was disappointed, but I didn't ask her. And she didn't ask me about Mick.

Eventually we left the house and found the nearest bus stop. It would be a desperate rush back to the hostel to pack our bags and then on to catch our midday trains: hers to Cork, and mine to Kilkenny.

We eventually caught a double-decker bus into town, and lied about the fare. We sat near the front in our soiled party clothes, Viv and I, and after all the chatter and laughter of the week, we didn't seem to have a word to say to each other.

# MARY RUSSELL

# ON THE STREETS OF BAGHDAD

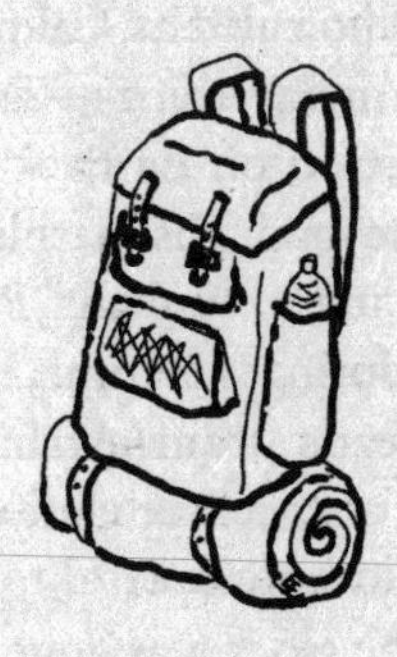

*Iraq and its brutal dictator, Saddam Hussein, became a focus of world attention when the US targeted them in the war on terrorism. While the regime has been accused of manipulating the Oil For Food Programme to fund the military, in October 2001 Mary Russell found the people of Baghdad blaming the West for their suffering.*

At 2 a.m., the border-crossing between Syria and Iraq is stark: big brutes of lights, trucks with their engines running. In the customs shed, my palmtop computer and camera are examined carefully, though it's the mobile phone that gives me most grief. I should have left it behind in Damascus but word had reached me that there was a shared taxi leaving right away and, fearful of missing it, I had thrown everything into a bag, paid the Syrian middleman sixty US dollars and set off on the 800-kilometre journey to Baghdad.

The phone is wrapped and sealed, leaving only the matter of the compulsory AIDS test: fifty dollars to have it, sixty dollars not to have it. And the baksheesh. One dollar here, ten there. Tip generously, I'd been told; their wages are abysmally low.

After two and a half hours, we're away, speeding along a smooth, six-lane highway towards a brilliant sun rising over the vast scrub that is the Iraqi desert. And then Baghdad, city of Alif Layla wa Layla – the Thousand and One Nights – and of Haroun al Rashid, who ruled as Caliph in 786.

They called Haroun many things – including Peacock of the World, Shadow of God on Earth – for he was the man who put Baghdad on the map. His marble palace shone white in the moonlight, pink in the sunlight. People he didn't like, he locked up – but during his time, the city prospered. Merchants brought pearls from Arabia, gold dust from Africa, slaves from Turkestan. Baghdad was the greatest city between China and Constantinople.

By 1258, however, the glory was gone – the city sacked by the Mongols. Two hundred years later, Tamerlaine struck. Fast forward to 1921 and Faisal, the Saudi prince – promised Damascus by the colonial powers, but shifted to Baghdad – is on the throne, ruling over a country in which Britain has a huge stake.

Independence erupts and is followed by the boom years with oil the new gold. In the 1970s, there's massive investment in health and education but the eight-year war (1980–88) with Iran – a war between a secular Arab country and an Islamist one, in which Iraq was supported by the US, the UK and the Gulf States – drains the coffers. In 1990, owing twelve billion US dollars to the Kuwaitis and disputing their common border, drawn up by the European colonial powers, Saddam Hussein launches his invasion, an ill-judged action for which the people of Iraq are now paying dearly.

Dr A.K. Al Hashimi, former Iraqi ambassador to Paris, is a small man, expansive and ebullient. Iraq's troubles are a result, according to him, not of Saddam Hussein's dictatorial regime, but solely to the UN sanctions. 'Kuwait,' he says, offering me a cup of coffee in his office in Baghdad, 'has nothing to do with all this. The UN – and that means the US and the UK – simply wants to control us. We were the second biggest oil producing country; now we are allowed to produce only what the UN says. Everyone wants to trade and we will do business with anyone – except Israel, of course. But New York is sitting on the contracts. The largest number of contracts being held up are for drilling equipment, because, they say, the parts have dual use. But what doesn't? With your pen, you can write a love poem – or an equation for a nuclear weapon.'

He is in full flood, figures at his fingertips, passion fuelling his arguments: 'The UN wants us to be a democracy.' He shakes his head in disbelief: 'Like America, with only two parties? People making holes in a bit of paper? Look at us. Are we a police state? Are you stopped by police everywhere you go? No. The sanctions are about collective punishment. We crossed a barrier, a red line, and that's not allowed.'

Not only has a terrible hole been made in the Iraqi economy but the people's pride has been wounded, leaving many of them, mainly the wealthy middle-class, angry and bitter. The poor, on the other hand, are simply worried to death.

Next day, however, driving out along the highway to see the ancient ruins of Babylon, there are seven checkpoints to negotiate; residents of Baghdad cannot leave the city without the correct papers. Access to the Internet is through the government.

Saddam, who has many fine residences, though no one knows which one he occupies at any one moment, is rarely seen in public and when he is, his armed aides scan the surrounding area with binoculars.

But there are portraits everywhere of the Great Leader: Saddam suave in a suit, oriental in Arab dress, courageous in army fatigues.

Driving over the bridge known as Leader Bridge, I ask the taxi-driver: 'Which leader?'

'There is only one leader,' he replies wearily.

Meanwhile, the buses run (red double-deckers, bodies made in China, engines in Germany), there are traffic snarl-ups, people go to work and children to school. But look closer at the traffic. Among the battered cars and taxis – scratches and dents patched over, door-handles missing, windscreens cracked – there are some very smart cars indeed, including Toyota Coasters and sleek, curtained Mercedes.

There's money about. You can see it in the palatial homes and in the opulent mosques being built. Building a mosque is a smart move for a businessman, guaranteeing his next development will go ahead tax-free. Saddam likes to keep both the military and the moneyed classes on-side. On the old racecourse, ten tall cranes mark the spot where the biggest mosque in the world is being erected – funded by the government.

One evening, I meet Mazeem Sahib, political editor of the government-sponsored *Al Juhumuriya*. 'Before the sanctions,' he says, 'there were people who disliked Saddam but not now. Since the bombing and the sanctions started, Iraqis have rallied behind him.'

'Before the sanctions' is a mantra I hear so often that I write it in shorthand: B4. Before the sanctions, there was free school-milk. Before the sanctions, Iraqis pursued their studies abroad, travelled to Europe, took two holidays a year. Before the sanctions, you could buy a large car for three thousand dinars. Now, all you'll get is a bunch of plastic flowers. When I changed ten dollars, I was handed a wad of notes thicker than a 300-page book.

The average monthly wage of a government employee is two thousand dinar, and people, desperate for more, subsidise this as best they can. Waiting to go into the press centre – housed in the same building as the Ministry of

Information – I watch money change hands as people seek to make appointments with government officials.

Driving to the Saddam Central Children's Hospital, we pass a crowd of men milling about outside the Libyan Embassy. A demonstration, I ask? No, they're queuing for visas. Once in Libya, they can earn money to send back home. Anti-US demonstrations are more orderly, I'm told, because they are organised by the ruling Ba'ath Party.

At the hospital, I meet Dr Ehab Raad. He is short, rotund, curly-headed and when he laughs, his whole body shakes with delight. In Haroun's time, he'd be reclining on a silk-covered divan, sipping wine, being fed grapes by a beautiful dancing girl. But this is Saddam's time and Dr Raad has the task of caring as best he can for the many children suffering from exposure to depleted uranium.

'We're short of everything, even the paper on which to write our prescriptions. It is a crime.' He lays his hand on the hairless head of a small, emaciated child. 'Some of these children are in remission. When they go into remission for the third time, we stop the chemotherapy.' Postponing death is costly. The supply of hospital medicine is limited and when it runs out, parents must buy it privately – if they can. One village mother from the south sold her washing bowl to help to raise the cash.

Dr Raad spent his childhood in Dublin. His mother worked as a doctor in the Rotunda and his father in St Vincent's Hospital. 'Tell me, how is Ireland? Gay Byrne, is he still there? I went to school in Saint Benilda's in Kilmacud and I loved it. I love Irish people.'

I don't have the heart to tell him that the Irish Government supported the bombing campaign on Afghanistan. Iraqis, after all, expect to be next on the list.

Dr Raad shows me a collection of drawings done by children on his ward. 'I get them to draw pictures so that when they die, their parents will have something to remember them by.' When they die, not if . . .

On 13 February 1991, 394 people died in the Al Amiriyah shelter in Baghdad constructed during the Iran/Iraq war. At 4 a.m., a two-ton laser missile, fired from a US F117A Stealth bomber, burst through the reinforced concrete roof and plunged into the people sleeping in the shelter before blasting its way to the floor below. A second bomb neatly targeted the ventilation system, closing off the air supply so that the temperature inside reached four hundred degrees. The guide points out the shape of a hand here, a foot there, the flesh seared into the concrete. A baby, born at midnight, was dead four hours later, and next day issued with a death instead of a birth certificate. 'This is the result of American terrorism,' she says.

The US accused Saddam of using people as a human shield, saying the shelter was really a command post.

'What was the floor below used for?' I ask the guide.

'A hospital, in case anyone in the shelter needed a doctor,' she replies.

But when I ask can I go down to verify this, she says no, she can't take me down because there are no lights. It is likely that, in fact, the shelter did double as a command centre, though no one told the local people, so what they thought was a place of safety turned into a deadly incinerator.

The courtyards of the golden-domed mosques are packed with devout Shia women, shrouded in black, picnicking with their children. The Iran-backed Shia – seen as a threat by the Ba'ath Party – live in Saddam City, a huge, working-class complex on the edge of Baghdad where they keep their heads down and concentrate on survival, for the canopied gardens, the sweeping staircases, the pillared mansions of the well-to-do are as remote to the poor of Baghdad as is their seldom-seen leader.

I ask another taxi-driver if the people of Saddam City suffered much in the bombing.

'The people there suffer from everything,' he says. He is a Christian and many members of his family have already emigrated to the US. Although he doesn't say so, he clearly dislikes the controlling influences of Islam, the fact that Christians are not always welcome in the mosques, the pervasive five-times-a-day call to prayer. As soon as his family sends the money, he will take his wife and children to the US.

One day, I take a walk through the old souk, its collapsing balconies and decaying pillared walkways a reminder of the Ottoman occupation. The UN has devised a monthly ration of food that people can buy for two hundred and fifty dinars and which provides them with 1,800 calories per day. There is no meat, fruit or vegetables in this diet. In the souk, however, the stalls overflow with fresh fruit and vegetables. Since the sanctions, Iraqis have returned to growing their own food, and if you have the money, you can buy it. Other stalls are stacked with cheap plastic goods, mostly from China. There have been protests about this. Under the Oil for Food Programme (OFFP), the Chinese have been importing Iraqi oil and exporting goods in return. Not a fair exchange. But Dr Hashimi is right: everyone wants to trade with Iraq, especially the Russians who are owed fifteen billion US dollars.

Sixty countries are represented in Baghdad. Some can't afford an embassy of their own while others prefer not to be too visible, so diplomacy comes into play with the Algerian embassy hosting the Syrians and the Indian embassy, until last year, hosting Egypt.

Under the OFFP, carefully orchestrated in New York, China has been awarded the contract to provide mobile phones, France will provide land-lines, and India will continue to sell rice and wheat. But there is also the Free Trade Agreement whereby countries make their own bilateral arrangements. Syria, Jordan, Tunisia and Egypt fall into this category.

Then there are even more informal arrangements. Turkestan buys Iraqi oil but sells it on, clandestinely, to Turkey, while a number of countries from the former Communist bloc sell their rusty, old weaponry left over from the Soviet era.

But to trade and to rehabilitate itself, Iraq needs hard currency and that can be earned only by selling more oil, which the UN Sanctions Committee controls. It's a no-win situation.

The country, however, is not without friends. India is one of them, lauded because its embassy remained open through the worst of the bombing. The British Labour MP for Glasgow Kelvin, George Galloway, is another. His London double-decker bus, emblazoned with its 'No sanctions' banner, stands like an icon of hope in the gardens of Mustansiriya, the Arab university that pre-dates Oxford. NGOs such as Voices in the Wilderness – an organisation supported by the former UN humanitarian aid co-ordinator in Iraq, Denis Halliday – work tirelessly to keep the issue in the public eye. And UNICEF is there, doing its best under fearful conditions, not least a budget shortfall of forty-five per cent.

After eleven years of sanctions, however, Iraqis are bemused. How can it be, they ask, that they are being punished – in the name of democracy – when Israel's bombing and illegal incursions into Palestinian land continue unchecked; when the military regime in Pakistan is now being courted by the US; when Syria, home to at least three militarily active political parties – a.k.a. terrorists – is not being bombed into submission as Iraq now may be?

'The US would like us to have a new leader,' says Dr Hashimi. 'But Saddam is not running a one-man show. It's a whole system. And we can't give up anything more. If we do, we cease to exist. We must survive.'

In the Besan primary school, Baghdad, the children jump to attention when I come in, and shout out a greeting: 'All praise to our great leader, Saddam. May Allah be merciful to him. Victory to us!' Then they sit down again, three to a desk.

A little girl bursts into tears when I enter her classroom. Seeing my notebook, she thinks I'm the doctor come to give injections; some school health programmes are still in place.

The broken windows, pot-holed playground, missing doors, however, remain unmended. And I wonder about money being diverted to build the biggest mosque in the world.

The children are bright and eager, smart in their uniforms. They're learning English, fractions, the Koran. Inevitably, the little boys want to be pilots when they grow up.

Outside in the sunshine, the temperature a cool thirty-seven degrees, reminders of Baghdad's glorious past are everywhere: the remains of the old Wastani Gate that led out along the camel route to Samarkand; the statue of Abu Nawas, poet and drinking companion of Haroun; the River Tigris, flowing south to join the Euphrates. In the evening, as the sun flames across the water, ropes of coloured lights come on along the embankment and people start to gather, to talk – as Arabs love to do – and to remember what it was like before.

# ANITA NOTARO

## LIFE'S A (NUDIE) BEACH

You know the feeling: it's day one of your much-longed-for holiday and you step outside your apartment to get the all-important daylight glimpse of the three months' salary view. What's the very first thing you notice? The cerulean sky? The soothing lap of the smoothie-like frothy sea? The masses of marshmallowy bougainvillaea creeping up every snow-white wall? Afraid not. At least, not on this holiday. There was only one thing, or group of things, commanding my attention this time. Penises.

It all started when I had my seasonal conversation with myself, the same one I've had every year since I turned thirty. Could I possibly get away with one more summer wearing a bikini? Usually, the first thing I do is head for the shops for a look at the latest offerings. I always start off by being sensible and make straight for the 'sexy yet elegant' one-piece swimsuits – at least that's how one of the hottest fashion editors always describes each season's newest creations. And, of course, I regard their every word as gospel. I stopped wearing floral prints when my favourite magazine listed them in their top ten no-no's for women over thirty-five. In the last few years, they've made me so conscious of my crow's feet, sagging boobs and bleeding lips that I'll barely leave the house without wearing a burka.

What is it about one-piece swimsuits that makes them all look like the stretch covers your granny used to have on her good sofa? I tried several on. They mostly had 'discreet support', which, unfortunately, failed to contain my sinking bosoms no matter what size I tried, so that I looked like I had an extra roll of fat round my middle. Also, they all had belts, or buckles, or bows at the waist and I resembled an Easter egg. Not good. I went for cappuccino and a Danish and considered my body. This is always where it all starts to unravel for me. You see, on a good day I reckon I could be mistaken for J. Lo's older sister with a slightly more rounded bottom. On a not so good one, I'm Jo Brand having a bad-hair day. I abandoned this pointless thought process and headed for the changing rooms once more.

Tank top bikinis, a.k.a. tankinis, were beginning to appear in the shops, aimed at women like me who were permanently in crisis mode when it came to swimwear. However, whenever I see the words 'tank top', I've only one picture in my mind – Frank Spencer. They always seem like a one-piece you've grown out of and had to cut around the waist to avoid causing yourself permanent damage, thereby exposing a little wedge of milky-white, squidgy flesh. Not for me, thanks.

Bikinis were ... well, skimpy. The tops appeared to be all held together with chicken wire, and the bottoms were, frankly, dental floss. Ice-pop orange and lurid lime green were the most muted colours I could find, so as it was almost lunch-time, I retreated for fish and chips and started to imagine what it would be like not to have to bother with any of this. To have the courage to go topless – and bottomless. No strap marks, no sagging, waterlogged behind as you emerge from the pool, no trying to read and hold your top in place at the same time. To be a confident, liberated, sexy, voluptuous woman in her prime. The idea of a naturist holiday was born. It seemed so bohemian, so daring and soooo scary.

The two friends I called to discuss 'casually' the idea had to receive medical attention. One choked on her chicken tikka wrap and the other laughed so hysterically that she was taken off the DART and confined to bed for months with the straps firmly tightened. I abandoned the ludicrous notion, bought the most sensible black bikini I could find, and joined a spinning class with a week to go.

But the mad idea never really went away, and eventually I did it, felt wild and crazy and brazen and fabulous, and never told a soul.

That was the end of it until I was asked to write about an unusual travel experience. I was going to tell you about the ice-blue splendour of the Canadian Rockies, or the dramatic, unspoilt beauty of Zanzibar, or the night I spent in Dracula's castle in Transylvania, but I guess I secretly wanted to be grown-up enough to admit to having had a very unique holiday experience (and stop those bitches – who at dinner parties still recall that famous phone call – from giggling at my expense).

It all seemed such a good idea when I visited the website, safely tucked up in my pink, flowery, flannelette pyjamas. Hundreds of bronzed torsos, all having fun with their arms folded, or the table tennis bat positioned precisely at crotch level, in order to discourage the perverts. Masses of tanned limbs and carefully tousled hair and Julia Roberts smiles, each one inviting you to enjoy 'the ultimate freedom', make a 'lifestyle choice' and experience the *joie de vivre* that apparently comes only with taking your clothes off in the open air. I was determined to try it out, purely in the interests of research, you understand. I wasn't researching anything at the time, but felt sure it would greatly assist me in later life, make me a more rounded person, encourage me to give alms to the poor. You know the sort of thing – any excuse, basically, to justify doing something you're secretly not sure is such a good idea at all. Well, to cut a short story short, I did it and never for one moment thought I'd be sharing it with the world.

Problem number one was finding someone to go with. You've no idea how many of my friends were washing their hair, or starting an embroidery class on the first day of my holiday. I almost gave up but, eventually, I bribed someone and I'm still paying for it – another reason to come clean. I can't stand the hold he still has over me!

At least it was dark when we arrived at the huge complex. Palm trees swayed in the gentle breeze of a balmy, tropical summer evening. The air was heavy with the scent of oleander. It all looked so ... normal. The good-looking guy at reception was polite and friendly and never leered at me once, unfortunately. When they buzzed us in past the main reception and we heard a sharp click as the door locked behind us, it finally sunk in where we were. Suddenly I wanted my mother.

Our apartment looked ordinary enough, cool and spacious and pleasantly, if sparsely, furnished. It took me a while to notice that there wasn't a door anywhere once you got inside. Not even into the bathroom. I decided not to panic completely by thinking about that one. I needed a drink and so, apparently, did my accomplice.

'Fancy a pint?'

'No, at least, yes, of course, but do we have to go out? I mean, wouldn't it be nice to just stay in and unwind?'

'But it's nine o'clock on a Saturday night and, besides, we don't have anything to drink.'

'We have that bottle of black rum that you bought in duty free. That could be delicious with ice and, em, tap water.'

He grabbed my hand and the rest of me was still attached to the bedpost when I realised that he was heading off with all his clothes on.

'Oh, I see, you mean *out*. Like *this*. You don't want me to change or anything? Fine. Let's go.' I was out the only door in a flash.

'I hardly think they'll be naked in the bar,' he told my retreating ass. Obviously, he'd done a bit more research than I had.

The bar in the complex was the first major surprise. It was, well, ordinary. The barman was wearing a dicky bow, if you'll pardon the pun. The band was lousy, but fully clothed. And the men and women could have been my relations. In fact, think wedding. Country wedding. Irish country wedding. Perms. Strappy dresses. Handbags. And the Macarena.

Before I could catch my breath, the music changed and a human centipede wound its way past, a hundred legs and arms all shooting out in different directions. The torsos all had clothes on and looked relaxed and happy. Two minutes later, the music came to an abrupt halt and the train collided and carriages became derailed before everybody was back on the floor, hands on shoulders, then crossed, then on waist, hips thrusting like copulating mongrels. I gave in and abandoned all thoughts of my ultra-cool CD collection, my passion for The White Stripes and Ms Dynamite lost in a gush of the Birdie Song. A large jug of sangria and four beers helped enormously.

Next morning, I jumped out of bed, grabbed my sarong and followed the signs for the supermarket, passing a gym, sauna and beauty salon en route. It looked just like any other fairly exclusive development. Orange juice and croissants were my main preoccupation, so it took me a second or two to focus properly, ten to realise that I was hung over, and the longest thirty seconds of my life to come to terms with the fact that everyone was shopping in their birthday suits, bags for life being the only accessory evident. Have you ever tried to buy breakfast while a handsome stranger beside you climbed a ladder, naked, in order to reach the cornflakes, or a pair of voluptuous breasts opposite weighed up some fruit and tested plums for ripeness? Trust me, it's mortifying, but I was the only one in pain. Everyone else simply strolled about happily. I grabbed a baguette and make a quick getaway.

By four thirty that day, I could no longer plead that 'the sun's too strong for me'. I'd no other option but to leave the ninety-six-degree apartment. Clutching my sarong defiantly – just in case – and wearing high heels, a hat and a humungous pair of D & G glasses, I felt it to be a defining moment in my life. Somehow I managed to get to the sunbed with my head focused firmly on the growing ant population and my bouncing white whatsits largely hidden by my chins. Lying down had never seemed so inviting, and there was no way I was moving – to hell with the sun cream and my now pinkish virginal white bits.

Two hours later, I plucked up the courage to open one eye and survey the fabulous pool area. A penis was showering to my right. To my left, a breast sat up to lick her ice-cream cone, and directly in front of me, the rear of a very large hairy bottom was diving into the pool. I dived for cover once more but was secretly dying to have a really good look.

Penises and testicles, dicks and balls, willies, *cojones,* whatever. They were everywhere. And once you realise that you're not in any immediate danger, they, and their owners, can provide you with hours of endless fascination.

The *Bunty* equivalent of your schooldays, the *Jackie* of your spotty, teenage years, and the *Hello* magazine of your dreaded dentist visits. And for me this was much more exciting than the hottest bestseller, and the reason was simple. This was forbidden fruit; it was daring, exciting, bold. And most important, it was real life.

Eventually, sunstroke threatened to overwhelm me, so I half sat up and felt my way blindly along the towel, groping for my Factor 50. Even now, I can't bear to think what I must have looked like. I tried to feign nonchalance as I endeavoured to cover myself in a thick film of cream, struggling to reach previously unexposed parts. Suddenly, I saw myself in a contorted, not-very-attractive-even-when-dressed position, so it was back down flat on my stomach quick, and to hell with a few minor burns. Much later, and only after two ice-cold beers from a passing, strangely disinterested waiter, did I open my book – upside down, as it transpired – and sneak a proper look around.

Just as men come in all shapes and sizes, so do their privates. There were tiny little dangly things, short stubby ones and a couple that stretched almost to the knee, or so it seemed from where I was sitting. Some were smooth and even, others pink and wrinkly. And if you've ever doubted how much men love them, just watch them in action naked. They strut about. They fondle and flick and seem inordinately proud of their package. And even more surprising, most seemed relaxed and oblivious to those around them. I wasn't ogled once. I was slightly peeved.

After a quick sulk, I turned my attention to the competition, and I discovered that, for a woman especially, the way you wear nothing is key. Confidence is everything, and a bit of style, regardless of age, helps a lot. Sounds like a contradiction in terms of nudity? Well, it isn't.

I saw a fifty-something woman, with a reasonably good figure, struggle to move around in four-inch-high patent red sandals, a huge red straw hat, and a bright gold chain belt around her middle. A thirty-something, heavily pregnant woman looked serene and content. A dark-haired beauty who must have been a relation of Selma Hayek arrived shortly after me and sat down nearby. She was truly scrumptious to look at, but obviously didn't think so herself. She spent the entire time examining her skin, brushing away imaginary specks and looking around with her mouth turned firmly downwards. She sighed and pouted frequently, and her magnificent hair was heavy and just another source of irritation. Her apparently constant struggle for perfection eventually made her not so easy on the eye. For me, that first, momentous day, the most attractive female by far was a forty-something, voluptuous brunette who moved around with total confidence, completely oblivious to the rest of us, and wearing nothing but a mane of glossy dark brown hair and painted toe-nails. She oozed sexiness and a sense of being perfectly at ease in her own skin. I longed for her calm, sensuous way of moving and envied her tranquillity.

As for me, it took a while but I eventually got sort of comfortable in a don't-look-at-my-fat-bum kind of way. In spite of myself, I came to enjoy the freedom of it all, adored swimming naked and, in the end, relaxed enough to wander nonchalantly (almost) for an ice-cream. I never fully got to grips with the shopping experience. When resting, I daydreamed about sashaying to the water's edge, feeling sexy and liberated, but sadly, in reality, my self-esteem never allowed me that pleasure.

Would I do it again? Definitely. I fantasise about returning with a slim, toned, tanned body, and driving every man mad and not noticing. Meanwhile, I've got a WeightWatchers class and a trip to the gym today, followed by a facial, a manicure and a visit to the hairdresser, and all because a couple of spotty builders' bottoms are coming to my house to work tomorrow. I guess I've still got a bit of a way to go.

# KATHRYN HOLMQUIST

# WHERE THE SUN ALWAYS SHINES

The birds are the ones that really own this place. As I sit in my nightdress on the deck, writing beneath the pines, a cardinal bristles its red crest and lands inches from my laptop to investigate. It is 6 a.m., and I am in heaven. Cockle Cove Meadows, Chatham, Massachusetts. My home. This is where I want to be.

The sky is the kind of innocent, promising blue that makes you want to cry if you live in Dublin. A morning dove is crooning five jazz notes, minor key, ignoring the dissonant contrapuntal chorus of robins and sparrows. A woodpecker plays percussion. Rabbits, squirrels and chipmunks come looking for their breakfast.

Today will be hot again. The sand will burn our feet. And I will spend the day halfway between laughter and tears, knowing that this is all too good to be true. Summer never lasts. In my case, it lasts three or four weeks in the time I can afford to take away from work in Dublin.

This is my mother's house. She died here. This is where I nursed her and mourned her. The house is so infused with her that I cannot help but think that this house is my mother. An old friend once described it as a tomb, but I don't think so. We have brought our own children here, and their laughter has cleansed the place of morbid memories. Because we know that while my mother may have died here, what she really did was live here. And she is still alive in the sounds of birds, in the smells of bay, geranium and rosehip.

Yet the children have to know that up the road a way, their grandmother is buried by the seaside. They plant flowers for her, and dance disrespectfully (I'm glad to say) around the red roses adorning her grave. Roses that bloom with determination, despite the neglect of children who live in New York, Washington, Dublin.

All of this makes Cockle Cove more than a place. Cockle Cove is grandmother to my children and solace to me. Nearly half a century in my family, this house is (I sometimes think) the only solid thing I have to rely on.

Somehow I think that our friend Alex knows this as she greets us, on our first jet-lagged morning, with a plate of freshly baked blueberry muffins, hot out of the oven by 8 a.m. Alex is more than just official meeter and greeter in our little compound of cottages.

Later in the day, Alex and her husband, Jack, who restores antique sloops for a museum at Newport in his spare time, have another gift for us. Jack has built a tiny white skiff from a single plank of plywood. The boat is to be named 'Finn', my six-year-old son's name.

Hilary, Alex and Jack's daughter, has chosen the name. She's been studying at Oxford the past few years, but still comes back – just like I do. You can't help but come back. You can travel the world, but nothing else is ever good enough. Not Spain, or France or Portugal or Greece. Chatham gets in on you and takes you over. You will always want fried clams, not calamari.

Standing on the lawn by the boat in the yellow evening sun, Jack helps Finn to place the black letters on the stern: FINN. My son is chuffed and we take pictures that we'll all share later, over the Net.

This is what coming home means. It's people who have known you all your life. People who give you homecomings created of bear-hugs and home-made strawberry jam and make you feel that you never left. People who may, for a second, help with the illusion that you will never leave, even though you know you will have to.

As I sit at my laptop, my children are playing on the lawns between our houses. This is a place with no gates or fences. We have all been here forever – the Driscolls, Ryans, Kellys, Dunnes. All Irish names and faces except for ours: Holmquists.

As my children tumble down a grassy hill, Alex says to me: 'What would your mother have thought?' It is enough, for me, to keep my mother's thoughts a mystery and simply to know that this woman beside me remembers that my mother was an insightful woman. Between us, without a word, Alex and I can quietly imagine what my mother would have thought. My rangy, wild, middle daughter is just like me – that's what.

We are in the attic, my three children and I, looking for the fishing nets. There is a box: 'keepsakes', it says. Translation: special objects that remind us of our mother, who died nearly a quarter of a century ago when we were in our teens. I daren't open it. 'Why not?' asks my daughter. 'A box is nothing to be afraid of!' Sometimes it is. Sometimes a house is like a box that you open, only to feel memories spilling out. It's best to keep it taped shut.

The years I haven't come here have been the closed box years when I couldn't bear to feel all that I had lost. Now, with my own children, I've done with adventuring and I come home as often as I can. It's the same with the other mothers on the beach. All of us played together as children, and now our own children play together. We all share in common parents with the foresight to have given their grandchildren and great-grandchildren Cockle Cove summers in perpetuity. Not that it's so cut and dried.

Sometimes we feel like we're hanging on for dear life. We're adults, not children. This place brings out the children in us, but doesn't erase real life altogether.

Beside the house, our boat is up on blocks. I can remember sailing with my parents, sunning myself on the deck as my brothers dipped their fishing rods into the water, trying to catch flounder. The boat has been there forever, unused. It's so much work to get it into the water. None of us has the time. My brothers and I come and go for a few weeks, revisit memories, then leave again. Life has changed from the days when we were children, and mothers spent the summer in Chatham, while their husbands came and went on tiny planes as fragile as toys at Chatham airport.

Everything changes here. When I was a child, the first thing my mother would do was take us to the beach to see how it had been remoulded by winter storms. Year after year, the beach was never the same. Just like life. Yet everything was the same.

Always, for me, there is this feeling that Chatham knows me better than I know myself. That I will one day be one of the many ghosts who cannot say goodbye. Not that I want to sentimentalise it. Chatham is a real, working town. Young people come here to build lives and families – people like Tim Wood, an award-winning journalist who edits the *Cape Cod Chronicle*, probably best described as a mini-*Irish Times*, with its liberal ethos, environmental awareness, political savvy and campaigning spirit.

Tim is among those fighting to help Chatham retain its small-town feel. He leaves a key to the small newspaper office hidden under a grey shingle by the editorial entrance, so that I can log on whenever I need to. He leaves his PC running for me and a note with his phone number just in case I have a problem. This is what home means. People who recognise you as one of their own and make you feel 'at home'.

You could take an outsider's perspective and see Chatham as something like the town in *Forrest Gump*, a kind of Disney-on-sea where nothing changes and no one ages. Where the white clapboard houses sparkle and there is never any pain or disappointment. Those of us who grew up here know that's not true.

We know pain. It's the bittersweet beauty of the place that makes us keep coming back. It's the memories and the family ties. We daren't feel smug about it. It's enough for us to know how lucky we are to give our children the kind of summers we once had – even if it's only for a few weeks.

Reprinted courtesy of *The Irish Times*.

# ARCHDEACON GORDON LINNEY

## ABOUT

Kisiizi Hospital is situated in the Kigezi Hills in the Rukungiri District, halfway between Kabale and Rukungiri in southwest Uganda. Kisiizi is a tranquil place with stunning scenery, like the dramatic thirty-metre waterfalls adjacent to the hospital. The climate is very pleasant because of Kisiizi's location 5,500 feet above sea level and almost on the equator.

The hospital was founded in 1958 by a young doctor, John Sharp, who was supported by an Anglican missionary society. He began treating patients in an old, redundant flax factory. Sadly John Sharp died quite young but the work continued and has expanded ever since. The hospital is still relatively isolated (two hours' drive from the nearest town) and patients travel from a large area, sometimes on foot, sometimes carried long distances looking for help, partly because other hospitals in the area often do not function fully.

Kisiizi Hospital deals with the whole spectrum of medical, surgical and obstetric problems, and for many patients, Kisiizi is the 'end of the line' as they cannot afford to travel to Kampala even if referred. Kisiizi does a fair range of general surgery (but not thoracic or neuro) and eye cases. Common problems include malaria, TB, typhoid, gastroenteritis, malnutrition, pneumonia and AIDS, plus some cases rarely seen in the west, like rheumatic fever and amoebic liver abscesses. Obstetric problems are also quite frequent.

There are almost two hundred beds in the hospital, including thirty-two medical, thirty-two surgical, fifty-two isolation, thirty paediatric and twenty-one maternity beds. Specialist departments include special-care nursery, theatre, physiotherapy, X-ray, laboratory, pharmacy and out-patients. There is also a college of nursing.

The mainly-Ugandan staff are augmented by a small number of Europeans, and medical professionals from the UK and Ireland regularly provide specialist services on a voluntary basis.

Among its many outreach programmes to the community, the hospital has a support scheme for thousands of AIDS orphans, providing mattresses and blankets and, on occasion, shelter, as well as medical aid.

The hospital has strong support groups in Ireland and the UK. The Dublin parish, St Paul's Glenageary, has been actively involved in the hospital since its inception. In 2002, two young students spent part of the summer working there, and currently a civil engineer from the parish, David Barrett, is supervising major building projects. The building of a new children's ward has been completed; a new maternity ward and other important building projects are underway. This has been part-funded by the parish and an Irish government aid programme. David is also hoping to develop a major hydroelectric scheme to provide electricity to the local community using the powerful Kisiizi waterfall. This waterfall powers a hydroelectric power plant that supplies the hospital with a limited amount of electricity.

Third-party support is significant for two reasons: firstly, the Ugandan government can provide only thirteen per cent of the hospital's budget, the rest comes from voluntary sources; secondly, it makes a real difference in a beautiful part of the world to a people who have been on the losing side for too long.

# LETTER FROM KISIIZI

*Dear Reader,*

*We wish we could describe adequately what it is like to live here at Kisiizi. There are beautiful, lush, green hills all around, with banana plantations rising up the steep slopes of the once-volcanic hills. Everything grows fast, and many things grow big. At this altitude there is a lot of rainfall, and the nights can be cool, so we wear long sleeves at times. Malaria is present, although we rarely see a mosquito, and by using anti-malarial drugs we hope to avoid catching it. The local people do suffer from recurrent bouts of this sickness though.*

*Forty-five years after it was founded the hospital is still growing and changes are taking place rapidly. One of the most recent is the new Children's Ward, opened in May with a service of thanksgiving for progress so far, and with prayers for what is still to come. Scaffolding remains around the building, as plans have already been laid to construct an upper storey, the new Maternity Ward. This work is now in progress.*

*The work of the hospital is varied. It has its own primary school and school of nursing, as well as a rehabilitation unit, outreach testing and counselling ministry on AIDS, and help to orphans. Outpatients is usually very busy. The Psychiatric Unit is a rare thing in Uganda, and does important work. The hydro-electricity generator, which has worked well for twenty years to supply the hospital, is still going strong; now there are plans to add another and to provide power to the surrounding villages. Even the mobile telephone network has arrived: Kisiizi now lies just on the edge of the area – we can telephone out if we find the right spot, and face the right way!*

*A good thing about being here is meeting the many visitors who pass through. They include medical students doing their electives, and visiting teams of doctors doing surgical 'camps'. One camp has just finished in which there were operations on over twenty children with cleft lips and palettes, with visible and life-changing results.*

*We thank God for his goodness shown in so many ways. The spiritual life of the hospital is at the heart of things. We see how our work is transformed by love-in-action. What else matters?*

*Yours sincerely,*

*Richard and Lorna Emmens*
*Church of Uganda Kisiizi Hospital,*
*P.O. Box 109, Kabale*
*Uganda*

*Email: kisiizihospital@hotmail.com*

# AUTHOR BIOGRAPHIES

OLUTOYIN PAMELA AKINJOBI is a bilingual secretary, caterer and writer. Over the years, she has written and published several articles and short stories in newspapers, journals and magazines in Africa and Europe. Her book, entitled *Her Story*, relates the true life stories, past trauma and struggles encountered by ten African women from different African countries before they came to live in Ireland. *Her Story* was published in Ireland in 2003.

NENA BHANDARI was born in Dublin in 1973. She moved to England when she was eighteen to study at university. After working for five years as a corporate lawyer in London, Nena recently gave it all up to pursue her dream of becoming an author. *Enduring India* is Nena's first published work. She is currently working on her first novel. Nena lives with her husband, Alexander, in North London.

ROSITA BOLAND was born in Clare. She has published two collections of poetry, *Muscle Creek* and *Dissecting the Heart*, and one travel book, *Sea Legs: Hitch-Hiking the Coast of Ireland Alone*. Her poems have been included in many anthologies, including the *Field Day Anthology of Irish Literature*. She has travelled widely. She lives in Dublin, where she works as a feature writer journalist for *The Irish Times*.

JEAN BUTLER, originally from New York, settled in Ireland after completing a BA in Theatre Studies at the University of Birmingham. Although best known for her work as a choreographer and dancer in *Riverdance* and her own show, *On Dangerous Ground*, Jean has appeared in several films over the past few years and has found time to write for Irish publications including *Image* and *The Dubliner*. She is currently the Artist in Residence at the University of Limerick, attending a Masters in Contemporary Dance. She lives in Ireland with her husband, Cuan Hanly, and their dog, Freddie.

ANNA CAREY grew up in the north Dublin suburb of Drumcondra. She studied German and History of Art at Trinity College Dublin before going on to do an MA in Journalism at DCU. After that, she worked as a features writer and arts critic for *The Sunday Tribune* for five years. She is now a freelance journalist, writing about everything from children's books to Belle and Sebastian for a variety of publications, including *The Irish Times*. She loves BBC Radio 4, 1960s French pop music, *Built By Wendy* clothes and *Buffy the Vampire Slayer*. She hates Avril Lavigne, Donald Rumsfeld and people saying, 'I'm not a feminist, but ...' Her summer in Berlin put her off yoga for life.

MARITA CONLON-McKENNA was born in Dublin. She enjoyed an eccentric roller-coaster childhood, split between the city and Wicklow. Her first children's novel *Under the Hawthorn Tree*, became an award-winning, international bestseller and established her as a strong new voice in Irish fiction. Obsessed with writing, and pictures in her head, more bestselling children's novels and picture books followed. Her adult novel, *The Magdalen*, a powerful story set in the confines of a Magdalen laundry, also topped the Irish bestseller list and was published in the UK, Australia and America. Marita now lives with her husband and family in Blackrock, Co. Dublin. She has a view of Dublin Bay from the upstairs of her home, where she likes to focus on the magic craft of using words and character to create good stories for all ages. She is the Chairman of Irish Pen and is involved in the Writers in Schools scheme, as well as a number of initiatives to promote reading and writing in Ireland.

MARTINA DEVLIN was born in Omagh, Co. Tyrone but left home at eighteen. After trailing round less than exotic locations, she wound up working as a journalist in London for the Press Association. Eventually she found herself back in Ireland and joined the *Irish Independent* as a reporter and columnist. She now works as a novelist and freelance journalist in Dublin. Martina started writing fiction in 1996 when she won a Hennessy Literary Award for her first short story. Her début novel, *Three Wise Men*, was published in 2000, followed by *Be Careful What You Wish For* in 2001, and *Venus Reborn* in 2003. Her fourth novel is due out in 2004.

CATHERINE DONNELLY was an award-winning copywriter with a Dublin advertising agency, before leaving to write. She was an occasional columnist for the *Sunday Independent* and a regular contributor to *Irish Tatler* magazine, before writing *The State of Grace*. She is currently working on her second novel.

CLARE DOWLING trained as an actress and began writing for theatre in 1992 with *Burns Both Ends*, produced by Glasshouse Productions of which she was a founder member. She went on to have six plays produced. She has subsequently written for film, television and radio. She has published children's fiction and drama for teenagers. She has written three novels, *Fast Forward, Expecting Emily* and *Amazing Grace*. She is currently a scriptwriter on RTÉ's *Fair City*. She lives in Dublin with her family.

CATHERINE DUNNE is the author of four acclaimed novels. Her first, *In the Beginning*, was short-listed for the

Bancarella, the Italian Booksellers' Prize. Her second, *A Name for Himself*, was short-listed for the Kerry Group Irish Fiction Award. *The Walled Garden* was broadcast as part of *The Book on One*, on RTÉ Radio. Her fourth, *Another Kind of Life*, was published in February 2003. She has also contributed to two anthologies, *Irish Girls About Town* and *A Second Skin*. Her first work of non-fiction, *An Unconsidered People*, was published in June 2003.

CIARA DWYER was born in Dublin in 1972. She is a journalist with the *Sunday Independent*. Her two great weaknesses are charity shops and beautiful men, in that order.

LOUISE EAST has been writing creatively about travel since she lied about her age to go on an archaeological dig in France at the age of seventeen. She has been digging for something that might be valuable and trying to tell the truth ever since. Since joining *The Irish Times* at the age of twenty-two, she has written features on eating reindeer in Lapland, being rescued by the Flying Doctors in Australia, losing her way in the Vietnamese Highlands and losing her dignity on a snowboard in Italy. She is also books editor for *Image* magazine. She is currently doing an MA in creative writing at the University of East Anglia.

MARY HENRY was elected to Seanad Éireann in 1993 and re-elected in 1997. Her involvement with the Red Cross led her to take a greater interest in women's health in developing countries. To promote the issue, she has visited several African countries on behalf of UNFPA, the United Nations organisation particularly involved in women's health issues. She is married to John McEntagart and has three children.

KATHRYN HOLMQUIST was born in Vermont, USA and has been a staff journalist with *The Irish Times* since 1986. She lives in Dublin with her husband, the writer and broadcaster, Ferdia MacAnna. Her book, *A Good Daughter,* was published by Raven Arts Press in 1991.

NIAMH HOOPER is a Dublin-based writer. Having worked for Independent Newspapers for many years as a feature writer and news reporter, she is now freelance. Her niche area whilst in Independent Newspapers was entertainment – she was the *Irish Independent*'s concert reviewer and regularly interviewed celebrities from the world of film and music. She now writes for numerous newspapers and magazines. In the past two years, Niamh has taken part in charity hikes that have raised more than €12,000 for the Dublin Simon Community, a charity caring for the homeless. The first was on the magical Great Wall of China, on which her contribution to this book is based; the second was in the wilds of Brazil.

ANN MARIE HOURIHANE is a writer and broadcaster. She was born and lives in Dublin. She does not like flying and is uncomfortable travelling below deck on boats. She is nervous in cars and does not like lifts. Her book, *She Moves Through the Boom,* examined Ireland's economic good times, and was widely praised.

MARIAN KEYES is the author of six novels: *Watermelon* (1995), *Lucy Sullivan is Getting Married* (1996), which was also made into a major ITV television series, *Rachel's Holiday* (1998), *Last Chance Saloon* (1999), *Sushi for Beginners* (2000) and her latest, *Angels* (2002). The royalties from Irish sales of *Under the Duvet* (2001), a collection of her journalism, were given to the Simon Community, a charity that cares for the homeless. She has sold over six million copies of her books worldwide.

CAUVERY MADHAVAN was born and educated in India. She worked for a newspaper and a hotel group before getting her first taste for writing when she drifted into advertising in her early twenties, working as a copywriter in her home town of Madras. She moved to Ireland fifteen years ago, arriving on Valentine's Day and, despite the Irish weather, has been in love with the country ever since. She has written two books, *Paddy Indian* and *The Uncoupling,* and is a regular contributor to the *Evening Herald.* She lives with her husband and three children in Co. Kildare.

CAROLINE MORAHAN began her writing career as a freelance journalist with the *Evening Herald*. After six weeks at the paper, she took over as the social diarist. Her own column, 'Caroline in the City' soon followed. But fashion has always been her principal interest and the dream of having her own weekly fashion spread in the paper was realised within a year. In 2001, an open audition at RTÉ was to change her career path dramatically. Caroline beat 2,000 hopefuls to secure the role of presenter for a new quiz show, *The Fame Game.* After a successful debut, RTÉ producers approached her to audition for their flagship fashion programme, *Off the Rails.* Caroline has just completed working on a second series and continues to contribute to a number of publications.

DERVLA MURPHY was born in Waterford, where she still lives, and is the author of twenty books about her travels on four continents, and the problems of various countries including her own. Her books include: *In Ethiopia with a Mule*, *Eight Feet in the Andes*, and *Through the Embers of Chaos: Balkan Journeys.* At present she is working on an account of a journey in Eastern Siberia.

ANITA NOTARO is a television producer, journalist and director, and worked for RTÉ, for eighteen years. She has directed the Eurovision Song Contest and the Irish General

Election, as well as programmes for the BBC and Channel 4. Her first novel is *Back after the Break*.

ANNE-MARIE O'CONNOR began writing short stories in 2001 while working as a PA in Dublin. After hiding them in a cupboard for a while, she finally plucked up the courage to send them to M6, a theatre company that was running a competition for monologues, and two were chosen to be staged. Her play, *You Can't Always Get What You Want*, was staged in 2002. She worked as a waitress while writing the novel, *Everyone's Got a Bono Story,* which was published by Tivoli in February 2004. She currently has work in development with BBC Radio 4 drama and is busy writing her second novel.

JULIE PARSONS was born in New Zealand but has lived most of her adult life in Ireland. Formerly a radio and television producer for RTÉ, she has been writing full time since 1997. Her first novel, *Mary, Mary,* was published in 1998, and was translated into seventeen languages. She followed it up with *The Courtship Gift*, *Eager to Please,* and *The Guilty Heart*, all of which have also been translated. She is currently working on her fifth novel. She is married and lives outside Dublin

SUZANNE POWER is an emigrant by nature. She is now resident in Dublin via London, Phnom Penh, the back of an Australian Ford Falcon car and Belfast. Her twin boys and partner, who is a special needs educator, are hopeful her itchy feet find camomile. When she is not moving, she writes fiction and is a columnist.

TERRY PRONE is a leading author on public communications. She has published six non-fiction bestsellers, including standard texts used in third-level journalism courses, *Write and Get Paid for It* and *Do Your*

*Own Publicity*. In addition to her work as an Executive Director with Carr Communications, Terry Prone has published six bestselling novels and a collection of short stories, one of which won the prestigious Francis McManus award.

MORAG PRUNTY edited several young women's magazines in London, including *More!* and *Just Seventeen,* before moving to Ireland in 1990 to relaunch *Irish Tatler*. She has written three novels, *Dancing with Mules*, *Disco Daddy* and *Poison Arrows*. She is now a full-time writer and lives in Dublin with her husband and son.

TINA REILLY is the author of three bestselling novels, *Flipside*, *The Onion Girl* and *Is This Love?* Her fourth book, *Something Borrowed,* is due out in 2004. In her spare time, she looks after her two kids, teaches drama, writes plays and co-manages an under-nines soccer team.

MARY RUSSELL was born in Dublin, and completed an Arts degree at University College Dublin. She had a variety of jobs in London including ward orderly, garage forecourt attendant and teacher. She was also an au pair for a time in Italy. In 1980, she did an MA course at the School of Peace Studies at Bradford University and started writing regularly for *The Guardian*. The following year, she travelled to Lesotho, the first of many such journeys. That year also, she wrote a four-part series on solo women travellers for *The Guardian*'s Women's page. Some of her stories have been published in different editions of the *London Magazine,* as well as in collections including *Nocturnal Emissions* and *The Phoenix Book of Irish Short Stories*. Her book, *Journeys of a Lifetime,* was published in 2002.

GAYE SHORTLAND was born in Cork. She has taught English literature at University College Cork, the University of Leeds, Ahmadu Bello University Nigeria and the Université de Niamey in the Republic of Niger. She lived in Africa for sixteen years, spending much of that time with the nomadic Tuareg of the Sahara, and eventually abandoned teaching in favour of managing a restaurant and recreation centre for the American Embassy in Niamey. She married a Tuareg and has three children. She began to write in 1994 on her return to Ireland, and is the author of five critically acclaimed novels. *Mind That 'tis My Brother* and *Turtles All The Way Down* are comedies set in Cork; *Polygamy*, *Harmattan* and *Rough Rides in Dry Places* are set in Africa. In 2002, Meridian Theatre did a successful stage version of *Mind That 'tis My Brother* for which she wrote the script. She has been editor at Poolbeg Press since 1998.

HO WEI SIM is a Malaysian Chinese woman living in Ireland. She has spent the past six and a half years trying to crack the code of the Irish. She lives in Summerhill with her husband, Donal, and her two daughters, Liadh and Ciara. Contrary to popular belief, she is not associated in any way with the takeaway business. She wrote television drama in Singapore before she moved to Ireland. Most recently, her short film was produced and shown on TG4 and at the Galway Film Festival. During the day, she spends her time pretending to be a solicitor. One day, she will finally capture, in a scattering of well-chosen words, the joys and heartache of settling in Ireland. She will never know whether it was the right decision, though in saner moments during the early hours of the morning, she has suspicions that it might be.

SARAH WEBB is the author of four bestselling novels – *Three Times a Lady*, *Always the Bridesmaid*, *Something to Talk About*, and *Some Kind of Wonderful*. Her new book, *It Had to Be You,* will be published in 2004. She lives in south Co. Dublin with her partner and young family.

GRACE WYNNE-JONES grew up in Co. Limerick. Having travelled extensively in Africa and America, she returned to Ireland, and settled in Bray, Co. Wicklow. She is the author of *Ordinary Miracles* and *Wise Follies*. She is also a freelance journalist, and her articles have appeared in many magazines and national newspapers, including *The Guardian*, *The Irish Times* and the *Irish Independent*.

**RUPERT BOGARDE**

**Daybreak into Darkness**

PAN BOOKS

***'If somebody had said to me, "Your wife will go mad, she'll go missing, you'll end up bringing up your children alone, you're going to search for her for years and years," I would have thought they were the ones going insane.'***

At the age of twenty-one, shy Rupert Bogarde – nephew of Dirk – fell in love with a nurse a great deal worldlier than he. Jacquie loved France and the couple moved there, married and bought a ruined chapel near Perpignan to turn into a business. Juggling restoration and building work with odd jobs, they eventually opened a holiday centre for young diabetics. With the birth of their two sons their dream should have been complete, but Jacquie had become obsessed with the business – working and partying for days and nights without sleep – while Rupert struggled to keep his family and marriage together. Jacquie's mania became alarming, until one evening she disappeared. Rupert, by now heavily in debt, was left alone with the children and a business in ruins. Jacquie's car was later found crashed and abandoned by the roadside and Rupert soon became the French police's number-one suspect. Rupert looked for Jacquie for years, learning to live with people's assumptions that he was responsible for her disappearance. Then, in 2000, seven years after his search began, Rupert finally discovered the truth.

'Unsparing in its raw honesty'
***You Magazine***

**JULIE PARSONS**

**The Guilty Heart**

PAN BOOKS

Ten years ago Owen Cassidy – eight years old, thick fair hair, bright blue eyes – disappeared. Everyone thought he was out playing with his best friend Luke. But later it turned out that Owen had left him in the middle of the afternoon. And never made it home . . .

His disappearance left his father, Nick, distraught, but also full of guilt. For instead of looking after Owen that day, Nick had spent the afternoon in bed – with one of their neighbours. It was an affair that would tear his family apart.

The aftermath of Owen's disappearance drove Nick away from his wife and home, to America. He moved from city to city, trying to forget. Now, ten years on, a sudden encounter forces Nick to return to Dublin to confront his demons. He arrives to find that the world he knew has moved on. But he is determined to face up to his past, and find out at last what happened to his only son. Little does he realize that his investigations will soon unleash further violence, taking him into a terrifying world that he barely knew existed . . .

'A mesmerizing tale of obsessive love,
harrowing loss and perverse appetites'
***Irish Independent***

## PETER SHERIDAN

## Big Fat Love

PAN BOOKS

***A delectable Dublin tale of life, love and redemption***

Philo's mouth is always getting her in trouble – it's either food going in or profanities coming out. But when she turns up at the Good Shepherd convent looking for a bed, Sister Rosaleen finds she can't say no. Philo needs to escape a troubled past and the nuns help set her on the right track. In the process, though, everyone's world is turned upside down.

With a heart as big as her waistband, Philo brings out the best in people. She makes even the stony-faced crack a grin and, through an unlikely mix of *Blind Date*, bingo and stock-car racing at the local day-care centre, puts heart back into a community that's looked on the point of extinction.

Alive with the sights and sounds of Dublin's dockland, Peter Sheridan's debut novel is bursting with character. In turns moving, hilarious, raw and heart-warming, this gem of a story is impossible to resist.

'Brilliant writing that matches the rhythms of a Dublin backstreet: sharp, ragged, jazzy, hilarious, and often painful'
**Frank McCourt on *Forty-seven Roses***

'Sheridan's writing is in a class of its own . . . fast-paced and endlessly witty'
***Sunday Express***

**SARAH WEBB**

## It Had to Be You

PAN BOOKS

***In the Irish village of Burnaby, life is about to change for three very different women.***

Molly Harper is the long-suffering manager of Ireland's only dedicated romance bookshop, 'Happily Ever After'. She can't stand Milo Jones, the super-smooth new owner but he does have a rather attractive son, Sam. Should she stay or should she walk?

Her best friend, Paige Brady, has problems of her own. She's just launched a general election campaign and is astonished when another candidate, Annette Higgins, starts to attack her in a very personal way. But Paige is determined to stay in the race.

Kate Bowan, shop assistant in the trendy Burnaby designer shoe shop 'Baroque' by day, runs the popular dummy dating service 'Dublin Dummy Dates' by night. But one particular client is proving to be more than a handful.

But all's fair in love, politics and business as the three friends are about to find out. Enter the world of Burnaby Village and you'll be glad you stayed, because sometimes finding yourself is only the start of the adventure.

'Perfect for curling up beside the fire . . .
this is one to savour'
***Irish Independent***

## OTHER BOOKS

## AVAILABLE FROM PAN MACMILLAN

| | | |
|---|---|---|
| **RUPERT BOGARDE** | | |
| DAYBREAK INTO DARKNESS | 0 330 48789 2 | £7.99 |
| **JULIE PARSONS** | | |
| THE GUILTY HEART | 0 330 48888 0 | £6.99 |
| **PETER SHERIDAN** | | |
| BIG FAT LOVE | 0 330 41337 6 | £6.99 |
| **SARAH WEBB** | | |
| IT HAD TO BE YOU | 0 330 41217 5 | £6.99 |